Towards Professionalism in International Theory:
Macrosystem Analysis

Towards Professionalism in International Theory:
Macrosystem Analysis

Morton A. Kaplan

THE FREE PRESS
A Division of Macmillan Publishing Co., Inc.
NEW YORK

Collier Macmillan Publishers
LONDON

The Free Press
A Division of Macmillan Publishing Co., Inc.
866 Third Avenue, New York, N.Y. 10022

Collier Macmillan Canada, Ltd.

Library of Congress Catalog Card Number: 78-65223

Printed in the United States of America

printing number

1 2 3 4 5 6 7 8 9 10

Library of Congress Cataloging in Publication Data

Kaplan, Morton A
    Towards professionalism in international theory.

    Includes index.
    1. International relations--Research. I. Title.
JX1291.K36   327'.01   78-65223
ISBN 0-02-916750-7

CONTENTS

PREFACE

This book is dedicated to those few international relations experts, such as Arthur Lee Burns, who already are true professionals and to the large number of younger scholars who are impatient to see the discipline achieve genuine professional status. I believe that it is obvious to most of them that in the area of qualitative macrosystem analysis the state of the discipline, with a few exceptions, is still preprofessional. The long initial essay on the art of criticism is designed to establish this point so surely that it will not be possible to doubt it. By demonstrating the poor state of the art of criticism, I hope to show that useful criticism is indeed hard work that requires careful analysis and attention to texts.

The initial essay has one further purpose that is quite important to me. My work has been consistently misinterpreted by the critics, and secondary sources claim that I say what the critics present as my position far more often than they report my actual positions. By virtue of a sustained dialogue with one of the very ablest of my critics, I hope to disentangle the existing framework of misinterpretations and to provide a critical "key" to the understanding of *System and Process in International Politics* (1957).

The second chapter, which is on systems analysis, is intended to be as concise a statement of that metodology as I am now able to make. It consists of a revised, reordered, and expanded version of materials that previously appeared in *Justice, Human Nature, and Political Obligation* (1976) and *Alienation and Identification* (1976). The third chapter, on international systems theory, is put together from three previous essays in revised and expanded form. It includes the six models from chapter 2 of *System and Process,* several mixed empirical models that consitute alternative projections of the contemporary international system, a statement of how the theories are engineered to take account of particular events, of how they are employed in macroanalyses of past international systems, and of how the computer may be used to explore the internal logic of "balance of power" theory. In addition, there is a more specific account of the assumptions underlying the models than occurs anywhere else. Thus, there is a further specification of the boundary conditions consistent with equilibrium.

The last chapter is a revised version of an essay that appeared in the *Journal of Modern History* (1975). It distinguishes the task of the historian from that of the political scientist, and demonstrates, I fear, that the field of diplomatic history also is in a preprofessional state. The essay, I believe, will be self-explanatory with respect to important methodological problems. The reader who is interested in a more philosophical account may turn to an earlier book of mine: *On Historical and Political Knowing* (1971).

I am aware that I have repeated quotations in whole or part in different places. Given the state of confusion with respect to the issues I am discussing, I much prefer the risk of redundancy to that of lack of clarity and incisiveness. The reader will note also that some arguments recur. This is because the principles involved in correct explanation are fewer in number than the confusions that result from their misapprehension; and it is the latter that I am trying to clarify. Moreover, I believe that the principles will become even clearer because of this procedure.

ACKNOWLEDGEMENTS

Portions of Chapter 2 are taken from Chapter 1 of *Justice, Human Nature, and Political Obligation*, and Chapter 3 of *Alienation and Identification*, both published in 1976 by the Free Press, a division of the MacMillan Company. Portions of Chapter 3 are taken from *International Political Communities: An Anthology*, published by Anchor Books, 1966; *Macropolitics: Essays on the Philosophy and Science of Politics*, published by Aldine Publishing Company in 1969; and *New Approaches to International Relations*, published by St. Martin's Press in 1968. Portions of Chapter 4 were published in the *Journal of Modern History*, a publication of the University of Chicago Press in volume 47, number 1, March 1975. The quotations from Winfried Franke were taken from his chapter in *New Approaches to International Relations*. Appreciation is expressed to the publishers of these books for the use of this material.

CHAPTER I

THE GENTEEL ART OF CRITICISM, OR HOW TO BOGGLE MINDS AND CONFOOZ A DISCIPLINE

PROLOGUE

CRITICISM AND THE STATE OF INTERNATIONAL RELATIONS THEORY

Although individual great minds may be responsible for spectacular advances in science, the progress of science requires community. Even the greatest minds solve problems that have emerged in the community of scientists and with tools and methods that are contemporary. If those working in a field fail to address themselves to similar problems, or fail to do so in a manner that permits genuine comparison, then it is possible neither to build on previous efforts nor to discover the inadequacies of current efforts. Rejection of, as well as development from, the past is an integral part of the scientific process. Formulation and criticism are opposite sides of the same scientific coin.

THE CURRENT STATE OF THEORY

The current state of theory in international relations is surely depressing because progress of any type seems absent; and this has been attested to by a wide variety of writers. In his recent article in the *Handbook of Political Science,* Kenneth Waltz writes: "Nothing seems to accumulate, not even criticism. Instead, the same sorts of summary and superficial criticism are made over and over again, and the same sorts of errors are repeated" (1975, p. 2).

1

Waltz's despair with the state of the literature shines through his survey, in which he chastises his colleagues in often funny asides that are punctuated with irony and exclamation points for what he regards as their egregious errors. It would be ungenerous to repeat his complaints concerning others; therefore, I shall let his comments on me stand for his withering assault on the contemporary corps of theorists.

Waltz says of my work: "Sadly, one must agree with Charles McClelland: Kaplan has both popularized systems theory and rendered it mysterious" (p. 63). Elsewhere he avers that a "former student" of mine was "surprised" when he discovered what Waltz characterized as a failure of my theories to accord with evidence. He finds several of my formulations "mind-boggling." He complains: "Here, as so often, Kaplan's language is loose and imprecise to the point of misleading the reader" (p. 60).

I am sure that Waltz was indeed sad when he came to the conclusion that he would have to paddle my behind so vigorously. In fact, his candor is both courageous and long overdue. Only a deep sense of professional obligation could have led a gentleman such as Ken Waltz, who is above the petty rivalries of lesser minds, to have made the harsh comments he did about his colleagues. The discipline, except perhaps for an occasional pompous exception, will respect his purpose, which is essential to its reconstruction; and the discipline will be grateful for the fresh air, and even the sense of humor, that he has let in.

Waltz, in addition to chastising his peers, also instructs us in how to reconstruct the discipline in a satisfactory fashion. How can we break this vicious cycle of poor theory? We must be rigorous. Waltz points out: "Taking stock of theories can lead to a fashioning of better ones only if evaluation is rigorous" (p. 6). He states correctly: "Whether one is offered a quotation from Plato or a number, one wants to know what it is for. How does it address one's logic? How does it establish a connection? How does it serve as evidence?" With this lucid and penetrating statement of the problem I can only agree. One wishes only that Waltz had taken his own good advice.

If one believes, as I do, that Waltz has left the state of the literature in a far more confused state than he found it in, it is indeed time to set things aright lest still another generation of students lose their chance to develop professional competence.

The key to the problem of analysis lies in Waltz's advocacy of rigor. More than rigor, however, systematic inquiry is required. It is not possible merely to pull sentences haphazardly out of a systematic statement and then to treat them as if their meaning is fully transparent or to refute them by poorly understood and controversial one-line quotations from philosophers of science, whose positions, in any event, may be mutually inconsistent. Nor, although one must admit the possibility that any writer, including this one, may say foolish or mindless things, is it safe to assume that this is the case without examining alternative possible—and sometimes syntactically required—interpretations of the text at issue.

Until recently, I had not ventured into the field of criticism because criticism of good professional quality involves a lot of hard work. And I was much more concerned with formulating my own position than I was with criticizing those of others. It has become clear to me at last that I can no longer present my own work to others unless I disentangle it from the web of confusions the critics have introduced. To undertake this task, it is important to understand the requirements of criticism.

Critics require skills as great as those of theorists, and to some extent the required skills overlap. One understands something best when he has attempted it himself. For this reason, I believe that critics should be cautious in their comments on theorists unless they have first bloodied their noses in the hard work of building or of applying theories. For the same reason, I believe that critics of critics should be careful about telling critics how to do their work unless they have first carried out a substantial task of criticism. Because I have done this only in the field of philosophy, an area in which many professionals in international relations may not read extensively, I hope that I may be allowed to show that I have "paid my dues" in this respect by quoting from a review of *Justice, Human Nature, and Political Obligation* in the *Review of Metaphysics:* "Proceeding on the basis of [the] methodology [in chapter 1], Chapter 2 offers a thorough and very useful critique of Toulmin's *Reason and Ethics*....[In chapter 3]...Rawls' *A Theory of Justice* is subjected to a similarly rigorous critique..." (1977, p. 119). Briefly, in the case of Rawls, I first showed on the basis of the methodology in chapter 1 that Rawls's theory could not work. I then showed by detailed analysis of his arguments that the expected failures were present. I then inquired as to whether the difficulties might be avoided by a reinterpretation of his position. Furthermore, I examined carefully the qualifications in his statements to see whether these would modify the judgment reached. Moreover, in the process, a systematic presentation of his position was given. Whether or not I was correct in my methodological and substantive criticism of Rawls, I wish to urge adoption of similar standards for criticism in the profession of international relations: for if such standards are not enforced by readers for journals or publishers and by the profession generally, we will continue to perpetuate a situation in which confusion compounds confusion.

I have no wish to denigrate any particular individual for following the existing standard of criticism in the area of international relations. Except for the neglected work of Arthur Burns, a few specific criticisms by William Riker, and some difficulties in my own position that McGowan and Rood have recently discovered, I am not aware of any criticism in international relations that even begins to meet the standard I am suggesting. The significant question is not whether we can expose the inadequacies of critics but whether we can raise the profession's standards. In that endeavor, this work is designed to show how the lack of rigor and systematicity makes nonsense of the art of criticism and confuses the state of the profession.

How shall we proceed in trying to remedy the situation? First, we shall do what Waltz did not do: we shall examine the state of criticism, for the profession's understanding of theory to a considerable degree is mediated through the critical literature. And we shall use Waltz's article as a paradigm for the critical literature for a number of reasons. In the first place, a systematic treatment of a particular author clarifies the fact that I am not dealing with particular lapses or quotations taken out of context but with a systematic failure of analysis that derives from a preprofessional style of analysis. Particular failures in interpretation of text or of methodological position may occur even among professionals. Consistent carelessness with texts and with theoretical arguments is the mark of the preprofessional; and it is important to document this state of affairs so thoroughly that future criticism, in self defense, will be directed to the real rather than the imaginary inadequacies of the literature.

In addition, Waltz's criticism is appropriate for this task because it is the most recent. He has mined thoroughly nearly 20 years' of critical literature on *System and Process* and has incorporated in his work those criticisms he believes can be defended while adding a number of original criticisms. Although it would be tedious and unrewarding to attempt to prove that Waltz is a superior example of the preprofessional critic and theorist, I believe that his skills are widely recognized. Stanley Hoffmann of Harvard, moreover, refers to Waltz's critique of the literature as "brilliant" in Hoffmann's review in the *American Political Science Review* (1977); and it appears in a handbook that is widely used. Moreover, his mistakes are so central to the most important problems of international relations theory that a criticism of them will permit us to advance the state of understanding as well as to show what genuinely professional criticism would encompass. Waltz's virtues—not his defects—make him useful for my purpose.

WALTZ'S METHODOLOGY

Much of what Waltz says about laws and theories is standard. With respect to his judgment that theories are weak in the area of international relations, I not only agree with it but have long argued for a number of reasons—including complexity, lack of independent measures, and so forth—that this is inevitable. I do not know that I would agree with him that a theory explains laws although some generalizations within theories may be derived from others and, in that limited sense, may be explained by them. I think it would be better to say that theories, including laws, are used to explain particulars.

I am somewhat troubled by Waltz's statement that "laws are 'facts of observation;' theories are 'speculative processes designed to explain them.' " They are neither facts in any simple sense nor are they clearly related to observation in any simple sense. Nor are theories processes in any sense that I understand. Furthermore, I fail to understand his comment that "experimental results are permanent" (p. 4). There are many putative "observations" being made in laboratories throughout the world today that are never reported because the scientists who make them do not believe them. Mitogenetic rays were repeatedly "observed" by scientists although they now agree that they do not exist. An "observation" is a fact only in the original Latin sense; that is, it is something that is made.

Moreover, despite Rudolf Carnap's (1928, 1947, 1950) extensive efforts, Willard van Orman Quine (1953) has shown that there can never be a protocol sentence that has a one-to-one relationship with observation. Therefore, it is not possible for a sentence simply to communicate an observation. In addition, psychologists well know that what we observe depends on our mind sets as well as on the character of external objects or events.

However, it is possible that I misinterpret Waltz's argument, for later in his article, he argues for the "close interdependence of fact and theory" and then states that "changes of theory produce changes in the meaning of words" (p. 11). Although there are ambiguities in this position also, it is certainly better than his earlier position.

As I am concerned with Waltz the critic, and less with Waltz the theorist, I shall not attempt to reconcile his positions, to discover whether he is contradicting himself, or to find out whether instead he is groping toward what I regard as an essential distinction between theory and praxis. It will be useful, however, to say something, if only briefly, about the relationship of theories (including laws) and observations.

It is so well known that it is somewhat tedious to repeat that theories in physical sciences are not simply confirmed by observations. The idea of a critical experiment has been jettisoned by almost every philosopher of science. Although I shall not be able to pursue the matter, this informs the position that Imre Lakatos calls "sophisticated falsification" (1970, p. 116), to which I refer in my discussion of Galtung.

Physics does have one clear advantage over the social sciences, however.

Because independent measurements with respect to forces, and so forth, are available to the physical scientist, laws employing equality signs may be employed meaningfully. Parameter conditions and starting states are measurable in a way that is not true in the social sciences. Therefore, even in the absence of a vacuum, it is possible to work out in detail and often determinately the path and rate of speed of a falling body despite atmospheric friction and other disturbances. In the social sciences, we cannot do this and our judgments concerning parameter conditions and starting states are qualitative. This is a reason why highly general theories that pretend to be true of all social or political systems turn out to be tautological or at best truistic. The fact, however, that high-confidence judgments may not be available to us does not mean that reasonable-confidence judgments may not be available under some circumstances.

The former condition is not so different from some aspects of physics. For instance, it is simply beyond our abilities to predict the path of a falling feather. This does not mean that we can make no statements about it; however, the statements we can make will be of a general and largely qualitative nature that relate the path of the feather to air currents and so forth. This is not so different from the kinds of statements that can be made about the essential rules in my international systems.

Moreover, in those areas where the truth of particular physical theories is at issue, we must resort to a pattern of reasoning not so different from that of theories in the social sciences, although the tight relatedness of the elements in the field of knowledge in the area of physics provides greater confidence in its conclusions. Put briefly, and therefore in highly oversimplified form, we accept theories because they fit in with the general body of knowledge. If they did not, the evidence that confirms them would not seem nearly so convincing. Einstein's theory of relativity, for instance, came into general acceptance after the initial measurement of the bending of light about Mercury. Yet that measurement alone could not have been a decisive reason; for the expected measurement error was greater that the predicted difference. The measurement (that is, the "observation" of curvature) was accepted as valid long before the recent and more accurate cesium measurements, despite the estimated error margin, because Einstein's theories fit it in with such factors as the Michelson-Morley experiment, the development of neo-Euclidean geometries, and the Lorentz contractions.[1]

SCOPE

I believe that all the important critical issues will be surveyed if, apart from Waltz's own position on international theory, we restrict our attention to his criticisms of Johan Galtung and myself. Waltz's criticism of Galtung raises crucial issues in theory construction. If they are misunderstood, or understood as Waltz understands them, it will do considerable damage to a generation of students.

Waltz's criticism of my own work is useful for a number of reasons. I am more familiar with it than I am with the work of other people. And the variety of confusions he has introduced is of great theoretical interest. Furthermore, I think it will be possible to use Waltz's criticism of my work to gain a more systematic understanding of how criticism should be carried out, of how it can contribute to the development of international relations theory, and of the actual state of international relations theory; for Galtung's structural theory of imperialism—although it deals with an important issue—does not cope with central issues of macroanalysis in international relations.

WALTZ ON GALTUNG

Waltz comes to Galtung as the last in the line of his examination of theorists of imperialism. His examinations of Hobson and Lenin may be sound, although I must admit that I have not been sufficiently responsible to reread Hobson and Lenin in a way that would permit a mature judgment with respect to this issue.

REDUCTIONIST THEORIES

There is a great deal of confusion in the literature over whether reductionist theories work and even over what they are. Surely we wish to clarify this point if we are to understand how theory can operate in international relations. Let us see how Waltz, as in the case of so many other critics, misunderstands this issue. Later in this chapter we shall see its relevance to his discussion of systems theories, including mine.

According to Waltz, "imperialism, in Galtung's view, is a relation between more harmonious and richer states, on the one hand, and less harmonious and poorer states, on the other" (p. 26). This makes it a reductionist theory, he says, and, therefore, faulty.

To examine this question, let us first examine Waltz's definition of reductionism: "Theories of international politics that concentrate causes at the individual or national level are reductionist; theories that conceive of causes operating at the international level are systemic..." (p. 16). This definition is inadequate; but, even if it were adequate, the inferences that Waltz draws from it are wrong. Waltz continues: "with a reductionist approach, the whole is known by knowing the attributes and interactions of its parts. The effort to explain the behavior of a group through psychological study of its members is a reductionist

approach as is the effort to understand international politics by studying bu-
reaucrats and bureaucracy. Perhaps the classic reductionist case was the once
widespread effort to understand organisms by disassembling them and applying physical and chemical knowledge and methods in the examination of their
parts'' (p. 16).

Even the inexpert will see that although the second example is reductionist,
the first is not; and the last is reductionist not primarily—or even necessarily,
depending on the content of the propositions—because it employs physical or
chemical terms but primarily because it attempts to reduce the complex physical and chemical systems to the behaviors of the part systems, considered
separately. Although it is inherently implausible that biological theories can be
reduced to chemical and/or physical theories, it does not follow that physical or
chemical theories can not explain some behaviors of organisms.

There are in fact different types of reductionist explanations; and the
reader can see that Waltz at times refers to them although not all fit his definition.
One form of reductionism is that in which the laws of one science, for instance
chemistry, are derived from that of another, for instance physics, under appro-
priately stated parameter conditions. If this could be done, we would not state
that the laws of physics caused, even in Waltz's sense of concentration, the laws
of chemistry. Another form of reductionism is that in which the characteristics
of the whole are inferred directly from the characteristics of the parts; it can be
contrasted with a nonreductionist example in which the relevant characteristics
of the parts are employed in a theory that deals with relations among the parts.

Waltz in fact conflates the reductionist example in the last sentence with a
nonreductionist explanation that employs relevant characteristics of elements
of systems in terms of their relationships with each other. Even worse, he quickly forgets his definition—a concentration of causes in the parts—and argues:
"Because Galtung includes a national attribute in his international structure, his
approach becomes reductionist" (p. 26). Now mere inclusion of an actor attribute, Waltz says, make a theory reductionist. It is impossible, however, to
interpret a concrete system without some reference to the characteristics, as well
as the interrelationships, of the parts.

Consider a simple example that will illuminate the confusion in Waltz's
position. Suppose we wish to understand the characteristics of a necklace made
of pearls. Pearls are fairly rigid objects. A reductionist argument would derive the
characteristics of the necklace from the characteristics of the pearls. It would
state that the necklace is rigid because the pearls are rigid. In this case, it is easy
to see that the reductionist argument is false,for the necklace is flexible. However,
let us compare necklaces made of pearls, of paper clips, and of four-inch metal-
lic objects, each necklace being of the same size. It is now immediately apparent

that the necklaces can be ranked in order of increasingly rigidity and that this ordering is related to the structural characteristics of the components.

We cannot derive the characteristics of the whole from those of the parts. But neither can we understand the characteristics of the whole without reference to the characteristics of the parts. Thus, in the case of a necklace, it cannot be made out of soft wax. The elements must have some degree of rigidity if the band is to be flexible. Moreover, the relationships of the characteristics and the sizes of the elements to the size of the system are important in determining the degree of flexibility of the system.

Furthermore, according to his own account of Galtung's position, if Waltz wished to be consistent with either of the confused positions he has taken on reductionism, he instead should argue that Galtung is deducing national behavior from international behavior; for by Waltz's inaccurate account of Galtung, it is the discrepancy between the sizes and powers of states that increases the level of harmony in the big states and decreases it in the small states. Of course, this is not actually a reduction either; for Galtung, who, whatever his political beliefs may be, is an excellent social theorist, knows how to distinguish between including the entire actor in his theory and including merely those attributes relevant to his macromodel. In short, Galtung's theory is a systems "theory."

In any event, why should we abjure reductionist theories? The closest we can come to an argument against reductionist theories in Waltz is his statement that, although they may work well in other areas, reductionist theories such as that of imperialism fail in international relations because "at other times and places quite different types of states were also imperialistic" (p. 32). If this is an argument that imperialist states must always be of the same type, Waltz gives no good reason for this conclusion. Both fat and thin, rich and poor husbands may beat their wives. They may do so for a variety of reasons. This would be no argument against a theory that linked the type of husband to the type of reason for the beating. Whether such relationships exist is a purely factual matter. For instance, the argument that wars or imperialist politics responded primarily to national needs rather than to international requirements would be a reductionist position as Waltz employs that concept. And yet many different types of states might respond that way for many different specific reasons: economic needs; population control; geographic access; regime maintenance; feelings of grandeur; and so forth. Similar types of states might not respond that way in the absence of these motives or in the presence of other constraints. A theory that differentiates types of states and then explains the imperialistic behavior of each in principle could be both correct and reductionist in Waltz's sense. For reasons expressed earlier, I believe that global theories, whether or not reductionist, have only limited application in the social sciences.

If Waltz's argument against reductionist theories is an implication that the qualities of states are unrelated to behavior in the macrosystem, Waltz's agreement with Galtung that the terms of trade in general run against the economically weaker states refutes it, for this has an observable impact on behavior. If it is an argument that different types of actors produce the same responses and that similar types of actors produce different responses and, therefore, that these differences cannot be encompassed within the framework of a theory, it suffers from confusion. Boulders, pebbles, and feathers will continue serenely on their inertial paths in a vacuum. But a feather will be blown about by the wind and a pebble will be blown about in a typhoon. A boulder will not be moved by either. All of this is consistent with a nonreductionist theory that explains these varying, and superficially contradictory, types of behavior. Whether such theories are available is again a factual matter.

Waltz may be right, although I doubt it, that reductionist theories (as he incorrectly defines them) will not work in international relations. What is objectionable, however, is his failure to distinguish between a reasoned argument and a Delphic pronunciamento.

Waltz asserts that when differences in the actor produce difference in the outcomes, one should search for systems statements rather than general statements (p. 33). I admit this leaves me somewhat confused. The laws of physics —for example, equal forces cancel each other—are general, but the actual results depend on the relative size of the forces. Moreover, the work done by an energy source will depend on the efficiency of the engine. On the other hand, the laws applying to planets and suns do not apply to electrons and protons. Theories and systems explanations should be transformable into each other if properly stated. In the absence of a theory, there is no systems explanation, and vice versa. What is true is that every theory has only limited applicability and that we must be able to distinguish between those things for which a theory provides an explanation and those for which it does not. Living systems do not obey the second law of thermodynamics. But then it does not apply to them, but only to a properly stated physical system in which they are embedded.

What is necessary in the social sciences is that we be particularly careful concerning the reified use of language—for instance, "mother" may refer to a social rather than a biological mother—that leads to overgeneralization, a failure to employ formulations that relate generalizations to boundary conditions, and/or the use of inapplicable assumptions of additive or independently determinable and general measures.

But perhaps I misinterpret Waltz. Perhaps, despite his advocacy of rigor, he is merely being loose when he talks of imperialist theories. Perhaps he is merely talking about generalizations (laws?). He does say: "If the same causes lead to different effects and the same effects follow from different causes, then constraints must be operating upon individual variables in ways that affect outcomes" (p. 33). Although somewhat turgidly stated, this position is sound. Thus, a state such as Fascist Italy may dare to invade other states such as Ethiopia for reasons of internal regime prestige when other states need it to constrain a hegemonial power (Nazi Germany), but may not risk such activity when they do not need it. And a state such as France may engage in imperialism to gain access to external riches when the English navy is relatively weak, but may not when it is strong.

However, if that is what Waltz means, he should have argued against overgeneralization rather than against reductionism. If reductionism is as he defines it—a concentration of causes at the national level—the causes of imperialism in the cited cases are reductionist; and external or systemic considerations affect only the calculus of risk. If, on the other hand, Waltz had wished to argue that theories or generalizations should be properly stated—for both hold only on the basis of specified assumptions or boundary or initial conditions— he has certainly found an obscure way to make that point.

In the process, Waltz has obscured the theoretical understanding of reductionism. For instance, a boundary effect is fundamentally different from a theoretical explanation. If the sun goes into nova, biological life will be destroyed. However, the incineration accounts only for the physical and chemical processes. It does not contribute to an explanation of biological behavior, but explains only its absence. Similarly, if an internal state process produces imperialism, an explanation of this act does not reduce international behavior to national behavior. It explains only a parametric condition of the international system—perhaps from the standpoint of a theory of national behavior—and can contribute to a theory of imperialism at the international system level only if it functions within a theory that employs international concepts. If we assert that one man punches another in the nose because he is angry, that is a psychological and not a sociological explanation. Only within a theory that explains why anger is elicited in different types of social situations or how a society of angry men behaves is a sociological explanation possible. Thus, explanations of imperialism that "concentrate causes" at the national level are neither reductionist nor international. But they might be correct.

The correct question is: Are the differences in states theoretically relevant with respect to a theory of imperialism at the international level? If they are not, then Waltz has no valid quarrel with Galtung. If, however, they are theoretically relevant, then Waltz faults Galtung for the wrong reason. Given Waltz's incorrect use of the concept of reductionism, Galtung's argument in this case would have been insufficiently reductionist; that is, it should have made more extensive reference to the "internal" characteristics of states.

The confusions concerning reductionism that affect Waltz's analysis stem, I believe, from his systematic failure in practice to understand the use of theoretical terms. I think that we can illustrate this by referring to one of Waltz's criticisms of my work. Waltz says (p. 62): "Kaplan declares that his systems deal with any states whatsoever, that at the systems level the particular identities of states are of no account." Waltz cites no reference for that assertion; but the only relevant statement in *System and Process* begins on the very first page of chapter 1 of *System and Process:*

> It is legitimate to demand that propositions be independent of labelling. The laws governing the relationships of heavenly bodies should apply regardless of the names of the stars. But one does not expect these laws to apply to heavenly bodies regardless of their weight, size, distance from each other, or presence of other heavenly bodies. In the same way, the propositions of international politics should apply to international actors regardless of the labelling of the actors, but not regardless of factors which differentiate actors in other ways (p. 3).

The reader will note that I refer not to nations but to "international actors." Furthermore, chapter 2 states that the "balance of power" system is not role differentiated and that the only actors are essential national actors. However, in the loose bipolar system, for instance, national actors do not appear at all. Instead, we have blocs, bloc members, uncommitted actors, and universal actors.

Although Waltz, elsewhere in his chapter, does quote authorities who refer to theoretical terms, a recognition of the difference between a theoretical term and a concrete real-world participant seems to be totally absent from his discussions of the theories he criticizes, almost as if different people had written the methodological and the critical sections of his essay. Waltz shows no understanding that, in the absence of theoretically relevant actor characteristics, no theoretical statements could be made or any initial conditions specified for the application of a theory. That is probably why he regards any mention of an actor characteristic as a form of reductionism and why he fails to distinguish between the method for determining the value of a characteristic and its function in a theory. This likely is why everything that is theoretically relevant is "lumped" together under the concept of "constraint." That is why he is unable to distinguish one form of international system from another and why he is forced to regard the field as one of anarchy. This is also why he uses the model of microeconomics while failing to understand that microeconoimc decisions can be understood only within the framework of a macroeconomic system. We need to look "inside" an actor only when the "internal" characteristic is linked to systemic behavior in a regular fashion. But this is not a reduction, for we bring into the explanation at a theoretical level only those elements that have systemic theoretical relevance.

AUXILIARY THEORIES

The term "theory" is often misused in the international relations literature, and there is much confusion over how theories may be formulated or validated. Let us see how these confusions become manifest in Waltz's discussion of Galtung. Later in the discussion of my own work, many relevant aspects of theory will be explicated.

Waltz lumps together all neocolonial theories under the heading "self-verifying theories." This precedes Waltz's discussion of Galtung, who, he says, accepts the neocolonialist definition of imperialism. Galtung, therefore, according to Waltz, has a theory "in which the traditional economic theory of imperialism has been amended in order to cover recent practices" (p. 26). This, Waltz tells us, is an auxiliary theory:

> Imre Lakatos uses the phrase "auxiliary theories" to describe theories that are devised "in the wake of facts" and that lack the power to anticipate other facts.... Suppose...that I want to maintain my theory substantially intact, even though the activity explained, and those who engage in it, change a good deal over time. To reach that end, I need to do two things: first, redefine the old word to cover the new activity and "second" revise the old theory in order to cover new elements. The evolution of theories about imperialism nicely illustrates both procedures (p. 25).

Waltz then argues that Galtung's theory is an effort to "sav[e] Lenin's theory."

For reasons that will be explained shortly, I would be willing to accept an auxiliary theory as an acceptable form of theorizing even if the distinguished philosopher of science Lakatos had argued against axuiliary theories. Even according to Waltz's inadequate account of an auxiliary theory, Galtung's theory is not an auxiliary theory. However, since Waltz uses Lakatos and Kuhn indiscriminately, without giving any weight to the incompatibility of their positions, I think it advisable at least to examine what Lakatos said. On one of the two pages cited by Waltz, I find the following splendid sentence, which Lakatos places entirely in italics: *"Mature science consists of research programmes in which not only novel facts but, in an important sense, also novel auxiliary theories, are anticipated; mature science—unlike pedestrian trial-and-error—has 'heu-*

ristic power' " (1970, p. 175). Thus we see that Lakatos views auxiliary theories as a legitimate component of science.

In any event, according to Waltz's account of Galtung's position, Galtung's theory is not an auxiliary theory as Waltz uses that term. According to Waltz, in addition to a revision of a definition, the new theory must "revise the old theory in order to cover new elements" (p. 25). I take it that the words "revise" and "cover new elements" necessarily imply that the old theory is incorporated in the new theory, albeit perhaps with major modifications, as, for instance, Newton's theories of mechanics might be regarded as an approximation of Einstein's theory within solar distances or as the theory of the perfect market might be regarded as a special asymptotic case within Edward Chamberlin's (1948) theory of imperfect competition.[2] As Waltz presents Galtung, the latter does not incorporate a significant number of the elements of the theories of Lenin or Hobson; he primarily employs the same term. It is as if Waltz had argued that behaviorist theories of neurosis were attempts to "save" Freud's theory because they employed the concept and because they argued that those who were maladapted became neurotic.

But perhaps I misinterpret Waltz's intention. Perhaps he is arguing not against auxiliary theories but against any type of theory that is constructed in the "wake of the facts." Perhaps he just happened carelessly to misread a sentence in Lakatos that referred to auxiliary theories when Waltz was interested really in the general problem of theories that "follow in the wake of the facts." Let me show briefly, with respect to a mundane problem, what is wrong with this position. Suppose one has a stereophonic system. An expert now comes in and gives an account of how it operates and the conditions under which it does so, as completely as he is able to, and concludes that the music played by the system will be of a certain quality. Now suppose that instead of good music the set begins making odd sounds during the music although all the components upon examination are in exactly the condition the expert said they should be. The expert then says that the disturbance probably is caused by a new invention, the citizens' band radio. His explanation of how the system functions is now enlarged to include the interference effect of a nearby CB. Although this is not a theory in the strict scientific sense, it is an explanation of a kind involving at least a theoretical sketch—and it is a thoroughly legitimate technique. Moreover, physical theory has been revised on this basis many times, even when the revision has no further power to produce new predictions. Thus, this position of Waltz's is also wrong. Shortly, we shall see that this is the case with respect to a genuine theoretical problem in physical science: Galileo's problem.

Perhaps I am too hard on Waltz. Perhaps there is a passage in Lakatos, even if not used by Waltz, that would justify his misinterpretation. Lakatos does attack research programs that "unfailingly devise their actual auxiliary theories in the wake of facts without, at the same time, anticipating others" (p. 196). But why does he do so? We can find out if we go to the pages cited by Waltz. According to Lakatos, theories that are constructed in the wake of the facts are not "progressive" or "heuristic." A theory that is progressive or heuristic must have an excess empirical content over its predecessor; "that is, it will predict some novel, hitherto unexpected fact." Lakatos specifies what he means by a novel fact (f. 2, p. 118). He says that if one knows that a particular swan is white the statement that all swans are white represents no progress because it leads only to the discovery of similar facts. "A *new* fact must be improbable or even impossible in the light of previous knowledge." The statement "Some swans are black" would clearly meet this criterion if we had only observed white swans previously. A theory that predicted the existence of black swans thus would meet the Lakatos test. If it were proper to regard imperialism as a situation in which deliberate behavior by strong powers produces the exploitation of weak powers, then a theory that predicted the exploitation of weak powers by strong powers without deliberate actions on their part would be a theory that predicted a novel event. Yet this is the very feature of Galtung's theory that Waltz ridicules: "And a country is called imperialist by virtue of its attributes and aside from the acts it commits" (p. 27). However inadequate a rendering of Galtung this is, if accurate, it would establish Galtung's theory as progressive or heuristic according to Lakatos's criteria.

The stress by Lakatos on what may even seem impossible is perhaps best understood within the framework of the history of science. In 1772 the French Academy of Science, which included such famous men as Lavoisier and Berthollet, concluded that meteors did not exist because the falling of stones from the air is physically impossible. This emphasis by Lakatos is clarified by his comments (pp. 117ff.) on Karl Popper's position that a theory may be saved with the help of "auxiliary hypotheses" only if they "satisfy certain well-defined conditions." Here Popper is using the well-known distinction which rules out "*ad hoc* hypotheses," "mere linguistic devices," or "conventionalist stratagems." Then, as Lakatos points out, what is being tested is not an auxiliary hypothesis but a theory with its auxiliary hypotheses, initial conditions, and so forth, "especially together with its predecessors that we may see by what sort of *change* it was brought about. Then, of course, what we appraise is a *series of theories* rather than isolated *theories*." Then Lakatos says: "Let us say that such a series of theories is *theoretically progressive (or 'constitutes a theoretically progressive problem shift')* if each new theory has some excess empirical content over its predecessor, that is, if it predicts some novel, hitherto unexpected fact" (p. 118). Lakatos then goes on to say that a theory is also empirically

progressive if it does in fact lead to the "actual discovery of [that] *new fact*."
By this standard, Galtung's theory does predict a new set of facts, namely, the
relationship between the internal disequilibrium in the smaller states and the
terms of trade. It is also in this sense a theory rather than a reformulation of
Hobson's or Lenin's theories that employs auxiliary hypotheses.

We might find more authority for Waltz's interpretation of Lakatos on a
page he does not cite, page 187. According to Lakatos, "the sophisticated fal-
sificationist allows *any* part of the body of science to be replaced *but* only on
the condition that it is replaced in a 'progressive' way, so that the replacement
successfully anticipates novel facts." In this sentence, however, Lakatos again
is referring to the research program as distinguished from the theory. Thus, for
instance, if Galtung's position were that Hobson's or Lenin's theory of imperialism was incorrect, he might develop a research program designed to investigate
the relationships between large and small states with respect to the terms of
trade. In this case, there would be a novel fact: the impact upon the internal system of the small state that results from the unintended action of the large state.
This meets Lakatos's criterion for sophisticated falsification. It also establishes
Galtung's theory as a full and not auxiliary theory.

If, however, Lakatos really means what he appears to say here, he would
in fact—and incorrectly, in my opinion—rule out of account valid theories.

What does Lakatos mean by a new fact: something that was unknown before or something that is recategorized by a reformulated theory and brought
within the framework of an explanation that did not previously include it? Is he
arguing against the use of auxiliary hypotheses that respond to new categoriza-
tions without giving rise to additional predictions, or is his usage more restricted?
Because Lakatos is writing on the philosophy of physical science for philosophers of science, these distinctions become relatively trivial. However, let me
use an analogy from physical science to show that an interpretation of Lakatos
which requires not merely recategorization of known events but the incorpora-
tion of things never before observed is inconsistent with scientific procedure.
Suppose that before he developed his theories, Galileo had observed that bodies
fell toward earth with what seemed to be equal rates of speed. Suppose that
someone mentioned to Galileo that feathers were carried by the wind and that
Galileo then devised a new formulation "in the wake of these facts" by stating
that he was talking only about those cases in which the effects of atmospheric
friction were negligible. This would be a valid extension, but it is a trivial
distinction for physical scientists because they are usually possessed of highly
articulated theories that, in addition to recategorizing seemingly discordant
"facts," permit a wide range of new predictions. Thus, for instance, while the
physical scientist can use Newton's theory to predict only the general type of

movement of a feather, he can also use it to predict the specific path of a projectile. The matter is by no means so trivial in the area of the social sciences, where theories, or more properly theory sketches, have a much lower degree of articulation and where, for the most part, we are in the pre-Galilean condition.

Perhaps Lakatos's formulation is merely his own manner of objecting to the procedures whereby theories are added to in ad hoc fashion rather than reformulated. In this case, the reformulated theory does predict a novel event: the rise of a feather in the wind or even the rise of a much heavier object in a high enough wind. In this sense, it could be distinguished from Copernican theory, which Lakatos calls ad hoc because it merely redescribes phenomena noted by Ptolemaic theory without adding anything. This is a well-known position that has been argued ever since Ockham's razor. More recently, it has been argued on the grounds of probability theory by Rudolf Carnap (1962) and Hans Reichenbach (1949). Popper accepts simpler hypotheses as better because they are more easily refuted; that is, they exclude more states of affairs than more complex hypotheses. Others have argued for this position on qualitative or methodological grounds. Lakatos's footnote to the case of "All swans are white" would seem to reinforce this point of view. In this usage, the argument is methodological.

Furthermore, what is simple depends upon knowledge of and statement of a case. A brief example will suffice to illustrate this. We are well aware that most conspiracy theories are produced by paranoidal minds. However, there may be the case of a person against whom there is a conspiracy, perhaps to get control of his wealth, and then his assertions may well seem to mimic the symptoms of the classic paranoid. Only when we are in possession of independent additional evidence concerning the conspiracy can we recognize that the conspiracy theory is the simpler theory. Only after reconstruction based on the whole pattern of evidence can it be said to be not merely "in the wake of facts" in this interpretation of those words. Yet it may have nothing to offer in addition to the "facts" that are known.

Fortunately for us, we do not have to evaluate Lakatos to determine which position is actually his. No interpretation of Lakatos—whether with respect to theories, auxiliary theories, or progressive theories—will make sense out of Waltz's criticism of Galtung, who comes out unscathed on all counts.

If Waltz had had a better appreciation of the position Lakatos in fact takes, he would have been able to see the similarities between Lakatos's position and mine. Although *System and Process* was written long before Lakatos developed his present position, and although in my more recent writings I have stated the problems somewhat differently from the way he does, the similarities are clearly much greater than the differences. The preface and chapter 1 state what Lakatos would consider the research program: the search for regularities with respect to structure and behavior in the international system, including the specifications of variables and of other heuristic devices at a highly general level. Chapter 2 is more specific concerning the research program as it distinguishes among alternative international systems and offers at least initial hypotheses to be tested. Chapter 3 states a program for considering differences among states as a further factor in engineering the models more closely to the complexity of reality. Part II is a research program at a high level of generality, that is , one that is not yet specified in a way that would permit concrete research, but that indicates the importance of processes within systems. Parts III and IV are similar with respect to problems of values and strategy. The research program, including partial theory sketches, paved the way for comparative historical research—as in the papers by Winfried Franke (1968) and Chi Hsi-cheng (1968) on the Italian city-state and the Chinese warlord systems, respectively—and the computer program; and these may permit reformulation of the theory sketches.

DEFINITIONS

Are definitions arbitrary or natural? What makes one definition better or more appropriate than another? Again, there is much confusion in the literature. We shall see here how this confusion invalidates Waltz's discussion of Galtung. Later we shall see how it affects his discussion of my theories.

I share with Waltz his discomfort with Galtung's use of the term "imperialism." However, although I believe that a strong argument can be made against Galtung's use, Waltz has chosen the wrong argument. Among other things, it is not accurate in terms of Waltz's own presentation of Galtung's position to state that Galtung calls "a country...imperialist by virtue of its attributes and aside from the acts it commits." Galtung's position, as Waltz himself has stated it, is that a country's economic size by virtue of its relationship to the size of some other country leads it to behave in a way that has the unintentional consequence of worsening the other country's terms of trade and therefore its internal harmony. Evidently Waltz does not even read Waltz accurately or consistently, as we have seen previously in his haphazard use of his own definition of "reductionism."

Waltz does note a difficulty in Galtung's position: "Thus Galtung can say about Japan's role in Southeast Asia that 'there is no doubt as to the economic imperialism, but there is neither political, nor military, nor communication, nor cultural ascendency.' Imperialism, perfected, employs no military force whatsoever, neither direct force nor threat of violence" (p. 27). This is the correct focus, but before we can make that claim we must know why it is such; and we cannot learn that from Waltz.

I shall attempt to elucidate the problem in Galtung's use of "imperialism." Is the phenomenon he is describing sufficiently like that talked about by Hobson, Lenin, and other writers for the use of the same descriptive term? I employ a stipulated artificial example to elucidate the issue. A student of sociology studies a number of societies. He finds in all of them a process by means of which young people acquire the standards of adults. In all of them, he finds that this process is produced by punishment. He now defines socialization as a process by means of which adults inculcate acceptance of their norms by young people through punishment. Ten years later another researcher comes on the scene who discovers societies in which apparently the same process occurs but the result is induced by rewards. He now retains the term "socialization" but accommodates the new observation by expanding the definition to include "punishment or rewards." Ten years later another researcher comes on the scene who discovers a society in which the young acquire the norms of the old but neither punishment nor reward is employed. Instead, the process is one in which autonomous emulation occurs. He now restates the definition: "Socialization is a process by means of which young people accept the norms of older people because of punishment or reward or autonomous emulation." I find it difficult to believe that any sociologist would object to this broadening of the definition or that there exists any defensible standard in the philosophy of science that excludes it. In this case, the definition points to a metatheory—that is, the process by means of which socialization is produced—that is similar for all the examples.

Certainly Lenin and Hobson were aware that the forms of imperialism they studied were not universal. In fact, Lenin specifically restricts his account to monopoly capitalism. Galtung's structural theory seems less adapted to justifying either Hobson's or Lenin's theories than to asserting that in any world in which there are large (or, more properly, strong) states and small (or, more properly, weak) states, the interests of the stronger states will have untoward consequences for the weaker states. Moreover, his assertion of a "terms of trade" argument occurs at a level of analyticity and abstraction different from that in the former statement. The former statement is propositional. The latter statement could possibly be theoretical, but it is a specific theory that has relevance to a particular type of social and economic system. Because Waltz does not make this distinction, it is impossible to determine how his criticisms apply to Galtung's position.

Let us move to a constructed example where a definition does not point to similar processes in all cases. Consider the subject of prosperity. Suppose that a study of eighteenth-century Holland shows that its prosperity was related to the hard work and commercial acuity of its solid burghers. Suppose another study shows that the prosperity of nineteenth-century England was produced by the inventiveness and organizational factors that constituted the Industrial Revolution. Suppose a contemporary study of Saudi Arabia or Kuwait shows that its prosperity is primarily the result of its location on a rich bed of oil. In this case, all three societies are prosperous, but the explanation of prosperity in the third example is radically different from the first two. In this case, the phenomenon of prosperity does not seem to imply a common metatheory.

Let us now consider those cases in which a theory is "engineered" to different boundary conditions. Consider the case of a feather floating in a breeze, in which we employ the Newtonian explanation while modifying only parameters and initial conditions.

Which of these examples elucidates what Galtung is doing? Does Galtung have a definition of imperialism that involves the exploitation of the weak by the strong? Does he have a structural theory that applies to all cases of imperialism resulting from the greater force of large powers in a world of large and small powers? Does he try to find explanations for particular cases of imperialism that are the same for all cases or that vary for particular types of imperialism; that is, does imperialism, for instance, involve the export of capital in the nineteenth century and the terms of trade in the twentieth century? Furthermore, does Galtung link his theory to a programmatic position in a fashion so intimate that they cannot be separated, or is this a different phase of his analysis? Even if Galtung had conflated theory and prescription—and Waltz asserts only that such theories "also contain, *at least implicitly* [italics added], the wider assertion that there are no good international political reasons for the conflict and the warring of states" (p. 32)—the critic for the sake of clarity should keep them separate. We cannot determine from Waltz either what Galtung has said or to which of the previous categories his theory belongs. Therefore, we must consider the problem of formulating definitions.

It is now generally accepted that definitions are not unitary or, in Wittgenstein's sense, that they constitute a family of cases. I will not bother the reader with a reference to the publication in which I show that even Wittgenstein's conception is too narrow, for that is not relevant here. To answer the question whether a particular set of uses falls within a family of cases, we must employ a praxical mode of argumentation. One way of doing this is to construct a stipulated example. Suppose one nation were to conquer another, hold it in subjugation, and improve its standard of living, literacy, freedom of occupational and artistic choice, and local self-government. Would we deny that this is a case of imperialism because it is for the benefit of the subject population? I doubt that most of us would, although I do not wish to attempt a conclusive answer on this point. If by a number of examples of this kind we could establish that position, we could then show that exploitation, however defined, is not part of the definition of imperialism, although, in fact, it may turn out to be the case that all imperialists exploit.

My own belief is that rule over an external, or foreign, population is the common core of the concept of imperialism and that relations that are too far removed from this cannot be called imperialism without creating considerable semantic confusion. Again, I do not wish to attempt to establish the validity of my particular answer here, but only to indicate the methodology of arriving at an answer. Neither do I want to deny that in some cases a usage far removed from an older use may be legitimized if it permits the development of intellectual tools that are far more extensive. In any event, these are among the questions that have to be asked.

In addition to the prior difficulties in Waltz's treatment of definitional problems, he uses evidence against Galtung's definition in a way that is inconsistent with his own account of it. If Galtung's theory, as Waltz claims, really says that the phenomenon of imperialism can be identified only by the impoverishment of weaker states, how can Waltz possibly falsify such a "theory" by citing evidence? Anything that did not fit that definition would not be imperialism; yet Waltz claims he uses evidence to refute Galtung.

Waltz has elsewhere stated correctly that whether something is evidence depends upon the statement of the theory that is being tested. Yet, when he cites evidence against Galtung, he does not seem to understand his own earlier point. Moreover, the form in which he states his evidence is in fact irrelevant with respect to Galtung's theory, for it is stated in highly general terms not strictly related to Galtung's definition of imperialism and the structural aspects of the world to which his propositions are related. If someone had sampled monastic orders to refute the assertion that the poor tend to be ill-educated, he could hardly have done a more haphazard job than Waltz.

I happen to believe that Waltz is right in arguing that Galtung's use of "imperialism" is incorrect; but I would never believe this on the basis of the framework of argumentation employed by Waltz. Moreover, as a matter of fact, rich countries often self-consciously behave at a governmental level in ways that disregard and are injurious to the interests of poorer countries, although I think that the prescriptions of most of the third-world countries for a solution to this problem would be extremely injurious. I believe that the problem is in fact very real and that there is a responsibility to cope with it. In saying this, I do not mean that many third-world nations are not much better off than they were in the past. I do mean that they are confronted with problems that arise from their relationships within the international system and that it may be possible to cope with these problems in responsible ways if we at least admit their existence. I deplore as much as Waltz does the occasions on which Galtung ascribes the richness of the rich countries to exploitation of the poor, but I do not think that Galtung's rhetorical baggage should lead us to disregard the existence of a genuine problem.

POSSIBLE FAULTS IN GALTUNG

If we had a proper understanding of theories and definitions, we would be in a better position to critique Galtung's theories than was Waltz. Let us see how such a critique might run on the basis of the evidence Waltz presents. Subsequently I shall critique Galtung's position on the basis of his own presentation, for Waltz, like so many critics, is careless in presenting the positions he criticizes as well as incorrect in his discussions of the problems of theory.

The essence of Galtung's position, from Waltz's account of it, seems to be that the structural relations of the rich and poor countries produce a condition in which the poor countries do less well than the rich countries. Waltz does not dispute this conclusion but claims only that "Galtung has apparently drawn unwarranted conclusions from the long-lasting and *quite steady tendency* [italics added] of the terms of trade to move against primary products and in favor of manufactured goods" (p. 27). His only argument here is that perhaps Galtung's theory is not unreservedly true, that the trends "are not the same for all products nor do they last indefinitely." And he points out how well the underdeveloped Arab nations have been doing with oil. The most, however, that one can charge Galtung with on this basis is that he has not specified the conditions under which exceptions may occur. Such specification, particularly after adequate criticism, is one of the ways in which theories are developed and improved. As a general statement, however, although not a universally true one—and Waltz himself asserts that there are no strict laws in the social sciences—Galtung's position is, by Waltz's own statements and in terms of Waltz's position with respect to the status of laws, reasonably adequate. It is not as detailed or qualified as Waltz would desire, but the extent to which this is required depends upon one's research purpose. Galtung's position, as presented by Waltz, would be even stronger if he had analyzed the respective capabilities of large industrial states and of small states dependent upon particular commodity exports to maintain their domestic programs in periods in which there are rapid fluctuations in the terms of trade. Even though no universal statement is correct and although the states of western Europe have been particularly subject to distrubances flowing from the energy crisis, on the whole the peripheral and small states have suffered much more severely from these fluctuations than have the developed states.

I believe that a longer argument that would divert us here would show that Galtung has not integrated the terms-of-trade argument into his theory of structure. Although the terms-of-trade argument—that the terms of trade may go against Periphery nations—is correct in general, it is at least plausible that this is not produced by the structural situation he discusses.

As Galtung is presented by Waltz, the most we can infer concerning his position is that the disrepancy in size between large and small states in the international system increases disharmony in small national systems. Neither the degree of disharmony nor the conditions under which it can occur can be inferred from such a proposition, for that type of inference can be made only within the framework of an application of a theory in which.parameter conditions and starting states are taken into reasonable account. For instance, when Franke (1968) uses my "balance of power" theory to investigate the Italian city-state system, he is applying that theory to the real world. Because the theory—or more properly, theory sketch—is an equilibrium model that is related to boundary conditions, we can show that the stability of the first phase of the Italian system (which is presented in more detail later) was produced more by nonsytemic factors such as institutional or leadership discontinuities within cities and logistic constraints than by the features of the international system. If Galtung in fact presents his theory as one that makes direct statements about the concrete real world—as contrasted with statements that hold only under specified boundary conditions—this is not made evident by Waltz's presentation of his position. Nor is there even any indication in Waltz's discussion of Galtung that this distinction is of importance is discussing what Galtung is saying. It may be this ease with which Waltz slides from theoretical statements to direct statements about the real world—a distinction that at some points in his article he seems to understand and at other points to be utterly confused about—that may account for some of his misinterpretations.

GALTUNG ON GALTUNG

I believe that we have clarified some of the major problems of theory formation in discussing Waltz's mistaken criticism of Galtung. However, Galtung's theory remains a mystery, and we must turn to Galtung to clarify this mystery. Galtung says: "Imperialism will be conceived of as a dominance relation between collectivities, particularly between nations...which cuts across nations, basing itself on a bridgehead which the center in the Center nation establishes in the center of the Periphery nation, for the joint benefit of both [centers] (p. 81). Galtung warns that imperialism should not be confused with other methods for achieving domination, such as military occupation or subversion, although dominance may occur in those activities. Galtung uses the analogy between smallpox, which is a specific form of disease, and a theory of epidemic diseases. Thus, there are various kinds of imperialism, all of which, according to Galtung, possess the structural characteristics he cites. We now see that Galtung has stated the elements of a system, that his account of contemporary imperialism is not a general statement, and that nothing in his account at either level justifies Lenin's theory.

If we were to characterize Galtung's theory as reductionist, we would be more inclined to do so on the basis of his differentiation of center and periphery within the nation rather than his use of harmony or disharmony as a variable. However, this would be faulty also, for Galtung's macrosystem is dependent upon this degree of differentiation within nations for its analysis. When football coaches concoct their strategies for games, their study of the interaction between the two teams is dependent upon the tasks that elements of each team have with respect to elements of the other team. This is not reductionist, except as Waltz transforms his own inadequate definition in practice; it is simply more detailed than a more general account of football for the lay public might be. The contest is not reduced to the behaviors of the individual elements or actors, or even to their individual interrelationships within teams. The analysis is given its meaning and can be carried out only within the context of the notion of team-against-team play. (This point is covered at greater length in the chapter on systems analysis.)

Waltz charges: "Rather than being a hard-to-unravel set of activities, imperialism [as Galtung presents it] becomes an easily seen condition: the increase of the gap in living conditions between harmonious rich countries and disharmonious poor ones" (p. 27). Waltz refers to page 89 in Galtung for this interpretation. On page 89 Galtung does say: "In short, we see vertical integration as the major source of the inequality of this world, whether it takes the form of looting, of highly unequal exchange, or of highly differentiated spinoff effects due to processing gaps." The reader might think that this validates Waltz's comment. But all that Galtung is saying is that imperialism is a major cause of inequality. That is a proposition, not a definition. Moreover, Galtung says in the very next sentence: "But we can also imagine a fourth phase of exploitation, where the modern King Midas becomes a victim of his own greed and turns his environment into muck rather than gold.... This may, in fact, place the less developed countries in a more favorable position...." In either event, the gap in living standards is, according to Galtung, the product of imperialism, not the sign of it. It is genuinely subject to evidentiary analysis.

According to Waltz, Galtung defines structure in such a way that "behavior and function disappear; and a country is called imperialist by virtue of its attributes and aside from the acts it commits" (pp. 26-27). We have seen from our socialization example that it is possible to produce a result without intending to produce it. However, that is not in fact Galtung's position. Galtung provides us with an actual mechanism that produces his specified consequences: relations between the center of the Center country and the center of the Periphery country as affected by the terms of trade. In this case, even if the result were unintentional, it would not be unproduced.

The reader will remember that Galtung distinguishes between the theory of epidemic disease and the account of a particular disease. The general theory distinguishes between the centers of Center and Periphery countries and their relationships. The more specific account asserts the linkage of the terms of trade to this relationship.

Thus, Galtung has a definition at the general level, a general explanation at the general level, a more specific theory at the level of individual imperialisms, and possibly testable hypotheses; for one must examine the real world to find out whether the centers of the dominating and dominated nations are connected in the way he suggests and whether this does, in fact, produce asymmetries in favor of the dominating nation. This is both good systems analysis and good scientific methodology.

Waltz argues further that theories such as Galtung's are part of an effort "to save Lenin's thesis" (p. 25). And its "logic...is best seen in Galtung's essay" (p. 30). Let us turn to the record and then link this to the previous discussion.

Is Galtung trying to save Lenin's theory, as Waltz states? On page 89 (the first page in Galtung's article), he says: "Our view is not reductionist in the traditional sense pursued in Marxist-Leninist theory, which conceives of imperialism as an economic relationship under private capitalism...and which bases the theory of dominance on a theory of imperialism. According to this view [that Galtung has rejected in the prior paragraph], imperialism and dominance will fall like dominoes when the capitalistic conditions for economic imperialism no longer obtain." Galtung says more specifically: "Belief in a simple causal chain is dangerous because it is accompanied by the belief that imperialism can be dispensed with forever if the primary element in the chain is abolished, e.g., private capitalism" (p. 99). I hardly believe that Lenin or the current Soviet Union would praise Galtung for "saving" their theory of imperialism in this fashion.

The core of Galtung's argument is that there is a harmony of interest between the centers of Center and Periphery nations, even though the relationship on the whole is beneficial to Center nations and non-beneficial to Periphery nations. Clearly, this assertion is partly true, at least in terms of the relationships among the centers. If Galtung were to have argued that under most conditions the strong nations gain more from the relationship than the weaker and that under some conditions the weaker is injured, I believe that the data might support it.

When, however, Galtung asserts that "vertical interaction [is] the major source of the inequality of this world," he certainly is subject to Waltz's objection that he has provided no compelling reason for believing this. Just as it is a shame that Galtung's ideological stance has led him beyond what his theory or evidence could be expected to produce, it is a shame that Waltz, by conflating the problems of definition, theory construction, and methodology with factual issues, has succeeded in confusing every issue. There is a key issue of theory construction in Galtung: his failure to integrate his terms-of-trade argument into his general structural argument. There is a key factual issue connected with Galtung's terms-of-trade argument. And there is a key problem of definition. All, however, differ from Waltz's confused account of them.

AN EVALUATION OF GALTUNG

Apart from the fact that the only substantial evidence Galtung produces to link the terms of trade to relations between centers is that trade is organized between the centers, he has neglected to inquire whether the general worsening of the terms of trade for commodity-exporting nations is part of a much more general phenomenon according to which as industrialization progresses the price of labor rises more in urban areas than in rural areas. If he had inquired into this process, he would have noted that it is a general phenomenon connected with industrialization and that it affects relations even within industrialized nations. Historically, in countries such as Britain, Japan, and the United States, agricultural prosperity is the substratum that permits industrial development. As industrialization develops momentum, however, industrial and urban labor becomes more valuable than agricultural labor and industrial products become more valuable than agricultural products. This process is not one in which value is drained from the periphery but rather one in which value begins to increase geometrically in the industrialized sphere while increasing more slowly at the periphery. Prior to the onset of industrialization, labor is cheap and servants are plentiful. As it progresses, labor becomes expensive and machines become relatively cheap. However, primary good become relatively even cheaper. Thus the process is one of general enrichment, and it is notable in those third-world areas that are developing industrially: South Korea, Taiwan, Singapore, Malaysia, Brazil, Iran, and so forth. The hope for the Periphery countries is that they will be drawn more fully into this process. Their major problems arise from two factors: their internal failure to utilize wealth and human resources to create national economic progress, and their vulnerability to rapid fluctuations in the terms of trade. If Waltz had noted this in a coherent manner, he would have been able to avoid his confused and inappropriate criticisms of Galtung and to have exposed the central difficulty in Galtung's theoretical structure.

Thus, if we are to criticize Galtung, we would not criticize his choice of a structural theory. It is a useful and good theory. His recognition of the role of the factors that support dominance—military, political, economic, social, communication, and so forth—is a useful corrective to those in large countries who are unaware of how their impact upon the world produces changes that produce concomitant irritations and perhaps even social and psychological costs for others. My major quarrel with Galtung at the theoretical level is with his definition of imperialism; for I think it conflates a number of disparate phenomena and carries connotations that are unjustifiable in terms of the theoretical gain that is achieved. A more complex view of economic and political interrelationships could have been combined with the concept of international domination to achieve every one of Galtung's legitimate scientific aims without the use of a term such as imperialism, which carries so many misleading connotations.

Furthermore, Galtung does not inform us what distinguishes a Center nation from a Periphery nation. Was Rome a Center nation before it conquered Latium? Were only the results of Rome's conquests and not the conquests themselves imperialistic activity? And, if Galtung's theory is correct, how do we explain the rise of Periphery nations to Center status and their domination over the Center nations that previously dominated them? Are Macedonia, Sumeria, and the United States examples of the latter? Thus, at best, Galtung's "theory" can have reference only to a phase of more complicated relationships that it does little to explain; and at worst it is inadequate as an explanation even for an individual phase.

WALTZ ON WALTZ

A SYSTEM OF ANARCHY

Before continuing this critique of critiques, it will be useful to clarify Waltz's conception of the differences between his position and mine.

According to Waltz: "Kaplan perpetuates the perennial misconceptions about balance-of-power theory and makes it harder than ever to see that in international politics balance of power is simply a theory about the outcome of units' behavior under conditions of anarchy" (p. 63). Waltz regards balance-of-power theory as a theory universally applicable to all international systems. According to him such theory makes assumptions about "the interests and motives of states, rather than explaining them. What it does explain are the constraints that operate upon all states. To understand how motives and constraints combine to form policy, one would have to add the missing factor—the characteristics of the states themselves. To add the missing factor would take us beyond the realm of international-relations theory" (p. 41).

Waltz's initial assumptions are that states are "unitary actors who, at a minimum, seek their own preservation and, at a maximum, drive for universal domination" (p. 36). They may do this by alliances or by increases in internal strength, according to Waltz. He thinks that he can derive all necessary statements about balancing or the recurrent formation of a balance of power from this principle. And he identifies the system as a system of anarchy in which self-help is the basic principle.

Waltz defines a self-help system as "one in which those who do not help themselves or who do so less effectively than others, or fail to prosper, will lay themselves open to dangers, will suffer. Fear of such unwanted consequences stimulates states to behave in ways that tend toward the creation of balances of power" (pp. 39-40). In the first place, there is a sense in which every system is a self-help system. Even a slave-master system is a self-help system in certain respects, for if a slave does not behave in a way that maintains his relationship with the master, he will be injured. This is the reason why one of the most distinguished writers in the discipline referred to the balance-of-power principle as a universal principle that applies to all social systems. Of course, in this sense it tells us nothing about any system except that, if individuals or actors or organizations behave in ways adapted to maintaining a system, it will be maintained; otherwise it will not. They may accomplish this by anything that works, including cooperation with others, self-improvement measures, and so forth. This is a tautology in which we can discover the effective principle only from what works. Moreover, because it does not function within a theory, it is viciously empty.

The only advantage to Waltz in specifying a system of anarchy when he talks of a self-help systems—by which I hope he means the absence of a political subsystem rather than anarchy in a literal sense—is that he excludes all social systems in which there are political subsystems and therefore appears to be making a statement that is about international relations rather than about domestic systems. And he can appear to be talking about alliances and wars rather than about presidents, kings, citizens, and slaves. However, this position is still entirely open, as it does not give us any idea of what the appropriate forms of behavior should be, given the other elements of the system. Waltz talks vaguely only of external constraints. Clearly, in master-slave systems, slaves do not want to become too "uppity." But in certain types of international systems—for example, gunboat diplomacy in the nineteenth century—it also behooves small states not to get too uppity. Until we have some notion of what type of behavior produces what kind of response and why, we do not have a structured theory. Thus, when Waltz says that his analysis takes us as far as international relations theory can go, short of looking inside the actors, it has in fact taken us nowhere.

A properly stated theory sketch will take us considerably further than Waltz has gone, and I shall show this when I discuss Waltz on Kaplan. Such a theory sketch will distinguish the conditions under which it holds and the conditions under which its conclusions will be modified. It will also distinguish the conditions under which it is irrelevant. But it is best to discuss this when I discuss a genuine theory sketch, for then I can demonstrate this in practice.

Furthermore, Waltz has gotten into difficulty on several grounds. He appears to have taken a reductionist position against his own advice, for whether a state maximizes or not can be discovered only by looking inside the actor as well as at the external constraints. In the absence of a theory, moreover, he has no grounds for distinguishing between theoretically relevant actor characteristics and anything whatsoever. Second, if he really identifies self-help with external gain, he does at last have a position and not a tautology. However, in this case it is false, as I demonstrate when I discuss Riker's criticism (which Waltz misunderstands while praising it) of my work. I will show that maximizing behavior is counterproductive in international systems. This kind of demonstration is precisely what theory is about, and to lump it all under "constraints" or to call it "anarchy" is in fact to reject theory.

RATIONALITY

Many theories of political behavior, including theories of international politics, utilize rational models. Waltz, who misunderstands the role of rationality in theories, believes that he can dispense with the concept of rationality. He says that his "theory requires no assumptions of rationality or of constancy of will on the part of all of the actors. The theory says simply that if some do relatively well, others will emulate them or fall by the wayside" (p. 39). Here he is committing the very sin that he is accusing his opponents of: turning "an assumption into a truth" (p. 37). When John von Neumann introduced the assumption of rationality into game theory, he was not asserting that men were rational or that it would be rational to use minimax in a zero-sum game if one could predict a specific irrational choice of strategy by an opponent. He was investigating the conditions of rational choice in the absence of which it would not be possible to make a general analysis of the problem of choice in circumstances in which self-conscious opponents faced each other. In the same way, the assumption of rationality in economic theory is the basis for an analysis that permits us to understand what both rational and irrational economic behavior are. In the absence of a theory employing the concept of rationality, we would not be able to make general statements about economic behavior.

Although it is quite true, as Waltz says, that in a large market a certain amount of irrational behavior can be sustained without destruction of the system, this does not necessarily follow for a small market. Thus, in the absence of an appropriate theoretical analysis, we could not even investigate the question Waltz answers by fiat.

Although Waltz properly states the distinction between the theoretical assumption of rationality in economic theory and the factual state of affairs in the real world, he jumps illogically to the conclusion that we can simply dispense with the concept of rationality in formulating international relations theory. However, if we were to do this, we would not know how to distinguish one form of behavior from the other. We would be minus that general form of analysis that provides the matrix for our conclusions. If Waltz had genuinely understood this, the reason for the construction of equilibrium theories would not have escaped him.

Waltz, who distinguishes his approach from those that employ the assumption of rationality, argues that the latter (including mine) assume

> a necessary correspondence of motive and result...[and the inference of] rules for the actors from the observed results of their action. What has gone wrong can be made clear by drawing an economic analogy. In a purely competitive economy, everyone striving to make a profit drives the profit rate downward. Let the competition continue long enough under static conditions, and everyone's profit will be zero. To infer from that condition that everyone, or anyone, is seeking to minimize profit, and that the competitors must adopt that goal as a rule in order for the system to work would obviously be absurd (p. 39).

Apart from the gratuitous character of his example—surely we all know the history of such examples since Mandeville's fable of the bees—his use of it is inapt.

Let us now dissect the confusions inherent in Waltz's use of his examples. First, he has committed an elementary logical fallacy. Even a valid demonstration that individually rational behavior was collectively irrational in a particular case does not imply that this is true in all systems. Second, his own example would not be valid for anything unless there were an economic theory within which it was derivable. However, he has failed to note either that his assertions about the character of theory in international relations are false or that he has no right to use his example against theories employing the assumption of rationality, for the cases are apposite. Third, he has failed to note that he is talking about the average rate of profit and not the profit of any particular entrepreneur for that model within which his example does hold. I will not note the host of additional assumptions of a theoretical character that are required for his example to work, for this is sufficient.

In fact, Waltz's example is not one of individual rationality, producing collective irrationality, for in a sufficiently careful statement it will turn out to be both individually and collectively rational. However, let me distinguish the two cases—individual rationality and collective rationality, and individual rationality and collective irrationality—by means of examples I put into the literature in 1960 in a controversy with the philosopher J.C.C. Smart over the proper form of ethical behavior. Consider a community of ethical altruists in a period of water shortage such as New York City faced in the 1950s. The mayor asks all citizens to take baths rather than showers to save water. However, most citizens love showers and detest baths. By taking a shower, each will deprive his fellow citizens of less than a drop of water apiece—a not noticeable amount. And, as showers are taken in privacy, no violation of the request will set a bad example. Therefore, most take showers and water becomes short for critical needs. In this example—and it is a strong one, because even altruism does not negate it—individual rationality produces collective irrationality; and only a moral rule can prevent this type of outcome in this type of situation.

Consider, however, a community of three individuals under conditions of water shortage. Here altruism—and self-interest as well—will lead each to conserve, for the direct and immediate character of the relationship between use and shortage makes conservation both individually and collectively rational. One important function of theory in the social sciences is to link behavior to systemic conditions. In these cases, we are not looking inside the actors, except in that minimal sense required for any statement, but are deriving our conclusions from explanations related to the differences in the systems: in this case the small number of actors is sufficient to produce the difference.

This latter system, in which individual and collective rationality coincide, is one in which the actors have a definite incentive to observe those conditions of choice that make for equilibrium of the system. This suffices to demonstrate the inapt character of Waltz's example. However, it does not demonstrate that the "balance of power" system is one in which the actors have an incentive to observe rules that are consistent with equilibrium. This point is covered on a general level, in chapter 1 of *System and Process*. In chapter 2, there is a partial explanation of why the "balance of power" system is a system of this type. In further work, including *Macropolitics* and *New Approaches to International Relations* (1968), this explanation is expanded. The computer models that I discuss at greater length below in my treatment of Waltz on Kaplan will add to the understanding of this topic.

The essential rules of the "balance of power" system are clearly not inferred from behavior in *System and Process*. They are hypothesized as equilibrium conditions. The general reason for the irrelevance of Waltz's competitive-model illustration can be found in my definitions of system and subsystem dominance—terms that Waltz does not like. Waltz's example is of one special type of perfectly competitive market. My illustration for system dominance is "the perfectly competitive market [wherein], although prices are determined by the activities of all, they function as parametric givens for any single buyer or seller" (*System and Process*, p. 16). I argue in chapter 2 that the "balance of power" and bipolar systems are subsystem dominant, an argument for which Waltz attacks me. In chapter 1, I define a subsystem-dominant system in the following way: "a subsystem becomes dominant to the extent that the essential rules of the system cannot be treated as parametric givens for that subsystem." In chapter 2, I characterize the "balance of power" system as subsystem-dominant and point out:

> If an essential national actor does not internalize the rules of the "balance of power" system, it may be possible for that actor to upset the stability of the system. In the "balance of power" system the equilibrium or rules of the system are maintained by the complementary actions of the essential national actors. However, there is no external policeman who will or can act to restore the situation if the participants, that is, the other essential national actors, do not take countervailing action in time.... In the economic system under conditions of perfect competition, one firm may be able to swindle another. But soon its shady business practices will become known and countervailing action will be taken. In the "balance of power" international system, however, an initial deviant act may serve to insulate the deviant actor from reprisal.... Such transformations of the "balance of power" system become more likely if an essential national actor aspires to some form of international or supernational hegemony (pp. 27-28).

Even if Waltz had not read me with care, he attempts to cite Riker against me. One would have thought he would have noted that Riker argues that the "invisible hand" (perfectly competitive) model does not apply to "balance of power" systems. In addition, he should have paid more attention to the published computer results of the Chicago workshops, for these demonstrate that maximizing behavior in terms of interests narrowly conceived—as Waltz puts it, "not 'Will both of us gain?' but 'Who will gain more?' " (p. 39)—will be self-defeating and that application of the rules is required. The empirical case studies to which I refer later also demonstrate this. But the more important fact is that I can demonstrate the incorrect character of Waltz's unexamined hypothesis through systems analysis. When I discuss Waltz or Riker on Kaplan, I cover these problems of analysis in greater detail.

WALTZ'S TWO-ACTOR MODEL

How many actors are required for a stable "balance of power system"? This is an important theoretical issue. Unless we understand this issue, we shall remain confused about an important aspect of how questions are investigated within the framework of a theory.

Waltz seems displeased by the fact that Burns and I both set the lower bound of a "balance of power" system at five major actors. He does not even like a lower limit of three. Therefore, he finds a way for stabilizing a two-state model: the militarily weaker state grows economically. Waltz says: "in a two-power system the politics of balance continue, but the way to compensate for an incipient external disequilibrium is primarily by intensifying one's internal efforts" (pp. 36-37). The introduction by Waltz of economic growth in that particular form as a variable in his two-nation balance-of-power system is an upside-down view of how and why one contructs models. If one wishes to posit a world in which the weaker state with high probability can compensate for its weakness before the other state either attacks or grows, one can construct a stable computer model of the process. The computer would be instructed that, after a war in which the system is reduced to two states of unequal size, it should permit the weaker to achieve enough economic growth to compensate for this weakness before the other state can attack. This might actually occur in a particular case, but it is not an illuminating example. In this respect Waltz's two-actor model reminds me of nothing so much as one of those animated cartoons that children find so hilarious in which a fox is squashed flat as a sheet by a huge boulder and in the very next frame bounces back into its original form in a saucy and energetic manner. In any event, is not his model reductionist?

I don't believe such models are the appropriate way to use computers or to develop equilibrium models. Assumptions are chosen for their explanatory power. Although it is well known that counterfactual assumptions are often used in theories, they are chosen not for their counterfactuality but for their power in explanations. Waltz's assumption is merely counterfactual.

In my discussion of the number of actors in a "balance of power" system—a subject that I treat at greater length later—the instability of the two-actor model lies in the high likelihood that relative capabilities will change during some reasonable time period. Whether this change is produced by economic growth, asymmetric military technologies, or some other cause is not crucial. The theoretical knowledge that this is likely predisposes one against reducing the system too much unless one is willing to risk all to gain hegemony.

Waltz insists upon a two-actor balance-of-power theory, because otherwise he will have to admit that there could be different types of international systems, which would not then be anarchic systems. Waltz finds my own discussions of dyarchic systems irritating. He praises me for calling the rigid dyarchic system after 1870 a "balance of power" system but damns me for calling the postwar system bipolar.

However, my bipolar system is not a two-state system, and my rigid "balance of power" system is a system in which alliances form around two poles. This issue is discussed, among other places, in chapter 2 of *System and Process,* in *New Approaches,* and in *Macropolitics.* Except for the fact that Waltz keeps assuming that Kaplan keeps contradicting himself, he might have noted my reasons for employing a "balance of power"—rather than a loose bipolar—theory sketch for the rigid system after 1870 in Europe. The system accords with the model, except for a specific parameter condition. The model calls for external rationality in the formation of alliances. However, the quarrel between France and Germany over Alsace-Lorraine made this impossible. All the structural elements of the model are present, however, including types of actors, range of capabilities, and so forth. When the theory is employed under this changed-parameter condition, the reason for the great flexibility of alliances, and for the limitation of war—to optimize future potential alliances—is removed.

The reason why the system in the late 1940s and 1950s is called bipolar is related to striking differences in the ranges of capabilities; differentiated role functions in the system such as bloc leader, bloc member, uncommitted actor, and universal actor; and role-functional rules. In short, one case is called "balance of power" and the other bipolar because the systems differ in their major structural and functional characteristics. The fact that each system is otherwise dyadic is relatively insignificant in terms of the theoretical explanations. If Waltz had made simple note of this fact, much of his confusion could have been avoided.

CAPABILITIES AND FUNGIBILITY

Are politics and economics so dissimilar because money is fungibile and power is not, so that abstract theory is impossible in international relations? Unless we understand this issue, much of the controversy over international relations theory will pass us by. Waltz and Stanley Hoffmann are in disagreement on this issue.

In one respect, I should like at least partly to agree with Waltz against Hoffmann's criticism in the *American Political Science Review*. According to Hoffmann:

> Waltz demands more of theory in international relations than the field allows. He does not address himself to Raymond Aron's argument ...about the impossibility of achieving a single "scientific" theory of indeterminate behavior along the lines of economic theory: the concept of power differs from that of money; goal-oriented behavior differs from instrumental action; and while the permanence of a contest among units introduces elements of calculation and order, they do not suffice to provide the field with a rigorous theory. We can describe, in skeletal ways, the logic of state behavior, the main patterns of interaction and regulatory mechanisms, but making the field intelligible is not the same as disposing of an explanatory and predictive theory (p. 1636).

Hoffmann's position here is a curious mixture that is both sound and misleading. In a system such as a "balance of power" system, in which there is not merely no overarching political framework but no differentiation of role structure among the major actors, it is not impossible to get a well-articulated structure of arguments in which calculations concerning military force play a role. I would agree, as I always have, that this theory will not be rigorous. However, the mere fact that the elements that can be deployed in war cannot be given numbers in the same way as money is not overly significant. There are rough relationships of forces, and statesmen think in terms of them. And we can, and in my workshops we have, developed realization models (as we shall see later) that permit us to explore the sensitivity of the system to changes in battle-destruction ratios, tolerance for "balance," and a variety of other factors. This requires a far more articulated framework than Waltz uses. And even *System and Process* falls short of this goal, although its level of articulation was the requisite for the later development of the more complex and sophisticated computer exploration of actor relationships with respect to parameter sensitivities.

So far, the complexity of the bipolar system, with its differentiated role functions, has defeated our efforts to find a computer realization model in which capabilities play a dominant role. And we have not yet found any other mode of formulation that appeals to my sense of adequacy.

Hoffmann, who incorrectly denies the possibility of a capability-dominated theory of a "balance of power" system, is, however, correct in stressing in his review that Waltz places too much emphasis on changes of capabilities as a general explanation of changes in international systems. The fact is that many things in the environment may produce a change of a qualitative kind that produces a change in the nature of the system. Although I would never argue that my discussions of possible transformations in *System and Process* are more than heuristic, they do illustrate the wide variety of factors other than changes in capabilities that may produce changes in the systems themselves. In many cases these changes will also produce changes in capabilities, as, for instance, in the possible shift of capabilities to a supranational or universal actor. But some transformations will result from changes not directly related to capabilities, whereas in other cases there will be a far more complex relationship. The fact of the matter is that we cannot make general statements about change. Change may occur for an infinite variety of reasons, some of which may shock and surprise us if they actually occur. This is an additional reason why the investigation of change in systems should be relegated to the later stages of theoretical work or to a more empirical examination of concrete systems within which theory plays a smaller role.

Waltz on Kaplan

Waltz begins his examination of my work in a way that appears to bode well for his examination of the requirements of systems analysis. He recognizes that Hoffmann incorrectly "condemns Kaplan for overlooking the diversity of states, for endowing systems with wills of their own, for assuming that systems assign roles to actors, for believing that structures set needs and determine aims, and for neglecting domestic forces" (p. 56). He recognizes that "Kaplan naturally and rightly makes some simplifying assumptions and fails to write at length about national diversities and domestic forces. The important theoretical question, however, is this: How does he define, locate, weigh, and interrelate causal forces that operate in different parts and at different levels of the system?" (p. 57). He further recognizes that I made no claim to a completely deductive theory. From this point onward, confusion becomes all-encompassing.

THE FEATURES OF SYSTEMS ANALYSIS

What is a system? Does feedback occur within it? What makes a system political? Unless we can distinguish between definitions and propositions, or definitions and illustrations, we shall be thoroughly confused about the fundamental building blocks of theory. Because Waltz, as I have shown already, is confused about definitions, he is confused about the other elements of theory. In this section I show how this confusion leads him, as it does so many other critics, into fundamental misinterpretations.

On definitions

Waltz has considerable difficulty in handling definitions. Because this difficulty occurs throughout his critique, I offer in this section two specific examples of how his preprofessional approach to the subject of definitions produces both misinterpretations of texts and theoretical confusion with respect to the important topics of feedback and the character of a political system.

feedback

Waltz declares that I misuse the concept of feedback: "Kaplan's and everybody's favorite example of a thermostat...is consistent with Wiener's definition and with what it entails—a controller and a controlled instrument producing a given result. But in international relations, what corresponds to such notions? Nothing. Kaplan simply uses the word without worrying about its formal appropriateness" (p. 63).

How does Waltz attempt to define feedback? He says that the concept

> is borrowed from cybernetics where it is *defined* [italics added] as
> follows: "when we desire a motion to follow a given pattern the
> difference between this pattern and the actually performed motion
> is used as a new input to cause the part regulated to move in such
> a way as to bring its motion closer to that given by the pattern." By
> such a *definition* [italics added], feedback operates only within an
> organization: that is, the notion of feedback has no precise distinct
> technical meaning outside of a hierarchical order.

The reader will immediately see that Waltz's example of feedback, which he takes from Norbert Wiener (1948), is not a definition; and, of course, it was not presented as a definition by Wiener. Moreover, it is not even an illustration of feedback in general but of a specific type of feedback—negative feedback. Nor it is an illustration of the most general form of negative feedback but only of negative feedback under (homeostatic) equilibrium conditions.

Yet Waltz asserts that he can derive from "such a definition" that feedback "operates only within an organization: that is, [that] the notion of feedback has no precise, distinct, technical meaning outside of a hierarchical order."

Waltz does not tell us what he means by a hierarchical order and simply leaves us dangling in midair with the concept. I suspect that he loosely interprets that phrase with respect to the international system to mean that the international system will utilize feedback only if there is a political subsystem at the top of a hierarchy of authority; for he also asserts that there is "in international relations...nothing [that] corresponds to such notions [as] a controller and a controlled object producing a given result" (p. 63).

I will explore this more precisely shortly when I discuss serial adaptation. Here, I will simply use an example to dismiss that particular confusion. Consider a juggling act in which two jugglers toss in continual motion a large number of juggled objects to each other. The act will fail dismally unless negative feedback operates, for in the absence of feedback the jugglers will not catch the successively flying objects. Yet no hierarchy exists between the jugglers; they are coordinate, as in a subsystem-dominant system. This example is interesting for another reason. What is being kept constant can be denoted on different levels of abstraction: specific aspects of the coordination of bodies and physical objects and the rule "Do not break the flow of motion."

I suspect that some of the authorities to whom Waltz refers when he specifies hierarchy do so with reference to complex systems in which they posit a hierarchy of goals in terms of which the decision maker makes decisions. (Obviously, in simple systems, such as a thermostatic system, there may be a control hierarchy although there would be no hierarchy of goals but only a simple fixed goal of constant temperature and a series of fixed responses for environmental variations.) This latter concept of hierarchy is entirely irrelevant to Waltz's argument, for feedback in the international system is consistent with hierarchical and non-hierarchical codings. Therefore, I will not dwell on the inadequacies of the hierarchical concept here but merely note that it assumes a discrete coding system that is not context dependent and a strict hierarchy of values rather than a web. In these respects it is incorrect. The reader who is interested in pursuing this matter further can do so by reading *Justice, Human Nature, and Political Obligation* (pp. 22, 23, 44ff., 93, 263ff.).

Waltz at least would be close to a correct formulation when he argues for a controller and a controlled instrument if his formulation had permitted the plural form. However, even here, some qualifications are necessary. When Waltz draws the conclusion that there must be "a controller and a controlled instrument producing a given result," the truth of that statement, even for the case of negative feedback, depends upon what he means by a controlled instrument. In the example of thermostatic system, which regulates a furnace, the thermostat is clearly a controller and the furnace and the circuitry are presumably the controlled instruments, while the temperature is that which is kept under control. In another example given by Wiener (p. 14), picking up a lead pencil, it is difficult to put such an interpretation on it. For instance, the controller may be viewed as the central nervous system, the instrumentation as the anatomy. But what is controlled? Is it the pencil or the hand and arm? Or is it a combination of both? Or do the hand and arm function as controllers when considered in relation to the pencil and as controlled when considered in relation to the nervous system?

If we understand that a concrete element may have a different locus in different analytical schemata, we have no difficulty with the concept of negative feedback in international relations. In *System and Process* political systems are called ultrastable; all ultrastable sytsems include control subsystems (pp. 7-8). Where is the instrumentation? As the arm is an instrument in picking up the pencil, the national actor is an instrument in carrying out national policy. What is being controlled? Under conditions of stability, the actions of the national (or other) actors are designed to make sure that the state of the international system does not deviate too greatly from the conditions prescribed by the essential rules. When we come to Waltz's use of Alan Dowty (1969) against my position, we shall see that Waltz objects to my theory sketches precisely because they depend on feedback, that is, because I assert that essential national actors take the state of the international system into account in making their decision. Because Waltz believes that only systems in which there is a unique locus of control can be feedback systems, he does not—and cannot—understand feedback in international relations.

How does Waltz arrive at his incorrect interpretation of Kaplan on feedback? Waltz says that in Kaplan "the word 'feedback' then conveys *only* [italics added] that under certain obvious conditions some states are likely to change their policies in response to the moves of other states, whose further moves will in turn be affected by those changes" (p. 63). His reference is page 6 of *System and Process*. On page 6 I defined "feedback," and in the paragraph in which I do so, I say: "When systems, whether on the same or different levels, are coupled in two directions, feedback takes place. The foreign policy of the United States affects that of the Soviet Union and is, in turn, affected or influenced by the foreign policy of the Soviet Union." This constitutes a definition at a high level of generality of feedback, without specification of whether it is positive or negative, and an illustration at the same level of generality. I then get more specific: "Negative feedback operates in a direction opposite from that of the input. Automatic pilots that counteract deviations from level flight exhibit negative feedback. Positive feedback operates in the same direction as the input. The printing of money during inflation leads to still higher prices and the printing of still more money and so on." When I define negative feedback, I give an example that meets every legitimate criterion. When I give an example of positive feedback, my example meets the full requirements also. The reader will further note that keeping something constant is not part of a definition of negative feedback but a condition of a negative-feedback controlled system under equilibrium conditions, for the direction of the control is compatible with an inconstancy in the vital variable. Moreover, Waltz fails to distinguish between negative and positive feedback.

My theory sketches of international systems under equilibrial conditions accord with my definition of negative feedback. The process involved is that which Ashby discusses in his chapter on serial adaptation in *Design for a Brain*. I describe it more qualitatively in chapter 2 of *System and Process*, which contains theory sketches of six international systems. The equilibrium of the set of essential rules "is not a continuous equilibrium but one that results from discrete actions over periods of time" (p. 25).

Waltz's choice of authorities is peculiar, to say the least. Wiener's *Cybernetics* is the most seminal book on the subject. However, even apart from Waltz's misinterpretation of Wiener—resulting in part from his inability to distinguish between definitions and illustrations—he should have been aware that a lot of water has run over the dam since Wiener wrote his book: the concept of feedback has received significant explication since then. Waltz does refer to Arthur Koestler, who is a rather unlikely authority, and Bertalanffy, who is not highly regarded among workers in the field, but ignores Ashby, whose work he cites elsewhere. If he had paid attention to Ashby's concept of multistability, which involves multiple-control systems, he would have understood systems involving more than "*a* controller and *a* controlled instrument" [italics added].

Ross Ashby defines a multistable system as one that "consists of many ultrastable systems joined main variable to main variable, all the main variables being part-functions" (1952, pp. 171ff.). He then goes on to show that even the nervous system must be multistable. In effect, and partly oversimplified, this means that there are different control systems within the same organism—at least with respect to different main variables—because only with this kind of decentralization would extensive adaptation to a complex and varying environment be possible for a complex organism. Without attempting to place too much weight upon it, and recognizing that some though not all of these processes are serial in nature, at least in the nervous sytem, I find that this is merely another illustration of multiple-subsystem dominance.

As Ashby says: "This type of system has been defined, not because it is the only possible type, but because the exactness of its definition makes possible an exact discussion." Ashby then says that other systems that resemble it may approximate its behavior. If Waltz had been familiar with this discussion, he would have seen that there is no difficulty in thinking of the international system as one in which multiple-control subsystems of the essential national actors function simultaneously in controlling the states of variables of the international system. Although this process is too complex for us to define it exactly, the general pattern of this type of feedback operation is already adumbrated in Ashby. If one wants to advance this conception, one might refer to my concept of transfinite stability (*Justice,* pp. 19-20).

Furthermore, if Waltz had really understood the concept of feedback, he would have understood that no level of human or social activity can occur without feedback. Even in his own mistaken view of the international system as a system of anarchy—which I discussed earlier—negative feedback would occur; however, what would be controlled would be the specific outcome of wars under inherently unstable conditions.

Let me summarize the status of feedback in my theory sketches. Chapter 1 of *System and Process* identifies international systems as complex variants of homeostatic systems—that is, of systems whose equilibria depend on negative feedback. The theory sketches in chapter 2 analyze the feedback processes in terms of the relationships between three sets of variables: the essential rules, other system variables, and boundary conditions. The reader can see from the previous discussion that this set of interrelationships is a complex variant of multiple part (sub)system control of a complex serial adaptive process.

the political system

Waltz says that I contradict myself in my use of the concept of political systems. He asserts that my universal and hierarchical systems "have political subsystems and thus do not conform to [Kaplan's] own definition of an international system" (p. 78). He then cites pages 14, 21, and 45 of *System and Process.*

Let us see whether this complaint by Waltz is correct. I define political systems on page 14 of *System and Process.* In the paragraph in which I do so, I state, "In the *present* international system [italics added], the nation states have political systems, but the international system itself lacks one." Clearly, this is not a definition and the illustration is explicitly restrictive. The reader will see that I define political systems and international systems but that nowhere in *System and Process* do I place either concept in the definition of the other.

Waltz, however, fails to cite page 19, where a careless formulation might at least have seemed to support his argument. In the middle paragraph of that page, in a discussion of the then contemporary bipolar system, I do write: "One reason the international system is not a political system stems from the fact that, within the personality systems of decision makers, their role in the international system is subordinate to their role in the national actor system." I should have said, "this international system" instead of "the international system." However, the middle of a discussion of a then contemporary system would be a strange place for a definition.

Waltz also cites pages 21 and 45. Nothing relevant to his argument appears on page 21. Perhaps, however, he was careless and meant page 22. Page 22 is in that section of chapter 2 that is devoted to the "balance of power" system. On that page, I say: "The 'balance of power' system is *distinguished from other international systems* [italics added] by the following characteristics. It is an international social system without a political subsystem...." Page 45 is in that section of chapter 2 that deals with the universal international system. On that page I say: "The first thing to be noted about the universal international system is that it has as a subsystem a political system." Neither position "contradicts" the other.

ANALYTICAL SYSTEMS

The distinction between the analytical and the concrete is fundamental to an understanding of theory and the use of models. Unless it is kept clear, the interpretation of theory will be confounded beyond repair. In this section, we shall see how Waltz's carelessness in this matter has confused devastatingly his entire discussion of theory.

Models

Waltz, in an attempt to refute my use of models (p. 61), briefly quotes Abraham Kaplan: " 'When one system is a model of another they resemble one another in *form* and not in content.' " This implies both that the observation by A. Kaplan is categorically correct and that my usage violates it.

Waltz, at the least, should have noted that there is no standard usage in the literature of either philosophy or science of the term "model." I might, for instance, quote an authority to the effect that there are at least "five different senses in the confusing and often confused usage of the term 'model' ": (1) any relatively strict theory; "(2) a semantical model, presenting a conceptual analogue to some subject-matter; (3) a physical model, a non-linguistic system analogous to some other being studied; (4) a formal model, a model *of* a theory which presents the latter purely as a structure of uninterpreted symbols; (5) an interpretative model...." This authority would turn out to be the same A. Kaplan in the same book, *The Conduct of Inquiry* (1964, pp. 267-68).

However, I do not have any serious quarrel with Waltz's quotation from A. Kaplan. The variables in my theories are formal in A. Kaplan's sense. Let us see how he treats the question of form.

According to A. Kaplan, "A family, for example, may exhibit a hierarchical structure, and so serve as a model for, or be modelled by a certain abstract geometrical system. Presumably it is a hierarchy in terms of relations like those of authority or influence; matters of affection, loyalty, esteem, and their like are here exogenous" (p. 286). If I understand this correctly, we cannot speak of the family except in terms of the roles within the family, even though these may be modeled by a mathematical system. Thus we have, in a nuclear family, husband, wife, and children. The family is further identified by relations such as authority and influence. If we were to distinguish a nuclear family from an extended family it would be in terms of the different types of members and of how they are related in terms of authority and esteem.

This is precisely what I do with international systems. The "balance of power" system, for instance, has essential national actors within it who are not further role differentiated. The relationships among the essential national actors are those of equality with respect to such things as entering alliances, making war, and making peace, whereas in a bipolar system role differentiation occurs. The essential rules and certain conditions of information and capability specify the equilibrial conditions within the system, whereas the parameters do so for the environment.

The reader will remember that in my discussion of Waltz's attack on Galtung's theory as a reductionist theory I quoted Waltz's assertion that my theory is supposed to apply to states independently of any other characteristics. I made two points at that time. First, my theory sketches do not mention states, which are concrete entities, but actors of various types. A bloc member is not the same analytical entity as an essential national actor. Therefore, the same generalizations do not apply to it. In the second place, the application of a generalization to a real entity or event requires the statement of initial conditions, which means that a specific prediction must take into account the actual value of what in the theoretical statement may vary, depending upon the concrete case. Thus, two separate procedures are involved. The first is an identification procedure that determines whether the concrete entity is one to which a specific theory applies; whether, for instance, it is a solar system, to which Einstein's theory applies, or an atom, to which quantum theory applies. A second empirical procedure is that of determining the initial conditions and the boundary constraints, so that one can determine what the theory says about the subject matter to which it applies in a particular case.

There is a third distinction that needs to be made. In every one of the theoretical works I have written, I have stressed the point that a homeostatic system—and any social system is a homeostatic system—is one in which qualitative distinctions among systems necessitate different theories, unlike the case in physical science, where the existence of independent measures permits wide applicability of a generalization across many types of qualitatively different systems. For instance, Einstein's laws apply to single-sun or double-sun systems without further qualifications. Qualitatively, if we wish, it is possible to treat these two types of systems as behaviorally different. For certain purposes, this form of treatment will be more illuminating, while in the more general scientific sense it conveys less information. Because there are no independent measures of the types used in physics, in the social sciences there cannot be laws although there may be applicable generalizations. The theories or theory sketches used in social science are of the qualitative type rather than the lawlike type. This does not mean that they are concrete rather than analytical, for qualitative theory sketches about qualitatively different systems remain independent of labeling.

M. Kaplan's systems as models

The reader will note that my usage of models comes closer to A. Kaplan's first usage than to his own example of the family; for, in addition to roles and functions, it specifies other related variables and boundary conditions. Moreover, if I had not employed the distinction between form and content—if, for example, I had identified "essential national actors" with concrete nations— I could not have permitted my students Chi and Franke to treat Chinese warlords and Italian city-states, respectively, as essential national actors in "balance of power" systems (*New Approaches,* pp. 405-58). Because of the formal—but not the concrete—similarities between these systems and international systems, Chi and Franke could and did make successful use of a "balance of power" theory in an explanation of their cases.

Although Waltz quotes A. Kaplan, the analytical/concrete distinction has been around for a long time. Students of the social sciences have been acutely aware of this problem at least since Lewis Morgan pointed out in his *Systems of Consanguinity* (1970 [1870]) the distinction between social and biological mothers that became apparent to him as he investigated differences in language usage among Indian tribes.

The analytical character of my theory sketches is made abundantly clear in *System and Process.* For instance, apart from the general overview provided by the preface to *System and Process,* chapter 1 states: "A system is an analytical entity" (p. 18). When I prescribe how systems are coupled, I present an iterative analytical procedure for decoupling them:

> Systems are said to be coupled when the output of one system affects
> an input of the other system. Thus the personality of the secretary of
> state is an input for American foreign policy, and the foreign policy
> of the United States is an input for the international system. It is

possible to think of systems which are coupled as elements of a larger system. However, it is convenient to treat coupled systems separately. The United States and Great Britain constitute coupled systems. They are members of NATO and the United Nations; economic developments in one country affect the economy of the other; the policy of each serves as an input of the other. Consider, however, the difficulty in attempting to study the operation of the American political system with respect to foreign policy if one were to make a detailed study of every system to which the United States is coupled, for instance, a study of all external systems and all internal subsystems. It is far simpler from an analytic point of view to consider what the United States will do if Great Britain does x, y, or z.... It is convenient to consider how [the system] will behave if the inputs from other systems take arbitrary values (p. 5).

On page 16 I state: "A person may communicate an order as a consequence of his role in the system hierarchy and receive an order as a consequence of a different role. For instance, the federal government administrator may issue an order requiring cities to engage in an air raid drill but himself receive an order form a city official to cease keeping a goat in his back yard." Obviously this order is given to a man in his role as private citizen, not in that as a federal administrator.

This subject is clarified further in my discussion of role analysis: "A system is an *analytical* [italics added] entity. The same individuals may be members of a labor organization; employees of business; citizens of cities, states, and nations; and humans in the world community.... Each role has certain requirements that may, under some conditions, conflict with the requirements of other roles." (pp. 18ff.).

The preceding paragraph states clearly that in the systems theory or systems model we are no longer dealing with concrete entities but with roles. It is of course the concrete entities that have or fill roles. And, depending on the level of analysis, some of these concrete entities may be treated as subsystems in more inclusive systems. However, in the analytical model, as opposed to the real, concrete world, their characterization depends only upon the particular role that is being filled.

The fact that actors constitute an analytical concept is made fully evident in the last section of chapter 1: "The international system has among its subsystems a set of actors.... The set of international actors will be divided into the subsets 'national actors' and 'supranational actors'.... The subset of supranational actors will itself be broken into subsets of bloc actors and universal actors.

NATO and the Cominform are examples of bloc actors" (p. 20). If A. Kaplan in his discussion of formal systems, in particular that of the family, had said "John Smith is an example of a father," this would not have implied that John Smith in his concrete fullness was an actor in the formal model of a family.

On the same page, I point out:

> International action is action taking place between international actors. International actors will be treated as elements of the international system. Their internal systems will be parameters for the international system [note that they are explicitly parameters and they are not included in their full dimensions]; their outputs will be behavior of the international system. However, in the chapter on the international actors, the systems of the international actors will be treated as differentiated [but still analytical] systems; the international system will then be treated as a parameter for their systems of action.

Is this clear enough?

If not, I pursue the subject further in *Macropolitics*:

> [The models employed in *System and Process*] necessarily abstract from a far richer historical context. The theories therefore can be used for the derivation of consequences *only* under explicitly stated boundary or parameter conditions. For instance, statements concerning alignment patterns of the "balance of power" model in *System and Process* apply only at the level of type of alignment, and do not specify the actual actors who participate in specific alignments. And they specify even this broad consequence only for *stated values* [italics added] of the exogenous and endogenous variables (p. 213).

These statements—which mandate an empirical methodology that discriminates for the conditions that make a particular theory applicable and the extent to which the initial conditions are consistent with equilibrial conditions—do not permit the interpretation that Waltz places upon my methodology. He says: "Kaplan's method is in fact the classical one of examining the character and interactions of variables with the aggregate of their interactions taken as the depiction of the system" (p. 62). How can one possibly interpret an explicit equilibrium model that deals analytically in terms of roles and functions as one that employs concrete aggregative techniques?

Despite the foregoing, Waltz asserts: "Morton Kaplan fails even to be concerned with the problem of form. This unconcern follows naturally from his system-of-action approach. He does not think of different systems in terms of their different structures but instead ranges them 'along a scale of integrative activity.' This helps to explain his otherwise baffling statement that 'theory—in particular, systems theory—permits the integration of *variables* from different disciplines' " (p. 67).

This is typical of Waltz's preprofessional style. I shall overlook the fact that integrative activity in systems is so fundamentally different from the integration of variables in a theory that it is precisely their linkage by Waltz that is "baffling." Instead, I examine the evidence against this example of his "stream of consciousness" style of criticism.

Page 21 is the first page of chapter 2 of *System and Process*. In the first paragraph of that page, the six international systems discussed in that chapter are named. In the second paragraph, the statement that Waltz cites about a scale of integrative activity is made. The last sentence of that paragraph reads: "The subject of integrative activity will be discussed in chapter 5 and the closely allied subject of regulatory activity in chapter 4." In short, I specifically state that integrative activity is not the subject of chapter 2. The third paragraph states what the subject of the chapter is and avers that, for each of the systems, I will discuss the essential rules, the types of actors who participate in the systems and their other characteristics, the parameter values necessary to stability, the step functions that produce system transformation, and so forth; that is, the subject matter of the chapter will be the structures of the different systems. In short, Waltz asserts that the only thing I am discussing is what I specifically omit from discussion in this chapter and denies that I am discussing what I specifically state to be the subject matter of the chapter.

As to Waltz's puzzlement over my inclusion of variables from a variety of disciplines, this only signifies that the normal status of a discipline is irrelevant to the formulation of a particular theory and that one includes whatever is required for explanatory power. This refers back to my statement in chapter 1 that "the system consists of the variables under investigation. It has no absolute status" (p. 12).

Waltz and formal systems

I believe that this discussion of models finally places us in a position to disentangle the curious confusions that Waltz introduced in his discussions of reductionist and auxiliary theories. I was quite surprised, when it finally dawned on me, that Waltz, who indicts me for failing to distinguish between content and form—or, more accurately, the concrete and the analytical—repeatedly fails to make this distinction himself. However, that is why he had so many problems with the concepts of reductionist and auxiliary theories.

If one wishes to apply a formal theory or theory sketch to the real world, two procedures are necessary. One must be able to identify the real world as one to which the theory is applicable. That is, one must be able to distinguish an atomic system from a solar system or an extended family system from a nuclear family system. If one cannot do this, one does not know which laws or generalizations to apply. Second, one must be able to specify the initial conditions under which the theory is being applied; otherwise it is impossible to derive any specific conclusion.

Although one must look toward the real, concrete world to apply a theory, it is not correct to believe, as Waltz does, that one looks "inside the actors." With respect to the actors, one looks to their theoretically relevant characteristics; for instance, in the case of one of Morgan's family systems, a "mother" would be any female within a given age range, regardless of biological relationship. However, one may also look at any other theoretically relevant characteristic of the system, or at environmental conditions such as technology or state of the economy or wind resistance with respect to the application of physical theory to falling bodies, and so forth. Thus, the distinction is not between "system characteristics" and "actor characteristics" but between the formal model and the criteria for its application. It is not a form of reductionism to carry out the operations required for applying a theory to a concrete world situation; nor has one formulated an auxiliary theory or hypothesis when one has done so.

Because Waltz fails to make these distinctions, he reifies the concept, among others, of nation (which, after all, consists of individuals and organizations). Thus, he believes that any statement that refers to actors involves reductionism. What he has failed to understand is that no theory has applicability in the absence of criteria for its application. If all we had in the case of A. Kaplan's family model was a formal geometry, we would lack the criteria for either identification or application. The moment A. Kaplan identifies it as a family system he has introduced content. The determination that a theory is applicable and the estimation of initial conditions are direct applications of the theory and not a reduction to some other theory or to concrete actor characteristics. The reduction of a theory necessarily involves its derivation from some other theory. Waltz's failure to understand this is the source of his confusions and the reason for his reifications.

THEORIES AND RESEARCH QUESTIONS

If we understand how to interpret and apply theories, we are also alerted by theories to relevant data that otherwise we might misinterpret. In this sense, the theories are progressive or heuristic in Lakatos's sense.

For example, although it is not a decisive consideration, a study of Western German elite views on national security by Dietmar Schössler and Erich Weede discovered that "62.9% [of their sample] approve of the following proposition: 'the small and middle-sized Euroepan nations contribute to security in Europe if they accept the leadership of their respective superpower' " (ms. p. 28). Thus, individual Germans seem to understand that foreign policy conducted from the standpoint of "balance of power" theory is inappropriate in a bipolar world.

American responses in Korea in 1950 were related to a concept of a bipolar system. Although technically carried out within the United Nations, the American action in Korea was a direct American response to a perceived Soviet threat. The United States was woefully unprepared in terms of the situation on the peninsula and the resources it had readily available to bring to bear in that area. In a "balance of power" system, the threat would not have been so direct nor would the United States likely have intervened under those conditions of lack of preparedness. American leaderhip of NATO concentrated responsibility upon it in a way that would not have been possible within a "balance of power" system. This, it seems to me, is the major difference from the situation in the 1930s with respect to Ethiopia and Manchuria. In the latter case, it was not so much American absence from the League of Nations—for it is difficult to believe that the response in Korea would have not occurred even in the absence of the United Nations—as it was the concentration of responsibility upon the bloc leader that primarily accounts for the Korean action.

The situation in the 1930s was a "balance of power" one and not a loose bipolar one. The difference in roles and functions were the primary predispositive reasons for the differences in behavior. This is one of the primary reasons, in real "balance of power" systems, why actors who strive for predominance gain considerable headway before the antideviant coalitions form. There is no concentration of responsibilities. In the anti-Napoleonic coalitions formed by Great Britain in the nineteenth century, the costs of leading that coalition were eased by its island position and by its invulnerability to French attack. Otherwise, it too likely would have attempted to shift the costs of reaction to other actors. This behavior is in fact "mimicked" in the computer model, for in the absence of a specific antideviancy rule, some system "unbalancing" occurs before adequate coalitions form against the hegemonially inclined actor. Yet it is easy to see that in the real world even the effort to form such a coalition will involve an effort to shift the costs to other actors where possible. It would take strong situational reasons, such as the insularity of Britain or the particular vulnerability of a particular actor in the system, to compensate for this.

The Content of International Systems

Nothing is more elementary than the distinction between those things inside and those outside of a theory. If one is to understand the problem of theory in international relations, one must disentangle the confusions Waltz and other critics introduce.

Waltz asserts that I examine six systems and that I *"then* [italics added] identify five 'variables' that are sufficient for describing the state of each system.... The relative importance and the interactions of the five variables are not indicated and, because they are not, Kaplan's systems approach cannot be said to constitute a theory" (p. 57). Waltz's reversal of the order in which I discuss the variables and the systems may perhaps be a careless mistake on his part, although I suspect it reflects some of the confusion that is evident in his statement of requirements. Chapter 1, on systems analysis, discusses the variables that are included within the theories. It would be inappropriate to suggest their respective weights or their relationships to each other in this chapter, for to the extent that "weight" and relationships are specified, this must be done within a specific theory, not in general. If a physicist were to discuss the problem of a unified field theory, he would mention, among other things, that it would cover strong and weak forces and large- and small-scale phenomena. Only if and where he claimed to be presenting such a unified theory would specification of formulas become appropriate.

However, let us move back to square 1. Waltz talks about general systems theory. The title of chapter 1 in *System and Process* is "systems analysis," not systems theory. In later writings, I point out that there is no such thing as "a general theory of systems" (*Macropolitics*, p. 57). Later in that book I say:

> perhaps the first thing to be said about systems theory is that it is not a theory. It consists of a set of concepts. No propositions about the real world can be derived from it any more than propositions about physics can be derived from the infinitesmal calculus or from the methods of science in general. Advice to a political scientist to use systems theory to solve a problem, even when it is the appropriate methodology, would advance him as far but no farther than would advice to a physical scientist to use the methods of science (p. 71).

I then go on to say: "when the concepts of systems theory are used to construct theory in the area of political science, they can be most helpful; when they are used to evade the problems of substantive theory, they can be misleading or harmful. There is no such thing as theory in general; there is only theory about some specific subject matter."

The subject matter in chapter 2 of *System and Process* consists of six international systems. It does not follow that the "weight" of the particular variables will be the same in the different systems or even that we can speak of 'weight" in a precise fashion rather than in terms of an articulated qualitative set of relationships.

The six systems covered in chapter 2 of *System and Process* differ from each other. They do not constitute theories in the strict sense. Initially I called them "introductory theories." Today, I would call them "theory sketches." They do permit the articulation of relationships among variables that are theoretically relevant. They can be used in certain types of reasoning processes that I make explicit later. And they can form the basis for future research that presumably will lead to improvement of the theories.

System and Subsystem Dominance

We have already gained some insight into the problem of system and subsystem dominance from the discussion of serial adaptation in multistable systems (feedback). Chapter I of *System and Process* introduces the concept of subsystem dominance. In later sections, I show explicitly how these concepts are central to understanding international systems and to distinguishing "balance of power" and bipolar systems from those in which the rules of the system operate only as "constraints," to use Waltz's term. His failure to understand the relevance of these concepts produces Waltz's confusion when he discusses change, as I show in my discussion of feedback. In this section, I state Waltz's objection to the concepts and deal with it only at the level of common sense. Waltz argues: "Kaplan's language is loose and imprecise to the point of misleading the reader. On one and the same page he writes of subsystems sharing dominance and of essential subsystems entering 'into an equilibrium somewhat like that of the oligopolistic market.' The mind boggles at the thought of subsystems being dominant, let alone sharing dominance. What could subsystem dominance be other than the negation of systems approach?" (p. 60).

I am sorry if I made Waltz's mind boggle. However, I will attempt to clarify the matter for him. Let me use ordinary idiomatic usage to begin my investigation of the problem of subsystem dominance, although I make no claim that ordinary usage necessarily will be determinative. Suppose that the president of Ghana states that the United States, Russia, Japan, and the western European countries dominate the international system either politically or economically. I do not think that any of us would have any trouble understanding what he means or the concept of shared dominance.

Thus, the concept of subsystem dominance accords with common sense. We should be careful, however, not to reify the term. For instance, the international economic system, and its political subcomponents, is subsystem dominant from the standpoint of the large states but system dominant from the standpoint of the small states, except on those few occasions when, for example, small states can create a cartel with respect to the use of a vital commodity, as in the case of oil.

System, Boundary, and Identity

System and boundary are merely the old subject of content in slightly different form. However, when Waltz relates them to the question of system identity, he introduces a confusion at the theoretical level that is fundamental and that must be clarified if we are to understand theory.

Waltz finds no fault with my definition of a system of action as "a set of variables so related, in contradistinction to its environment, that describable behavioral regularities characterize the internal relationships of the variables to each other and the external relationships of the set of individual variables to combinations of external variables." He says, however, that I fail to define the system, to indicate the system's environment, and to delineate the boundary between them, "and, second, to define the system structure so that the identity of the system will be distinguishable from the variables within it and from their interactions. These two problems are not solved.... Kaplan merges, or confuses, international systems with their environment" (p. 59).

The reader will note that Waltz has lumped two different subjects together: the "identity" of a system that is distinct from its variables and their interactions, and a differentiation between a system and its environment. Waltz does not see what can possibly come from outside the system in my theories because, he says, "all of the things important for international systems are within them." Therefore, nothing can be outside of them.

If I had done what Waltz suggests, I would have put the sun, the earth, air, and food in my systems models because clearly they are essential to the existence and functioning of international systems. However, for some strange reason I failed to do this; in any event, I will show what is inside and what is outside my systems models.

The five sets of variables—actor types, essential rules, transformation rules, information, and capabilities—are inside, and they are listed in chapter 1. They are given specific content for each of the six systems in chapter 2. The environmental changes that are likely to trigger system change—that is, to invoke the transformation rules—are adumbrated for each of the six systems. They include such things as technological change, population change, economic change, opinion change, and so forth. They are outside of the system; that is, they are not included within the set of five variables that constitute the systemic framework.

Because Waltz does not distinguish what is inside from what is outside the system when he examines my work, he becomes thoroughly confused. Let us examine one of the more interesting of his confusions. Waltz states: "Kaplan declares that as systems deal with any states whatsoever, that at the systems level the particular identities of states are of no account. If, however, the system is so vaguely conceived as to offer little if any explanation of the behavior of states, then the question that is crucial for Kaplan—whether or not states will follow his rules—will depend overwhelmingly upon what those states are like!" (p. 62).

Waltz has now compounded two errors. One reason an actor may behave differently from the prediction of an equilibrium theory is because conditions are not at equilibrial values. This point is elementary, but I will come back to it. A second reason may be that the theory is inapt for the situation to which it is applied: the real world and the analytical categories of the theory may be grossly different.

Economic theory, for instance, is independent of the identities of particular economic actors, apart from such classifications as "person" or "firm" and so forth. But French firms in the 1940s did not follow the prescriptions of neoclassical economics, and they did not fail. This was not a refutation of economics nor did it show that the economic model was insufficiently stated. The French system— in which paternalistic stagnant firms conspired to freeze out innovative dynamic firms—was different from that described by the standard economic theory. Modern economic theory cannot explain the failure of farmers in certain areas to grow a second crop, although their behavior is quite rational in a society that is not competitive and in which wants are very limited.

With respect to the first reason—variations from equilibrium conditions— we cannot predict what an actor will do until the environment and system conditions are fully specified. The actor may be deviant (environmental) or unable to act because of economic constraints (environmental). Regime considerations may preclude required external actions (environmental). The actor may misunderstand the state of the system (systemic deviance).

All that a theory can specify in general is what will happen under equilibrium conditions. It cannot be used for a concrete prediction until the starting state and parameters are taken into account. An engineer, for instance, can tell us what will make a certain type of motor behave in a certain way when it functions in a certain kind of car and with a particular kind of fuel. If someone puts sugar in the gasoline, the car will not function; yet no one will criticize the engineer for not specifying this as part of his theory or claim that what he has done is too imprecise. The problem with Waltz is that we never know whether he is talking about theory, the concrete world, particular applications, or something entirely different.

System change

System change is a fundamental theoretical problem that requires elucidation. It is one thing to discuss change within the framework of a theory and another to discuss change as a real-world fact. I will discuss real-world change soon. Here I attempt to clarify the problem of theory and change.

Waltz, who does not see how change can occur in my theories, also accuses me of linking changes to actor decisions. Of course, I do. Unless actors respond to boundary changes, change could never occur in actor-action—that is, social —systems. The problem of change in my models is more general than the previous sentence allows. However, because Waltz specifies actor-induced change, I shall reverse the natural order and discuss it here.

According to Waltz I

> frequently [ask] what the effect of the behavior of states upon the
> international system may be. He cannot put the question the other way
> around, for he has no concept of the system's structure acting as an
> organizational constraint upon the actors, a constraint that would vary
> in its expected effects from one system to another. Since he cannot
> say how the system will affect the actors, his explanations or pre-
> dictions can only be about the system itself—its equilibrium condi-
> tions, the extent of its stability, and the likelihood of its transforma-
> tion (p. 62).

Here again Waltz seems to be making a metaphysical distinction between the system and its parts in their interrelationships. If my theory does everything that Waltz says it does, I fail to see that it does not specify how actors are affected. If it does not specify how actors are affected, how in the world can it do the things Waltz says it does? Where and what is this mysterious system that does not affect the actors? If I have explained, as Waltz here asserts, "the system itself—its equilibrium conditions, the extent of its stability, and the likelihood of its transformation"—I would have explained what he elsewhere denies I explain: the system's structure in a formal sense, for the former are intimately related to the latter.

There are so many related confusions in this expression of Waltz's position that I will not further confuse my readers by enumerating them but will attempt only to clarify the methodological problem. First, there is no system above and beyond the actors in their relationships. If, however, the reader refers back to my discussion of system dominance, for example, a perfectly competitive market in economics, the system can be treated as a parametric given— in Waltz's terms, a "constraint"—to which the actor adjusts. If one can explain how this system operates, then ipso facto one has explained how its existence affects the actors' behavior. However, one cannot ask how the actor affects the system. The actor's influence is infinitesimal. Only some gross macrosociological or cultural change could reverse this sign. This is the very opposite of Waltz's complaint.

If, however, the system is subsystem dominant, as are my "balance of power," bipolar, and unit veto systems, both questions—how the system affects the actors and how the actors affect the system—are applicable. When U.S. Steel modifies its prices, it must take into account the competitive behavior of other large steel firms, unlike the situation in a perfectly competitive market. It must ask both how its decision affects the equilibrium in the market and how disturbances in that equilibrium will feed back into its situation. When the economic theorist treats the latter problem in its general, rather than its specific, or applied, form, he has an analytic or formal theory. He specifies the structure of the system and the relationships between the system in its formal or normalized aspects and the actors. That is what my "balance of power," bipolar, and unit veto systems do; and they are different in their structural aspects. Waltz has one further argument against the possibility of such theories: the argument that oligopolistic systems are indeterminate. I analyze that problem later.

However—and this is an essential distinction Waltz fails to make—the system, that is, the normalized set of roles and functions, is not the only thing that affects the actors. Changes outside the system—technology, drought, and so forth—affect the actors also. The influences from outside the system may cause actors to act in ways such that other actors may compensate, or they may introduce changes so great that restorative actions cannot be taken, even when, in the absense of these changes, the actors would be motivated to take them. However, because Waltz does not make the previous distinction between what is inside and what is outside the system, he cannot understand the difference between the implications of a theory or model and real-world applications of a theory. This explains his confusion over the ways in which, and the reason why, actors produce change.

Let us see the specific form this confusion takes in Waltz. On page 60 he says: "In fact, for [Kaplan] the source of change in the international system lies in the behavior of the actors, specifically on their breaking the essential rules.... For Kaplan, then, states in one of their aspects are the international system's environment!" International actors are part of the international system; they are not part of its environment. But those aspects of concrete entities—

whether nations, warlord systems, or whatever—that are not included in the theoretical specification of essential national actors are part of the international system's environment.

Waltz states: "The states, being whole systems themselves as well as being subsystems of the international system, can be viewed as the systems in which disturbances originate" (p. 60). In this formulation, Waltz obliterates the distinction between the analytical category and the concrete entity. He utterly confuses form and substance. If international actors—as opposed to states—were whole systems, they and the international system *would* include everything. In that case, I would have a system so complex that I could say nothing at all about it, except in a completely arbitrary or ad hoc and partial manner. Of course, the reader is aware that if a system is analytic, so is a subsystem, and that the only part of the subsystem included in the system is the analytically relevant part. Thus, neither—nor both together—could possibly include the whole concrete system.

Waltz, who is correct in believing that actors produce change through their actions, fails to understand or to interpret this phenomenon correctly. Essential national actors (not states) are the only actors who can change the "balance of power" system, because they are the only actors in the system. However, it is a non sequitur to argue that states are "the source of change in international systems" without at least recognizing that other factors are required in explanations that account for deviant behavior by national actors.

The reason for this is quite simple. Although national actors are the only actors—and therefore no one else can break (or follow) the rules—the reasons they decide to break (or follow) the rules lie partly in the environment of the international system, which includes everything that is not included in the analytical theory and which, thus, includes all other aspects of national systems, of nature, of technology, and so forth.

The sources of change are multiple.

The reader will further note that it is not possible for an actor to attempt either to apply the essential rules or to deviate from them without taking into account the state of the system at a particular time. Is the state of the international system one, for instance, in which a particular actor is becoming predominant? One cannot interpret rule 4 of the "balance of power" system, which specifies combination against a hegemonially inclined actor, except in terms of an analysis of the state of a system.

Roles, functions, and change

The problem of change is explicitly discussed in *System and Process*. I point out in the very first chapter that

> a man may have a role as head of family and as a bookkeeper in a business. This is a relatively simple situation with only two roles directly involved. Yet even here conflicting requirements may arise. Each one of these systems is subject to diverse influences arising from parameter changes. The baby becomes ill and more money is needed. The father has made a fool of himself before his friends and feels the need to increase his prestige, perhaps by being able to spend large sums of money. The business suffers reverses and may not be able to meet the payroll, or the supervisor of the bookkeepers may be engaging in some private graft. The equilibrium is delicate and can only maintain itself as a dynamic, never as a static, process since each role responds to distinct needs in the particular system in which it functions, and since each system is subject to a different set of parameters, many of which undergo continual or rapid change. Deviancy of the individual who holds these rules...occurs in terms of the needs of the system that happened to have dominance under the existing parameter values. Systems and subsystems in the international systems have roles, and these roles have different functions depending upon whether they couple activity within the subsystems of a larger system or between system levels. Deviancy, accommodation, assimilation, conflict, and other forms of change occur as the functions of the roles change in the various systemic typological economies (p. 18).

I discuss the specific application of this methodology to international systems in chapter 2:

> Apart from the equilibrium within the set of essential rules, there are two other kinds of equilibrium characteristic of the international system: the equilibrium between the set of essential rules and the other variables of the international system and the equilibrium between the international system and its environment or setting. If the actors do not manifest the behavior indicated by the rules, the kind and number of actors will change. If the kind or number of actors changes, the behavior called for in the rules cannot be maintained. In addition, the essential rules of the...system may remain in equilibrium for a number of values of the other variables of the system (p. 26).

There is nothing mysterious about change. My discussions of role conflict and of the sets of equilibria within systems provide the key to understanding change. To illustrate the application of these keys, I shall make use of an analogy from law. In a simple law case, it is merely a matter of choosing a norm and reasoning about how to apply it. In conflicts of law cases, the problem is one of finding the right set of rules to apply, or perhaps of making modifications in the decision that give weight to both sets of rules. Similar problems arise for statesmen with respect to the application of essential rules: choices must be made of which system of rules to apply—in very simplistic terms, whether to give more weight to international or to domestic rules—and decisions made concerning how to apply the rules in concrete cases.

Why equilibrium theories?

My theories, like so many theories in the social sciences, are equilibrium theories. These have been the cause of much confusion in the literature. Waltz thinks that he can disentangle the real questions of systems theory from my equilibrum approach. Let us see why this is not so.

According to Waltz, the real questions of systems theory are:

> How does the arrangement of parts, and how do variations on the arrangement, affect the behavior and interactions of those parts? What is the expected fate of systems of different structure? Those are the structural questions, and systems theory is useful if it can help us to understand them. What systems theories seek to reveal is often misunderstood by their critics. Some claim that systems theory seeks only to define equilibrium conditions and show how they can be maintained, that systems theory deals only with systems as wholes. Others claim that systems theory seeks to show how systems determine the behavior and interaction of their units, as though causes worked only downward. Because some theorists have limited themselves to the first purpose or adopted the second one is no reason for limiting or condemning systems theory as such (p. 47).

Waltz's first two questions, which he calls structural questions, are in fact good questions, although they are not well put, for they imply the existence of a structure apart from the actors and their relationships. There is no such structure; there is only an analytic distinction between the normal or equilibrial form of behavior and its concrete and particular manifestations. The structure is the normalized form of behavior at the appropriate level of abstraction. It is a coded subroutine within the control systems of concrete people and concrete institutions.

It is used in a complex feedback process in the production of decisions and/or actions that are designed to maintain it or other systems to which it is linked, to adapt them to changed circumstances, or to transform them. Because the normalized mode is the form in which analytical or formal systems exist, an analysis that does not take into account this aspect of such systems cannot rise to a theoretical level.

Waltz fails to recognize that if we understand the equilibrium of a system —that is, if we have specified roles, functions, and environmental parameters —we have not only specified a full answer to the first question but have provided a procedure for answering questions concerning how systems can be changed or even transformed. As I point out in *Macropolitics:*

> If we can construct a theory for a system or type of system, as a system in equilibrium, we can then inquire how individual variations in parameters will produce deviant or unstable behavior. To know why a system changes, develops, or breaks down it is surely helpful to know why the conditions of change are inconsistent with the prior states of the system. If we cannot answer this latter question, it is doubtful whether we have correctly assigned the reasons for instability or change (p. 58).

The reason I start with an equilibrium model rather than a dynamic model stems from

> the principle of economy. Many more systems fail to persist through time than those that do persist. Although the parameter values that produce instability are large in number and differ in multivarious ways from case to case, the conditions producing stability are much more limited in number. Thus, concern with stability, *at least in the initial stage of the inquiry* [italics added], focuses attention on a relatively small number of systems, a limited number of variables, and a limited range of variation. Although the problem of inquiry may still be most difficult, it is much more focused and manageable than a concern with problems of instability [or change] (p. 58).

However, Waltz's second question, even though correct, is misleading without further explanation, which he does not provide. We certainly want to know the fate of different types of systems. However, no theory of a particular system can explain this, for reasons I provide below. This is why we should engage in comparative analysis. Systematic comparative analysis might enable us to link systems more concretely to their parameters—a process that is far more difficult in the social sciences than in physics, although even there it is not as obvious as many people suppose.

What I do not understand is why Waltz pays no attention at all to his own two good requirements: First, to trace the expected careers of systems of different structure by, for example, indicating their likely durability and peacefulness. Second, to show how the structure of the system affects the interacting units and how they in turn affect the structure" (p. 47). If international relations is a system of anarchy that is treated merely as a constraint by the actors, who behave according to microeconomic principles, it would not be possible to carry out either task.

Perhaps what he has in mind is an empirical evaluation of a concrete system in which one engages in trend analysis. Trend analysis of a particular concrete system, however, in the absence of an equilibrium model, resembles brute empiricism more than it does a genuinely theoretical approach. It will suffer from the fact that, because all the environmental constraints will be operating simultaneously, it will tell us very little about similar systems unless one starts with an equilibrium model, as Chi and Franke do. Unless one operates as they do, it will not be possible to recognize other systems of the same type in a way that permits a consistent framework of investigation.

Blocs and Alliances

Structures and attributes

Waltz argues:

> One must then carefully keep the attributes and interactions of the system's units out of the definition of its structure. If one does not do this, then no systems-level (or structural) explanation can be given. One cannot not even attempt to say how the system affects the units.... [Kaplan] often...is inconsistent. Having explicitly denied attributes a place in the structure, he in effect smuggles them in through his rules. In his balance-of-power system, relations are apparently not included in the systems level.... Yet his loose and tight bipolar systems achieve their special identities precisely through differences in relations, that is, through differences in the cohesion of blocs (pp. 63-64).

Waltz then draws his damning conclusion: "One can scarcely derive a part of the explanation for the formation, the importance, and the durability of blocs or alliances from consideration of type of system [if Kaplan's methods are followed]" (p. 64). Waltz is at least partly correct. It would be a serious methodological error to attempt to derive the existence in the real world of an actor from a theory in which that actor has a role and functions. Whereas an alliance is a product of a "balance of power" system, a bloc is a precondition for a bipolar system. It is possible, however, that the theory will help to explain why, in existence, the role of a bloc is reinforced.

Actually, in addition to its methodological confusion, Waltz's question conflates a number of separate issues. Suppose we attempt to ask how blocs operate in Congress, for example, the farm bloc or the labor bloc. One set of questions will ask how blocs trade off votes against each other. Another set of questions will inquire into what it is that motivates congressmen to organize a bloc, that is, a long-lasting relationship as distinguished from shorter-lived voting alliances. In this case, we might search for microexplanations for bloc participation. Yet the answers to this set of questions may not contribute to an explanation that differentiates between Congresses in which blocs exist and Congresses in which they do not. These types of Congresses might well manifest differences in forms of behavior that are related to differences in the types of units that participate in them rather than to the factors that produce these types of units. We can know how to proceed and how to formulate our questions only through an analysis of the actual case. (Waltz at least here admits that I do posit structures.)

Waltz's confusion, which produces his insistence that we ask questions only at the microlevel, demonstrates that he really does not understand the question of formal structure at all; for the explanation of why blocs form in a Congress that lacks blocs—an explanation that must take into account a Congress that lacks blocs—may, and likely will, be different from an explanation of how a Congress that includes blocs operates.

When we turn to international systems, we do not know what questions can be put to a theory until we have specified the system's roles, its functions, and the conditions under which these roles and functions are interrelated. The formation and transformation of alliances is a product—not a precondition—of "balance of power" systems in which actors arrange and re-arrange themselves in such groupings before, during, and after wars. Structure in this system is nonhierarchical and fast-changing. The interactions of the actors produce these forms; and they match the general characteristics predicted from the essential rules if other system elements and environmental conditions are at their equilibrial values.

The loose bipolar system, however, is role differentiated and partly hierarchical in structure, for example, bloc leaders, ordinary bloc members, and nonbloc members. The arrangements are relatively fixed—and the interactions that produce these arrangements are given by the application of the rules under equilibrial conditions—although not as fixed as legislatures, executives or dictators, and ruling parties in certain kinds of political systems. Just as different types of legislatures and executives may produce (be preconditions for) different types of political systems, different types of blocs may produce different types of bipolar systems.

Concepts and real-world applications

The distinction between the concrete and the analytical arises in another form when concepts are applied to the real world. My prior discussion begins to elucidate this matter. Now we can uncover the source of the confusion in Waltz's statement that I discuss things contradictorily by talking of a rigid "balance of power" system, which is dyadic, without mentioning the attributes of national actors, but specify attributes when I mention blocs in the bipolar system. This is merely a variance on his earlier confusion made manifest in his statement that my theories apply to any states whatsoever, in which he identifies the concrete "state" with the analytical "national actor."

A bloc is not an actor attribute in the bipolar system; it is a role. In principle, the term could be displaced by a symbol. However, it would not have been useful to produce a purely formal system without any interpretative framework for the reader to use. Attributes are relevant only to a decision concerning whether a role can be filled by a particular actor. Thus, given the explanation of the role of a bloc leader in the bipolar system, the real-world attributes of France do not permit France to fill the role of bloc leader. In A. Kaplan's model of a family system, the role of father can be filled by any adult male. If we particularize the son that the father is father of, then the determining attribute is either the biological one or the legal one, in terms of adoption, whereas in a system discussed by the nineteenth-century anthropologist Lewis Morgan, the necessary and sufficient conditions for being the mother of any child were adult womanhood and tribal membership.

The "theory" of either the family system or the international system explains why the roles and functions fit together as an equilibrial system. They do not explain why there are actors that fit the roles. And they could not do so, for the explanation of this must necessarily come from outside these particular systems. The theory of oligopolistic competition, in any of its forms, will not specify how or why oligopolies develop although there are economic theories that do specify the preconditions for an evolution from competition to monopoly within an industry.. It can be expected to explain how monopolies function with respect to each other and with respect to smaller firms within a basically oligopolistic system, in terms of such things as sharing the market and so forth. If one wishes to discover why oligopolies form, then one should look at the empirical or theoretical circumstances that lead to their development, attempt to develop a dynamic model of a more competitive economy to show why it will produce oligopolistic concerns, as Marx attempted to do in *Capital,* or investigate the environmental parameters that will transform the system.

On the other hand, the theory sketch of the bipolar system—precisely because it does explain how and why blocs function within the system—will explain the subordination by bloc members of their short-term interests to their long-term interests. Such an explanation is provided in *System and Process:*

> International political conditions within the non-leading...actors of a bloc must permit them to contribute to the proper functioning of the bloc. Otherwise, the bloc will become unstable. The instability of one bloc, while the other bloc remains stable, will constitute a factor tending to produce a hierarchical international system if the stable bloc is hierarchical or mixed hierarchical. If the stable bloc is non-hierarchical, the international system will tend toward a "balance of power" system, or possibly toward a universal or mixed form of international organization. On the other hand, if both blocs become unstable, there will be a tendency to the reestablishment of a "balance of power" system or to the establishment of a universal system (pp. 41-42).

Now I admit that it is not entirely irrelevant in a world in which blocs are less familiar than acquisitive individuals to say something about why blocs exist even if we cannot derive their existence from bipolar theory. In fact, I do do this in *System and Process:*

> The monolithic organizational principles of the Communist bloc of actors and informational inputs concerning the foreign policy aims of that bloc were the parameters chiefly responsible for the developing of bloc actors such as NATO. Leninist principles of organization constituted a major factor responsible for the organization of the Communist bloc. The parameters operated in a more complex fashion than this account indicates, but an examination of this complexity would not be relevant to the purpose of this chapter (p. 36).

I will ignore the question of whether my theory sketch is a good one, or even an acceptable one, and hark back to the methodological problem. "Balance of power" theory cannot explain the rise of the Communist bloc, for the organizational principles of Leninism, the particular characteristics of the Soviet state, and the circumstances of World War II provide this explanation. The world never can be derived from any particular theoretical frame. The explanation of system change—except in the case of a self-transformative system—must always refer back, in part at least, to real-world features that are not predictable from the theory itself. Because Waltz does not, in any articulated manner, distinguish between the types of things a theory can and cannot predict, he consistently compares apples and oranges.

Have I contradicted myself? I earlier criticized Galtung because he did not account for the transformation of Center nations into Periphery nations. Now I am arguing that the theory of the "balance of power" should not be faulted because it does not predict the emergence of blocs. Let us see if this is justified.

Galtung's theory incorporates a positive-feedback process in which the interchanges between the centers of Center and of Periphery nations stabilize and even intensify the differences between them. Therefore, the identities of Center and Periphery are central to the theory itself. If some process at the boundary is powerful enough to reverse this process—and there have been many historical instances of Periphery nations that have become Center nations as Galtung uses those terms—no fair examination of Galtung's theory is possible in the absence of some statement concerning this process.

In principle, the theorist should state all boundary conditions. In practice this is impossible. Even so, I did state the conditions that likely produced blocs and bipolarity even though these were *derived* from neither "balance of power" nor bipolar theory. Galtung, however, because of the very character of his theory, was required to say something about some specific boundary conditions that might contraindicate his predictions. Otherwise the historical evidence creates too many problems for fair application of the theory.

This discussion is useful for still another reason. It illustrates the impracticability of throwing generalizations about without careful application to specific cases. Although in practice no one will be careful without exception, a systematic absence of such careful discrimination is a mortal danger to any discipline.

Real-world transformations

Obviously we should not expect a theory sketch of a particular international system to predict its replacement by another system any more than we should expect a theory of the competitive market to predict the emergence of a controlled economy upon access to political power of a Soviet-type political party. However, we can modify that statement in one respect when we are in possession not of a single theory sketch but of a series of comparative theory sketches such that each sketch is linked to the specific factors that make for equilibrium within the system. This is what the transformation rules in my international systems models are intended to do, although I would make only weak claims for them.

We can see how a transformative process may function if we examine the situation existing at the end of the World War II. From the standpoint of a theory of international relations, it is an accident that the Eurasian land mass was dominated by the Soviet Union at the close of the war. It was also an accident of history that the states of western Europe were highly populous, possessed significant human skills, and had great potential economic importance. Furthermore, it was an accident from the standpoint of international systems theory that two of the key states in the system—France and Italy—had large Stalinist parties that might have been able to take advantage of economic turmoil, political instability, and failure of will in the face of the Soviet mammoth. Later on, when many of the political and economic conditions were corrected, it was an additional accident from the standpoint of international systems theory that technological change, particularly in the military area, had reduced western Europe from an arena within which defense in depth was possible to an arena that had no military depth. These accidents, however, were the very parameter features that indicated that the "balance of power" system could not be restored.

In the face of the Soviet Union and its control over its bloc partners, either western Europe forged a virtual defense union with the United States, in which case a loose bipolar system would develop, or all of Eurasia would come under Soviet control, in which case there would be an incipient hierarchical system.

In general, in a "balance of power" system the essential national actors decide on their policies in full independence and,.on the whole, in terms of short-term interest. True, there was some modification of the short-term interest consideration with respect to the operation of rules 3 to 6, which Riker agrees are necessary for stability. However, the dominant mode of operation was an independent one, and it was short term in terms of interests. In the loose bipolar system, genuine independence on the part of the bloc members is not possible, at least in the same sense as in the "balance of power" system. Moreover, the subordination of short-term interest to long-term interest and of national policy to bloc policy is a profound aspect, even if not without exceptions, of a loose bipolar system.

Except in the tautological sense that nations are still pursuing their interests when they subordinate short- to long-term interests and national to bloc interests, it is easy to see that the orientations, functions, and roles of the two systems are distinctive. One does not treat the loose bipolar system as such merely because it is dyadic, that is, a system centered around two actors, but because of the logic of the interrelationships.

System persistence under anomalous conditions
When we analyze the concrete world, we can see some of the conditions that sustain equilibrium even under abstractly nonequilibrial conditions. For in-

stance, it was an accident, in systems analysis terms, that the United States had a dominating strategic advantage over the Soviet Union at the time the Soviet Union had the greatest control over its own bloc. In the contemporary period, the eastern European states, with the possible exception of Germany, have interests that set them partly at cross-purposes with the Soviet Union. Although they have an interest in a strong Soviet Union and a strong Warsaw Treaty Organization— for, in its absence, their regimes might succumb to popular hostility—they have no interest in an extension of Soviet dominance over all of Europe. Such Soviet dominance would be a threat to their own partial autonomy, for the greatest deterrent to the current exercise of such control by the Soviet Union is the price that the Soviet Union would have to pay in terms of its confrontation with NATO. Its allies would be totally hated regimes dependent upon extensive measures of internal control, even beyond those now employed, and whose economies would likely become a drain on the Soviet Union for reasons of sabotage and apathy. Just as Finland's restricted degree of autonomy depends on the existence of a strong NATO in Europe, as well as the Finns' well-known stubborn fighting ability, so do current developments within the eastern European nations depend on the constraints that the existence of NATO places on Soviet domination.

Genesis of Usage

Although the term "bipolar" had entered into common usage well before I employed it in *System and Process,* the ideas that gained theoretical expression in that book came to fruition while I was working on the first draft of the Brookings book *United States Foreign Policy: 1945-1955* (Reitzel, Kaplan, and Coblenz, 1956). As I was working on that draft, I was also reading Ashby's *Design for a Brain.* As the concepts in this book filtered through my mind, I was also working through the reasons why the policies of John Foster Dulles with respect to uncommited states and of the Truman and Eisenhower administrations with respect to the United Nations were erroneous.

The consequences were serendipitous. As I was writing the first draft of the Brookings book and thinking about possible distinctions between "balance of power" and bipolar systems, I developed the basic ideas that went into *System and Process.* These ideas led me to investigate the system constraints under which the interests of uncommitted states and universal actors should both be taken into account and be appreciated in terms of long-term national goals. Although I do no wish to argue, and I would be wrong if I did, that these are the only reasons why Dulles's extensions of alliances were inadequate diplomatic devices, I do believe that useful statements can be formulated concerning these problems that are related to the conception of a bipolar system in terms of its equilibrium conditions. It is ironically amusing to me that a statement that was developed in opposition to the then accepted cold war views is now so often called a statement of a cold war position.

The essential rules

The essential rules are key elements in my theories. Waltz casts aspersion on my use of them in a way that confuses the character of theory in international relations. Let me clarify this matter.

"On different pages," Waltz complains, "Kaplan says that the six rules all have the following characteristics: they are descriptive and prescriptive; they are essential, interdependent, and in equilibrium with each other; and as prescriptions for the actors, they are inconsistent and contradictory. They do indeed have the latter qualities, as William H. Riker has conclusively shown" (p. 58).

Let me try to disentangle what Waltz has turned into a veritable puzzle. The essential rules are essential in the sense that in the equilibrium model or theory they are conditions for equilibrium for posited values of other system variables and of the environment. In this sense, they are neither descriptive nor prescriptive; they are analytical and theoretical. If the environment and the other variables of the system assume the equilibrial values, they are predictive in the sense that the theory predicts that essential national actors will follow the essential rules. As these predictions have existential reference, they are, in this sense, descriptive. If the environment and the other variables of the system take the equilibrial values, the rules are prescriptive in the sense that they optimize the interests of the actor—a conclusion that receives further specification in the following section. There are, thus, three sets of equilibria: within the essential rules, between the rules and the other variables of the system, and between the system and its environment. There is no possible inconsistency in any of this, as we can easily see from the following examples. "Two plus two equals four" is an analytical proposition. "John adds two apples to two apples and has four apples" is a descriptive statement. "If John has two apples and wishes to have four apples, he should take two more apples" is a prescriptive statement.

The fact that these positions are in principle consistent does not mean that they are in fact consistent—there may not be, for instance, two more apples for John to take—or that the elements of a particular theory employing this methodology will be correct in terms either of its internal compatibility or of its compatibility with real-world facts. The reader will note, however, that Waltz has substituted ridicule for analysis.

Rules and Contradictions

According to Waltz, "William H. Riker has *conclusively* [italics added] shown" (p. 58) that the essential rules of Kaplan's "balance of power" system are contradictory. The reader might infer from Waltz's phraseology that Riker agrees with Waltz that the "balance of power" model—as opposed to the world —is unstable and that the problem lies in Kaplan's rules. If this were the case, I should be seriously concerned, for Riker is one of the most profound and original thinkers in political science. Before I turn to Riker, however, let us first see what *System and Process* says about contradictions in the rules. For once, I must take some part of the blame for Waltz's miscomprehension.

System and Process was written before publishers were willing to produce completely analytical works in the international relations area. Thus, my statement of a theory sketch—which was too analytical for many readers—is followed by a variety of real-world illustrations, many of which represent nonequilibrial conditions. Specifically, my discussion of possible contradictions in essential rule applications occurs during my discussion of transformation rules. Transformation rules, as the reader knows, specify the changes that will occur when the environment or other system variables are in a nonequilibrial condition. For example, I point out:

> Positive feedback may occur although the various national actors have no intention of overthrowing the "balance of power" system. The wars against Poland corresponded with the rule directing the various national actors to increase their capabilities. Since Poland was not an essential national actor, it did not violate the norms of the system to eliminate Poland as an actor. The Polish spoils were divided among the victorious essential national actors.... Nevertheless, even this cooperation...had an "unbalancing" effect upon the "balance of power" system... (p. 33).

I also state: "If national objectives become supranational, weapons and transportation developments which permit successful occupation of vast modern industrial areas may permit successful deviance..." (p. 59).

A simple example will illustrate the difference between a lack of contradiction between the essential rules in an equilibrium model and a contradiction in practice when a real-world system is in disequilibrium. Consider a nuclear family consisting of a husband and wife before women's liberation. Among other rules, the essential rules might have included: (1) that the husband provide for himself and (2) that the husband provide for his wife. In that system, we can see that both rules are essential: the family in that form will not persist unless the rules are followed. They obviously do not contradict themselves in any formal sense.

Consider the same husband and wife adrift on the ocean in a small boat that will be swamped by the high seas if they both remain in it. The two rules now give rise to contradictory prescriptions. That, however, does not contradict the assertion that they are both necessary for equilibrium or the assertion that such a family will be in equilibrium under a wide range of parameter conditions if the rules are followed.

Riker on contradictions

It is quite true that Riker asserts—mistakenly, as I shall show—that my rules are contradictory. It is also true, however, that he agrees with my statement of the rules. Before turning to Riker's actual statements, let me first comment on Waltz's assertion concerning what Riker has "conclusively shown."

Riker, of course, conclusively demonstrates nothing substantial—nor would he argue that he has—let alone a contradiction in the essential rules of my "balance of power" system. Waltz has a rather peculiar notion of what a conclusive argument is—using the term as a form of verbal magic in which adamant assertion or an exclamation mark makes it so—although one would have thought that the continuing debate on Riker's theory of a minimum winning coalition would have at least caused Waltz some reflections before he used an adverb such as "conclusively."

Riker's style of criticism is in fact a good model for the critic to follow; it illustrates how careful critical analysis can advance theoretical understanding. According to Riker: "On the basis of this evidence from other sources, we can, I believe, feel some confidence in Kaplan's *precise* [italics added] statement of the rules of the system. Furthermore, we can be *thoroughly* [italics added] certain that rules 4 through 6 [the rules that Waltz wants to get rid of] are the essential features of a balance" (1962, p. 165).

Waltz, moreover, fails to note that Riker specifically rejects the "hidden hand" theory of the "balance of power" (p. 171) upon which Waltz's approach is dependent. Riker tells us that, unless each of the rules is followed, disequilibrium will occur. In this, he is surely correct, as our workshop's computer algorithm demonstrates.

Riker does attempt to show that there are theoretical, and not merely practical, cases in which the rules contradict themselves (pp. 170ff.). He attempts to make this showing upon the basis of several tables that he has developed for his theory of coalitions. These tables apply only to the zero-sum case and only for a division of the spoils as the result of a single play. Within these limitations,

Riker employs the same von Neumann solution for the oligopoly problem that I refer to soon.

The reader will immediately note several aspects of Riker's analysis. In the first place, the rules give rise to contradictions, even with respect to Riker's examples, only in those special cases in which one of the actors is already very large and another very small. Is Riker's example situational rather than formal even within his own framework? If we think back to the example of the married couple adrift on a small boat in a stormy ocean, that special situation is not an argument against the formal consistency of the set of equilibrium rules for the marriage under equilibrium conditions.

In this case, I believe that Riker is correct in regarding the matter as theoretical, although I would have to make an exhaustive analysis of his tables to prove this. If the result is theoretical, it follows from the particular model Riker employs rather than from any general principles. Riker's tables incorporate the zero-sum case. He posits a contradiction in the rules on a payoff distribution that does not take into account the effects of the distribution on the system itself. This is an artificial restriction that is less than general. If the players' interests in part at least are served by avoiding threats to the system, Riker's table is misleading. In the third place, the fact that his model requires that each decision be reached as if only the single-shot decision style applies exacerbates the misleading tendencies of a zero-sum example in a repeated-play game. In Riker's "contradictory" example, the weakest player, by joining a nearly predominant strong player, only creates a condition in which he will be the next victim. This is clearly irrational and is the artificial by-product of Riker's ad hoc model.

In any "balance of power" system whose starting state is not one of such grossly unequal distribution, the players would not allow the system to get into such a situation of disequilibrium except under conditions in the environment that depart from equilibrial values. When we come to an explication of my computer model, I will demonstrate that this is the case. Furthermore, the algorithms of the computer model are sufficiently sensitive to changes in parameters that they can specify those conditions under which a "minimum" coalition will be formed and those in which it will not be formed. These results of the computer project were not available to Riker when he wrote *The Theory of Political Coalitions*, but Waltz, who fails to take these results into account, cites books in which they are available.

In any event, it is surprising that Waltz failed to notice that Riker did not quarrel with my statement of the essential rules but instead asserted that a "balance of power" system would prove inherently unstable. That, of course, is the very opposite of the point that Waltz wants to make. He wants to show that the system is stable and that it does not depend for its stability on my rules.

Riker was arguing that the system is stable only as long as the rules can be followed but that in the case where one of the actors has gained virtual predominance, the rules will not be followed. We will pursue this question further soon.

Size of the system

Riker examines specifically, as Waltz does not, the question of the upper and lower bounds for the system. He agrees "with Kaplan that 'the gain from potential coalition partners is still great enough above the number five to justify some additional number of nations' " (p. 166).

Riker, however, disagrees with Kaplan, with Burns, and also with Quant on their various reasons for rejecting a three-actor system as a stable system. He argues:

> The argument offered for rejecting a minimum of three is...pointless as long as the third or sixth rule is obeyed. In effect, this argument is not a reason for requiring more than three actors but a reason for believing that, when there are only three, some may be tempted to ignore the third rule. While I wholly agree that the temptation is very great to eliminate some members in a three-partition division, still [there is] no reason to exclude a system of balance among three actors when the third and sixth rules are inserted precisely to prohibit the temptation (p. 166).

Riker is, of course, correct in asserting that if all the rules are followed, a three-actor system will be stable. However, the position of both Burns and Kaplan is dependent upon there being a reason for the actors to follow the rules. Riker agrees that temptation to disobey the rules rises when the number is reduced to three. His careful criticism led me to spell out more clearly than previously that a three-partition division is supported by so narrow a range of parameter conditions that such a system is potentially highly unstable in real-world situations. An otherwise "balance"-oriented victor in a war in a three-power system would have to contemplate the possibility that, in some future war in which he would be the loser, one of the parties would not be inclined to maintain the prevailing number of actors and the other victorious actor might not behave with external rationality. In addition, recursively, each of the victors would have to take into account that this might occur if they are the losers, thus reinforcing their incentive to preempt, that is, to behave in a destabilizing fashion, even though their original inclination might have been to behave in a "balance"-oriented fashion. Only if there are at least five essential national actors in the system are the permutational possibilities of alliance sufficiently great to prevail reliably against the preemptive option.

Although Riker and I agree that there is an upper bound beyond which the argument to maintain defeated actors would lose its force—clearly this would be so if there were 1,000 essential national actors in the system—we do not know how to specify where it occurs. Participants in my workshops did develop a point theorem that gives some insight into the problem, but I have only limited confidence in it.

The computer program

We resorted to what we call a "realization model" on the computer because we could not find any strictly deductive technique that would permit theory development for a system as complicated as an international system. The simplest international system is the "balance of power" system. We, of course, did not place the essential rules of the system in the computer, for it obviously would have produced behavior consonant with the rules had we done so. The realization model involved "building some features of the theory into the computer program as parameters of that program. These parameters can then be varied to explore the sensitivity of the computer program to changes in the parameters. Thus it is possible to explore changes in the numbers of players, the battle-exchange rations, the motivations of the players, and so forth" (*Macropolitics*, p. 210).

There are a number of problems in developing such programs. Every computer equation is particular rather than general in form. There is, therefore, a very real danger that it may be an artifact. Thus, in our Chicago workshops we spent months on single features of the program in an attempt to make sure that minor differences in the program that could not be related to some relevant real-world characteristic did not produce the computer results.

The computer model optimizes only over one war cycle. The iterative procedures are far too complex for the computer to engage in long-run optimization. However, given the utility schedule of the actors—without such a schedule they would have no motivation, and in the absence of motivation action would not occur—we could play the algorithm out and see whether the style of play established by the program produced outcomes that "matched" the players' utility schedules or whether some other style would do better.

One element in the computer program is a tolerance for "balance" among the other actors. This can be set very high, or it can be placed as low as zero, in which case the actors only have to concern themselves with increasing their capabilities. The last case is a special one correponding to Waltz's system of anarchy, in which states act to increase capabilities, taking only external constraints into account. It is also consistent with Riker's model, in which there is a zero-sum optimization over one cycle only. When the preference for "balance" is very high, wars do not occur in the system. When the preference for "balance" is moderate, the system goes through repeated war cycles while remaining absolutely stable. If even one actor has a very low tolerance for "balance," the system quickly goes into instability.

At this simple level, the computer example illustrates what our comparative historical examples have already revealed. If actors do not self-consciously take system stability requirements into account, a "balance of power" system will be stable only if some extrasystemic factor—for example, logistical or regime difficulties—prevents a roll-up of the system. On the other hand, only if an actor desires hegemony, even at a very high risk of destruction, will it be motivated to violate the essential rules.

The system is stable in that case in which, for extrasystemic reasons, an actor is willing to risk all in an effort to gain hegemony only if a counterdeviancy standard is built in. Even without this equivalent of rule 4—or of rule 6 if an actor is eliminated for some extrasystemic reason—it is not in the long-term interest of the hegemonially inclined actor to act as if it was so inclined; for in the long run, the actor will be a loser if it so behaves. Only some other anomaly in system conditions—the other actors do not interpret their situation correctly, or intraregime considerations prevent them from doing so—will permit the hegemonially inclined actor to succeed.

Thus, all the rules are necessary for equilibrium, and the set of rules is complete. And the rules are stable over a wide range of boundary shifts. We also explain the interests of the players in following the rules and why the systems of alliance have the characteristics that they do. We show why hegemonially inclined players follow the rules except when some extra-systemic reason provides them with a special opportunity for gain. Furthermore, the equilibrium of the system is dependent upon the fact that actors take the structure of the system into account in their decisions. Moreover, the system clearly is a non-zero-sum system. The computer model demonstrates that Waltz's objections to the essential rules are misconceived.

Waltz's analysis, moreover, is flawed in terms of his own examples. According to Waltz, if rule 6, which specifies maintaining the number of units necessary as the lower bound for stability (I have correctly reformulated Waltz's misstatement of my position), "were translated into economic terms, it would have to read: do not drive an essential firm into bankruptcy. The assumption that firms would conform to such a rule has no place in economic theory, for it is apparent that such a rule would conflict with the assumption that men or firms are profit maximizers" (p. 58). Without debating whether Waltz's statement is correct even with respect to economic theory, it is an unlikely conclusion to draw unless one is willing to argue for the isomorphic character of economic and international relations theory. However, there are important differences that are easy to understand.

It has been argued by some economists that General Motors refrains from driving Ford out of business—an act that, they argue, would maximize GM profits—only because it is afraid that Congress would break it up if it did so. In the absence of politics, an increase in profits is highly unlikely to backfire on an oligopolistic concern except in a special case: a combined economic assault by two giants on a third that leaves one of the winners so much better off than the other that it achieves a size-efficiency ratio that enables it ultimately to drive the other winner out also. This case, which is special in economics, is sufficiently likely in international politics for the ordinary economic metaphor to be inappropriate here.

Let me summarize what the computer realization model demonstrates. When I say "demonstrate," I do not mean "prove beyond all doubt," for an appropriate analysis both of the verbal theory and of computer model might make manifest problems that are not now apparent. On the other hand, I say "demonstrate" because there can be no reasonable doubt that the realization model in combination with the verbal theory sketch has reached a far higher state of articulation, exact analysis, and understanding of theoretical appropriateness than anything else in the literature.

The realization model demonstrates that there is no contradiction in the set of rules under equilibrial conditions. It shows that no rule is violated and that all rules except the counterdeviancy rule—which is not necessary in the absence of a hegemonially inclined player—are followed by the actors. The algorithmic realization model demonstrates that the system does become unstable in the absence of an antideviancy rule if a hegemonially oriented player is an actor in the system and if it acts upon that motivation. Because it demonstrates that the system then becomes unstable and hazardous for the "balance"-oriented players in that circumstance, it provides a sufficient reason for the addition of an antideviancy rule. It is highly stable in that or analogous cases. The computer model does not demonstrate the existence of a lower or upper bond for stability. It is too complicated a problem for the computer program, although we did develop a point theorem that sustains my qualitative arguments. That aspect of the theory reinforces rule 6. The computer model also demonstrates that whether alliances are three-two or four-one in "balance of power" systems depends on the costs of war and on whether side payments are permitted, and that Riker's size principle, therefore, is not general.

RULES, COMPUTERS, AND FORMAL SYSTEMS

I can now return to the question of fungibility and the relationship of theory to the real world in a more analytical fashion than in my earlier treatment. Now I can bring a modicum of theoretical clarity to the subject.

Oligopoly and Indeterminacy

According to Waltz: "An oligopolistic market...is not one in which firms dominate the market but rather on in which, contrary to the notion of dominance, the extent to which firms affect the market and are in turn affected by it is indeterminate" (p. 60). Waltz's assertion of an inverse relationship between the "notions" or concepts of dominance and determinacy—as distinguished from a specific relationship within the framework of a specific system—is a confusion at several levels. The explosion of a hydrogen bomb is dominated by the decision to explode it, and the general behavior of the materials is dominated by $E = mc^2$, but the positions of individual atomic particles are indeterminate. On the other hand, no firm is dominant in a fully competitive market; yet Waltz would agree that its operations are determinate. However, let us assume that Waltz was merely a bit careless and attempt to see whether he has an argument if we separate the notions of dominance and determinateness.

I show in earlier sections that Waltz's objection to dominance fails to hold on grounds of both common sense and systems analysis. A small steel firm would regard it as nonsense to be told that U.S. Steel, Republic, Inland, and other large steel companies did not dominate the market. An economist would regard it as nonsense to assert that the differences between a competitive market and an oligopolistic market—in which dominant firms make decisions on the basis of environmental factors and of expectations of how other dominant firms will react to their moves—are of no theoretical or systemic importance. I show in an earlier section how Waltz's neglect of such concepts has led him confusedly to talk of environmental "constraints" on actors' decisions to the exclusion of system-relevant concepts related to the anticipated behavior of other essential national actors. Now I will show how he misuses the concept of indeterminacy.

In the nineteenth century, the Edgeworth solution to the oligopolistic problem was considered indeterminate in the sense that it did not single out a particular unique point in demand-supply intersections as a solution, as opposed to the case in classical economics, which always has such a determinate solution. However, this does not mean that it was impossible to make any statements about equilibrial conditions.

Chamberlin developed his theory of imperfect competition in the 1930s. In his theory, the oligopolistic solution is represented by an intersection of supply and demand bands. Thus, Chamberlin's theory of bands is indeterminate with respect to the point in the band at which a solution will occur but determinate with respect to the area within which the solution will be found.

Von Neumann used set theory to approach this problem from a different standpoint. The n-person game is von Neumann's version of the oligopoly problem, and it has a solution. The solution—even though it is a zero-sum case—bears a resemblance in terms of form to the predictions that can be derived from my (non-zero-sum) "balance of power" essential rules concerning the characteristics of alliances. It predicts the character of the dominant imputation, but not the players who will benefit, just as my essential rules predict the form and character of alliance but not which actors will be in which alliances.

For instance, in an example used by Duncan Luce and Howard Raiffa (1957, p. 200), in which a full unit of something is to be divided if the division can be agreed upon, any of three imputations—(½, ½, 0), (½, 0, ½), (0, ½, ½)—is a possible solution. If, for any reason, players 1 and 2 agree upon (½, ½, 0), player 3 could propose to either of the other players that he join him in one of the other two imputations. However, neither of the other two players has any reason to leave the existing imputation unless the third player offers something like (¾, ¼, 0), in which case both members of the proposed new coalition would receive incremental benefits. In this case, as Luce and Raiffa show, (¾, ¼, 0) dominates (½, ½, 0) for the second and third players because both benefit; the imputation, therefore, can be enforced. However, if this imputation is formed, players 1 and 3 can form a coalition and enforce (½, 0, ½), which is preferable for each of them. Thus (¾, ¼, 0) is not a stable imputation. The initial imputation (½, ½, 0) is stable once it forms, because neither player 1 nor 2 can benefit ultimately by changing it and both run the risk of losing if they attempt to do so.

Von Neumann calls this particular type of solution set a "stable solution set." Whether a stable solution exists in principle depends on the characteristics of the world, but stable solutions are consistent with the existence of oligopolistic conditions.[3]

There are reasons to believe that it is easier to reach a stable solution when one is dealing with a qualitative distribution than when one is dealing with a strictly quantitative distribution. Although the example that I use to demonstrate this was originally developed by me in 1959 (*Some Problems of Strategic Analysis in International Politics*) to show the difficulties of a direct application of a particular game model to a real-world situation, I am now using it to show that qualitative determinateness may be even stronger than quantitative determinateness.

Some interesting, even fascinating problems arise in the noncooperative, non-zero-sum game, and consideration of these special cases can prove instructive. Consider, for instance, the prisoners' dilemma, a famous problem in the literature, the matrix for which is represented in figure 1 (p. 92). Clearly the players would do well to coordinate on their first strategies. Yet as long as they must make their decisions independently, they must choose strategies that will lead to the (1, 1) payoff. The reasoning is simple. The 2 strategies dominate the 1 strategies. That is, if player B plays strategy 1, player A gains from his strategy 2. If B plays his strategy 2, A still gains from his strategy 2. Thus A does better by playing his strategy 2 regardless of what B does; the same reasoning holds for B. Dominance is the strongest possible strategic criterion. Therefore, in the single-shot game, there is no possible way to avoid an undesirable outcome without communication.

Nor does it help if there is a finite iteration of the game. We might think that the players could at least maximize over time by playing their 1's; but clearly the last play, provided we can identify it, is equivalent to the single-shot game. Thus, in this case, the dominant strategy must be employed. If this is so, each player must protect himself by using the dominant strategy on the next-to-last play, which now becomes equivalent to the single-shot case, and so on recursively. In short, the dominant strategy must be employed in the very first game; therefore, both players get quite undesirable results. If the game is repeated indefinitely over time and if some discount factor is introduced so that there is a finite summation of the payoff, it becomes possible to produce a more desirable result.

In their discussion of the noncooperative game, Luce and Raiffa propose a strict-solution concept. According to Luce and Raiffa, there is a strict solution in the noncooperative game if an equilibrial pair exists among the jointly admissible strategy pairs and if all jointly admissible equilibrial pairs are both interchangeable and equivalent. An equilibrial pair exists when for any pair (x, y) there is no strategy pair (x', y) or (x, y') such that one of the players can gain from a change of strategies while the other player does not change his. A pair (x, y) is jointly inadmissible if each player prefers (x', y'). Thus (x', y') is said to dominate (x, y). A strategy pair (x, y) is said to be jointly admissible when no strategy pair dominates it. Two strategy pairs are equivalent when the returns to each player are equivalent, that is, when $M_1(x, y) = M_2(x', y')$ and $M_2(x, y) = M_2(x', y')$. Two pairs are interchangeable if (x, y') and (x', y) are also equilibrial pairs.

In figure 2 (p. 92), the pairs (x, y) and (x', y) are in equilibrium because neither player can improve his outcome by changing his strategy independently. The pairs are not equivalent, for A prefers (x', y') and B prefers (x, y).

Figure 3 (p. 92), presents a noncooperative game with a strict solution—that is, all conditions are met. Figure 3 presents problems that are related to the context of the game. It is therefore worthwhile to introduce an interpretation of the game in order to analyze these problems.

Suppose that two college students who are strangers to each other are seated in different rooms and that they are each placed at a desk with a buzzer connected only to an observer's room. Suppose they are told that each will receive $100 if neither presses his buzzer for ten minutes; that if either presses the buzzer within one second of the other, neither gets anything; and that if one presses the buzzer first, he gets fifty dollars and the other must pay fifty dollars. If the players are reasonably intelligent and recognize that the game has a strict solution, both will sit tight, without pressing the buzzer, and each will gain $100. Let us now double the sums and assume that each knows the other and each wants to date the same girl at the same time. This girl is a bit mercenary and will go out only with the student who can spend the most money on her. Thus only one student can get the date with her. Now each student will press the buzzer as soon as the game starts. If the other student has not pressed the buzzer, he is sure of the date. And if the other student has pressed the buzzer, the first student has at least prevented him from getting the date, and is no worse off himself. Of course the utiles in the boxes should have been changed, for they do not genuinely represent the preference of the players, but the outside observer may have been unaware of this.

Let us change the context just a bit more. Let us assume that each student wants to buy a new stereophonic set. Each would like to be the only student on campus with such a set but values having the set more than being the unique possessor of the set. The order of preferences is: (1) having set alone; and (2) having set and other also has set; (3) not having set. The set costs $500. (We must assume that there is no good alternative use of the money and no outside source of funds.) If the game is repeated indefinitely until at least one student acquires $500, each player knows that if he retreats from the strict solution on any play but the fifth, the other will spite him and he will not get the set. But then each must remain cooperative on the fifth play also. If we put the price of the set at $450, however, each will remain cooperative until the fifth play and then become hostile on this play. Without explicit cooperation they cannot get their sets. In politics such small differences as that betweeen $450 and $500 either might not be discernible or might be mistakenly discerned. Thus it is important to know the difference between the two models and equally important not to mistake the models for reality itself.

Although the prior examples were developed to warn against mistaking models for the real world, it is a real-world fact that fine distinctions are difficult to make with respect to the features of alternative alliances. Therefore, once formed for a particular purpose, they are unlikely to change until the situation has changed in a substantial way. Although we can no more predict the membership of particular alliances than the von Neumann solution predicts which particular imputation from a solution set will be chosen, the likelihood of an understandable, determinate, and stable solution that matches theoretical expectations is high. Finally, let me emphasize that this discussion is illustrative only, for other models exist for problems that are indeterminate in one sense but not in another.

Rules and the real world

The problem of relevance to the real world bears on another of Waltz's many objections to my procedures. Waltz argues: "In economics, because the concept of the market as the firm's environment is well defined, the extent of the influence of the market and of the individual firms can be investigated. In Kaplan no distinct and operational definition of the environment of states—no definition of such an environment as linked to and yet distinct from the states that form it—has ever developed" (p. 61).

It is not clear from Waltz's language what he means. I show in an earlier section that my international systems are distinguished from their environment. If this is what he means, he has been answered already.

If, on the other hand, "operational" is the significant factor in his objection, I would never attempt to give such definitions, unless possibly in the investigation of specific cases. What a national actor is and what a capability is are not the same in different times and places or for different systems. I have elsewhere written at length on the scientific universalism that is represented by such an operational approach. In the computer model, we were able to put an operational specification in the computer program because we were not talking about any concrete system. It would have been improper in a verbal qualitative theory sketch designed to apply to a number of real-world cases to offer an operational definition that was not differentiated for the infinite variety of systems to which it might have been applied. It would have been equally improper to attempt such differentiation of criteria in the absence of the concrete investigations that would permit some reasonable argument for the validity of the particular measures used.

In any event, the insistence upon operational definitions in all cases, rather than only when they are appropriate, is a hangover from a discredited positivism. As Popper notes: "Einstein told me in 1950 that he regretted no mistake he ever made as much as this mistake [the insistence upon an operational definition of simultaneity]" (p. 97).

The measures that were employed by my students in their historical studies were qualitative, although with some quantitative indications. Whether fully quantitative measures that are adapted to specific concrete systems are possible is a subject on which I remain an agnostic. But I am extremely skeptical of all existing measures and prefer reasonable qualitative measures to unreasonable quantitative ones.

In fact, in the real world, statesmen estimate capabilities without having operational definitions; and such estimates played important roles in alliance decisions in nineteenth-century "balance of power" systems. There is no need for capabilities to be fungible in the sense that money is for the concept of relative capabilities to be useful in guiding the actions of statesmen. The fungibility of money permits certain types of quantitative evaluations that have no direct counterpart with respect to the behavior of statesmen in international relations. That the form is rough, however, does not mean that it is not reasonably adapted to the requirements of statecraft or that it is not or cannot be employed.

The norms of any system, whether social, moral, or legal, are at a level of generality similar to that of the essential rules. It is this aspect of rules, whether juridical or essential, that led Justice Holmes to point out that general principles do not decide particular cases. This, however, does not mean that judges or statesmen cannot use them as "steering" devices. They provide a form of organization for thinking about problems that could not be thought about more precisely anyway.

Rules of thumb such as the essential rules can be employed successfully by statesmen for a variety of reasons. Most of the purely theoretical alternatives are eliminated by geography, previous decisions, specific sources of dispute, and so forth. Thus, decisions are no more unmanageable than that of the entrepreneur in locating a store—a decision that also would be unmanageable if he had to consider every theoretically possible alternative. The statesman makes rough calculations concerning potential gain in the immediate future, consequences for future gains or losses, and consequences for the state of the system. He "measures" proposed alliances, wars , and peace treaties against the criteria provided by implicit rules and, thus, gains an intellectual control over his decisions that would be absent if they were considered merely in terms of immediate gains.

This process is eased by a fact that I point out in *System and Process*: "The equilibrium of the set of rules is not a continuous equilibrium but one that results from discrete actions over periods of time" (p. 25). Although this may backfire and permit an unintended transformation, it also gives statesmen time to engage in restorative negative-feedback actions.

This last aspect of international systems is the factor that led me to discount greatly the cost of information. The failure to do this is what led Burns to set five as the number of actors making for the greatest stability in a "balance of power" system. In my opinion, he greatly overestimated the cost of information. Five is probably a lower bound for stability, but not an upper bound.

Waltz on Dowty

The question remains as to whether historical analysis negates the validity of my particular theories. I pursue this topic in this and the next section.

According to Waltz, Dowty, who looked at "states over a wide span of time and place," concluded "that in no case were shifts in alliances produced by consideration of an overall 'balance of power,' a conclusion which [Dowty] *correctly* [italics added] explains" (p. 79). Waltz regards this as a refutation of my position, according to which, under equilibrial conditions, actors take the system's conditions into account in determining their strategies.

It is difficult to understand why Waltz puts such weight on the data collected by Dowty whereas, in his discussion of J. David Singer, he makes cogent arguments against the type of inductive procedure used by Dowty:

> A datum is something given. But in international relations [and everywhere else as well (my interpolation)] the data are not given, nor can they be almost intuitively and directly grasped. How can we decide which data we should "make" when an infinite amount of data can be generated? No inductive procedure can answer the question, for the very problem is to figure out the criteria by which induction can usefully proceed.... We need a theory, or some theories [or at least some praxical coding procedures (my interpolation)] in order to know what kind of data and connections to look for. Knowledge, it seems, must precede theory, and yet knowledge can only proceed from theory (p. 9).

Apart from Waltz's mysterious treatment of international relations as different from other fields in the character of its data—almost as if he had force fitted the positions of two incompatible authorities into his first two (incompatible) sentences—this is an excellent statement. One wishes only that Waltz had remembered it when he used Dowty to criticize my theorical position.

Dowty examines 237 cases of conflict among 170 states from 2280 B.C. to 1914. This was not a long-range project and it resulted in a relatively short (seventeen-page) article. Dowty divides these cases according to four international contexts; the classical world (280-150 B.C.); India (A.D. 1347-1526); Europe (A.D. 1492-1559); and Latin America (A.D. 1810-1914). In a second table, he divides direct conflicts according to whether tensions or disputes existed and whether the dyadic arrangements that formed were homogeneous or heterogeneous. He then examines the relationship between heterogeneity and the incidence of tension; relates wars and peaceful settlements to the type of conflict (tension or dispute); and, finally, tries to establish a relationship between factionalism and inequality of conflict.

Apart from the fact that Dowty relies on the secondary literature and examines no case in depth, the reader will note that none of the periods covered by Dowty includes any system that I refer to as "balance of power" or bipolar, with the possible exception of the classical Greek period, which, in any event, environmentally does not match the posited equilibrial values of the theory sketches. Furthermore, and very importantly, the categories that Dowty uses for his data do not correspond to the categories of my theory sketches.

One can test a theory only by choosing an appropriate setting and by employing categories that are related to the theory, as Waltz himself points out in his critique of Singer. One would not regard the behavior of French corporations in the 1940s or those of Latin American corporations in the same period as refutations of modern economic theory. Nor would one infer from the fact that most falling bodies do not appear to obey Newton's laws—think of all the swirling leaves and particles of dust in the atmosphere—that the theory has been refuted. Only a procedure that is carefully designed to test a theory can give us even low-confidence confirmations or disconfirmations. It takes far more than a few isolated genuflections in the direction of theory to do this; and it literally would not have been possible for Dowty by himself, and in a short period of time, to have attempted to test my theory sketches for even a small fraction of the cases he covered in his tables. The tables are useful nonetheless, for someone who has a theory may get insights from them as to where he might get the greatest leverage for testing his theories if he examined particular areas or periods far more intensively and within the constraints of a theoretical statement than Dowty does. This is especially true if one wants to distinguish bipolar from "balance of power" behavior, the former not being merely a dyadic form of contention, as both Waltz and Dowty seem to think, but a far more complex set of interrelationships.

Dowty's study attempts to discover the immediate causes of war and alliance. My theory sketches do not constitute theories of the specific causes of wars, or of alliances, or of the details of peace. Behavior that conforms to the essential rules is not per se a confirmation of any of my theories, for the conforming behavior may be the product of extratheoretical causes. My explanation, for instance, for behavior in classical Greece that corresponds to "balance of power" rules is different from Dowty's but rests on extrasystemic causes: logistic considerations and the peculiar circumstances of the polity in Sparta. Franke's paper—to which Waltz refers and to which I will soon turn—demonstrates that logistical considerations were responsible for "balance of power"-like behavior in the first phase of the Italian city-state system. Likewise, behavior that apparently contradicts the theory sketch may be consistent with it if we can show a deviance from equilibrial conditions in the environment which, if taken into account in applying the theory, would predict what actually happened. I did this in my explanation of the rigid "balance of power" in Europe after 1870, to which Waltz otherwise approvingly refers.

In any event, Dowty's inferences from his data are directly related to his questions. He asks specific micro-questions. And he can get only specific microanswers from specific microquestions. It is one thing to ask why states X and Y entered an alliance and another to ask why the pattern of alliances took a particular form and why wars were limited in particular ways. This would be true even for nineteenth-century Europe, which I do classify as a "balance of power" system. I explicate this point in *System and Process:*

> Just as any particular molecule of gas in a gas tank may travel in any direction, depending upon accidental bumpings with other molecules, particular actions of national actors may depend upon chance or random conjunctions. Yet just as the general pattern of behavior of the gas may represent its adjustment to pressure and temperature conditions within the tank, the set of actions of national actors may correspond to the essential rules of the system when the other variables take the appropriate specified values. thus, by shifting the focus of analysis from a particular event to the pattern of events, seemingly unique or accidental occurrences become part of a meaningful pattern of occurrences (p. 25).

The specific, which is accidentally determined, is what Dowty discovers. Particular states may enter into alliances because of geographic configuration or because they are neighbors. They may have a conflict over a boundary issue. The analogy from economics would involve the specific place in which a businessman seeks orders or whom specifically he competes with. These are determined by theoretically accidental factors.

Both Waltz and Dowty should know better in any event, for the evidence that statesmen take the system into account in "balance of power" systems is available in any introductory textbook. It is widely agreed that nineteenth-century Europe—a period that Dowty strangely did not include in his study despite the great availability of evidence—was an arena in which a "balance of power" system operated. The specialized role that Great Britain played as "balancer" in the nineteenth-century "balance of power" system—a role that was related to the peculiar geographic and capability conditions of that period—clearly took the system into account. So did Lorenzo de Medici take the state of the system into account in the second phase of the Italian city-state system: a system phase that I characterize as "balance of power." This becomes clear in Franke's study, which I now turn to.

Waltz on Franke

Waltz refers to Franke's article and attempts to use it to demonstrate a weakness in what he claims is my practice of turning

> a dependent variable into an independent one...[t]he distinction be-
> tween laws that express a result and rules of action that produce
> one must be carefully made.... Kaplan write[s] as though actors will
> produce a given result only if they are motivated to do so.... A nice
> illustration of what erroneously doing so leads to is found in an essay
> by one of Kaplan's former students. To his surprise, he finds that the
> Italian city-states in the fourteenth and fifteenth centuries did not
> comply with Kaplan's rules one and four.

I must admit that I was surprised to find out that Franke was surprised to find what Waltz claims he discovered—for I went to great effort in my workshops to get my students to look for and to expect disconforming behavior in the real world. The surprising case in an open world would be where the essential rules are consistently followed. Nonetheless, I was prepared to believe that Franke had forgotten what I had taught him, for students have been known to do this. However, in rereading his article, I am at a loss to find any expression of surprise. Let us, therefore, see what Franke says:

> At first glance, the Italian city-state would appear to constitute as close
> a historical approximation of the model as we are likely to find *under
> the constraints of the real world* [italics added]. Whether this is
> actually the case may safely remain unanswered until a great many
> more comparative studies have been undertaken. It is clear presently,
> however, that the city-state system did not comply with the theoretical
> specifications of behavioral (essential) rules, other variables of the
> system, and parameters to the same extent. Moreover, one can dis-
> cuss successive phases which exhibit significant parametric and be-
> havioral differences (p. 427).

> The second phase can be distinguished from the first in terms of a
> new pattern of interaction, especially of alliances, as a somewhat
> delayed response to the changed conditions previously indicated. The

boundaries of the essential actors move closer together, and expansionary threats or other upsetting capability increases were more immediately registered as such and were more consistently counteracted (p. 441).

Moreover, the absence of successive violations [of the rules] is complemented by the deliberate and persistent exertions on the part of Florence (and of the Papacy to a lesser extent) to prevent a situation in which the violation of rules 3 to 6 might become probable (p. 443).

Apart from the environment complications, we may conclude that the internal equilibrium of the Italian city-state system increased further during the second phase.... This equilibrium was in large measure the result of the *conscious* [italics added] assumption of a "balancing" role by Florence, as the prior containment of Milan was largely the result of the Venetians' assuming a regulative role in the city-state system (p. 444).

The third phase, then, is distinguished from the preceding one primarily by the accession of deviant rulers in several actor systems and by the consequent changes in behavioral patterns: both the pattern of deviant behavior and the pattern of further adaptive responses (p. 446).

The third and final phase of the Italian "balance of power" system then compels us to draw apparently incompatible conclusions. On the one hand, most of the parameters that were favorable to equilibrium in the second phase persisted into the third phase: all essential and even nonessential actors were preserved; the territorial capabilities did not change greatly where some other essential capabilities, especially on the part of the Papacy and Naples, came close to parity; diplomatic activity and apparatus still rapidly expanded, while the new military technologies and techniques with their disadvantages for the defense, in particular for the defense of cities, continued to be eschewed. In addition, the absence of successful violations of the essential rules, the evidently increasing alignment flexiblity, and the level of regulatory activity would seem to make for a further stabilization of equilibrium. And yet, on the other hand, the equilibrium in fact became not only less static but also less stable. And the system ultimately disintegrated. That these conclusions are *only apparently* [italics added] in conflict is already plain from the frequent references that were made to the actors of the European environment. In recognition of that environment, the Medicean alliances from 1450 on explicitly had the double purpose of maintaining, irrespective of environmental developments, the internal Italian equilibrium and of minimizing whatever destabilizing influence could issue from that European environment (pp. 448-49).

However, as Franke then points out:

Florence was too weak and strategically too exposed to withstand the combined might of two superior actors located in the same hemisphere, at least if one or both allies from the opposite hemisphere could not afford prompt relief.... The flexibility requisite for such a neutral "balancing" role was wanting in the Italian system because of two circumstances already indicated: the existence of potentially interfering environmental actors simply, and the special claims which these had on two Italian actors. Had no such feudal hereditary relations existed and increased the likelihood of interference,...

the system might not have become unstable. Franke's conclusion is that the Italian city-state system had atypical parameters that were "less susceptible to remedial action by the...actors" (p. 456).

Let me summarize Franke's complex article, which is the distillation of a much longer work based upon massive documentation from both secondary and primary sources. In the first phase of the system, the rulers of the city-states had no comprehension of the nature of an international system. Although some changes did occur in membership within the system, the number was never driven below five. Franke does not relate the reasons for this, however, to the system-relevant characteristics of the Italian city-state system, nor does Waltz's formulation explain this either. The cities had no long-lasting administrative systems and were highly dependent on the personal characteristics of rulers. Thus several attempts that might have succeeded in gaining hegemony failed when particular dukes died. At other times logistical and economic difficulties made striving for hegemony impracticable. In the second phase, the "balancer," Lorenzo de' Medici, clearly understood the nature of the system and oriented the alliance behavior of Florence to the requirements of system stability. His self-consciousness concerning the character of the system was one of the most essential features of the stability of that period. The mercenary system also played a role. The specific character of the alliances, however, was determined in part by the particular geographic patterning of the peninsula. In the last phase of the system, Piero de' Medici did not understand the functioning of the system; and, although

I am greatly oversimplifying, his failure self-consciously to play a stabilizing role was a major factor in bringing in the French and causing the system to collapse.

In other studies in the workshops, it was possible to show that such statesmen as Bismarck, Castlereagh, and Palmerston did understand the character of the international system and did orient their actions toward that understanding. Although the elements that constituted this understanding must be pulled from documents and diaries, I have no serious doubts concerning the correctness of this statement.

We are all familiar with systems that do not need to be taken into account in their broader context by the actors if they are to be maintained. The perfect market that consists of a large number of sellers and buyers is presumably of this type. Simple maximizing behavior will for the most part suffice. This is not necessarily true for systems with smaller numbers of actors, depending on the specific features of the system. This is why, among other reasons, it is simply not possible to talk about "balance of power" as a universal theory without relating it to other structural elements.

The curious thing about Waltz's tunnel-vision reading of Franke is that he immediately footnotes Dowty: "looking at states over a wide span of time and space Dowty concludes that in no cases were shifts in alliances produced 'by considerations of an overall balance of power,' a conclusion which he correctly explains" (p. 95). But Franke shows in depth that this is not so and that an otherwise "balance of power" system does become unstable when it is not so.

EPILOGUE

Let me reiterate that the object of this essay has not been to demonstrate the inadequacies of Waltz's analysis. Were Waltz unintelligent or incompetent, this essay would not have been worth the effort I put into it nor would it be productive in terms of my purposes.

Ever since *Man, the State, and War* (1959)—the revised version of Waltz's doctoral dissertation—appeared, his work has received deserved attention from practitioners in the field of international relations. In the few short years since his essay in the *Handbook of Political Science,* Waltz's essay on the state of the discipline has been widely admired. Yet I have shown that at virtually no point in his treatment of Galtung on imperialism or of my own work—the portions of his essay (less than 20 pages) that I treat at length (about 90 pages) in this analysis—will Waltz's arguments withstand analysis. Its systematic confusion, I believe, demonstrates the preprofessional character of the field, for in no field in which a substantial number of the practitioners have achieved genuinely professional standards would it be possible for a distinguished scholar to produce such a work and for it to be published and admired.

Let me also reiterate that my objective in this analysis has not been to demonstrate that my conclusions in *System and Process in International Politics* —whether methodological or theoretical—are correct. On the contrary, I believe that if international relations were a discipline in which there were genuine professional standards, I would by now likely have been persuaded to modify my methodology and to correct my position on a number of substantive points. *System and Process,* after all, was offered only as a heuristic or introductory theory.

My regret that my critics have provided mostly wind and chaff is surpassed only by my regret that those students I have sent out to study historical international systems cannot get a hearing from a preprofessional discipline that is interested primarily in quantitative work or contemporary analysis. Apart from the things that we might learn from a computer project about the internal logic of theories, history is the only laboratory we have that permits comparative analysis on a systematic qualitative basis. The projects that we undertook in my workshops, I think, indicate strongly the types of information that would have been gained from such work if it had been possible to carry it out on a more systematic and sustained basis. In addition to comparative international systems analysis, the work was beginning to illuminate the reasons why some quasi-international systems such as the Holy Roman Empire and the classical Chinese state system remained international whereas others such as the Shogunate in Japan and the French system produced strong national kings. Moreover, the transition from the classical state system in China to the empire also illuminated this theme.

My disappointment over the tendency of the discipline to reiterate only the same old tired debates as a substitute for real theory was so great that I went on to other pastures myself. I still intend to leave the next stage of advance to younger scholars. However, the distinguished reputation and systematic care—at least by contemporary standards—of Waltz's work provided me with an opportunity to demonstrate the inadequacies of the present preprofessional stage of the discipline of international relations theory. Unless we move on toward a more professional and careful level of analysis, we will continue simply to throw arguments and authorities about as if they were brain-damaged soldiers in a haphazard war fought by drunken barons.

In the absence of genuine dialogue within the community of scholars, no discipline can advance. When the discussion that does exist falls as far short of professional standards as that in macrotheory in international relations, it is no wonder that the field is in a shambles. Younger scholars in this field must decide whether or not they are serious about it. Only if they enforce professional standards will the field lose its chaotic character. The choice is theirs.

Postscript: Now that I am reading reviews in political science journals of my two recent books in political philosophy, I am coming to the conclusion that I have been too harsh on critics in international relations.

FOOTNOTES

1. Important ways of thinking about a problem must sometimes be reoriented—as when phlogiston theory or the concept of the ether were rejected—although, interestingly, the recent discovery of traces of the possible original "bang" at the formation of the universe may provide a measuring standard that is independent of inertial systems but consistent with Einstein's relativity concepts rather than with Newton's concepts of absolute space or time.
2. As Lakatos uses the term "auxiliary theory," these also are new theories rather than auxiliary theories.
3. See Luce and Raiffa (1957, pp. 199ff.) for a technical analysis of this problem.

REFERENCES

Ashby, W. Ross. *Design for a Brain*. New York: John Wiley & Sons, 1952.

Carnap, Rudolf. "Empiricism, Semantics, and Ontology." *Revue internationale de philosophie* 4 (1950), 20-40.

———. *Logical Foundations of Probability*. Chicago: University of Chicago Press, 1950.

———. *Der logische Aufbau der Welt*. Berlin, 1928.

———. *Meaning and Necessity*. Chicago: University of Chicago Press, 1947.

Chamberlin, Edward. *Theory of Monopolistic Competition*. 6th ed. Cambridge, Mass.: Harvard University Press, 1948.

Chi, Hsi-cheng. "The Chinese Warlord system as an International System." In *New Approaches to International Relations*, edited by Morton A. Kaplan. New York: St. Martin's Press, 1968.

Dowty, Alan. "Conflict in War-potential Politics: An Approach to Historical Macroanalysis." *Peace Research Society Papers* 13 (1969): 86-103.

Franke, Winfried. "The Italian City-State System as an International System." In *New Approaches to International Relations*, edited by Morton A. Kaplan. New York: St. Martin's Press, 1968.

Galtung, Johan. "A Structural Theory of Imperialism." *Journal of Peace Research* 8 (1971): 81-117.

Hoffmann, Stanley. Review of "Theory of International Relations," by Kenneth N. Waltz, *American Political Science Review* 71 (December 1977): 1635-36.

Kaplan, Abraham. *The Conduct of Inquiry: Methodology for Behavioral Science*. San Francisco: Chandler Publishing Co., 1964.

Kaplan, Morton A. *Alienation and Identification*. New York: Free Press, 1976.

———. *Justice, Human Nature, and Political Obligation*. New York: Free Press, 1976.

———. *Macropolitics: Essays on the Philosophy and Science of Politics*. Chicago: Aldine Publishing Co., 1969.

———. ed. and contr. *New Approaches to International Relations*. New York: St. Martin's Press, 1968.

———. *On Historical and Political Knowing: An Inquiry into Some Problems of Universal Law and Human Freedom*. Chicago: University of Chicago Press, 1971.

———. Review article on diplomatic history. *Journal of Modern History* 47 (March 1975).

———. *Some Problems of Strategic Analysis in International Politics*. Center of International Studies. Princeton, New Jersey: Princeton University Press, 1959.

———. "Some Problems of the Extreme Utilitarian Position." *Ethics* 70 (April 1960): 228-32; "Restricted Utilitarianism." *Ethics* 71 (July 1961): 301-2.

———. *System and Process in International Politics*. New York: John Wiley & Sons, 1957.

Lakatos, Imre. "Falsification and the Methodology of Scientific Research Programmes." In *Criticism and the Growth of Knowledge*, edited by Imre Lakatos and Alan Musgrave. Cambridge: Cambridge University Press, 1970.

Luce, R. Duncan, and Howard Raiffa. *Games and Decisions*. New York: John Wiley & Sons, 1957.

Morgan, Henry Lewis. *Systems of Consanguinity and Affinity of the Human Family.* 1870. Reprint. New York: Humanities Press, 1970.

Popper, Karl. *Unended Quest: An Intellectual Autobiography.* Glasgow: William Collins Sons, 1976.

Quine, Willard Van Orman. *From a Logical Point of View.* Cambridge, Mass.: Harvard University Press, 1953.

Reichenbach, Hans. *The Theory of Probability,* translated by Ernest H. Hutten and Maria Reichenbach. 2d ed. Berkeley: University of California Press, 1949.

Reitzel, William, Morton A. Kaplan, and Constance G. Coblenz. *United States Foreign Policy: 1945-1955.* Washington, D.C.: The Brookings Institution, 1956.

Review of *Justice, Human Nature and Political Obligation,* by Morton A. Kaplan. *Review of Metaphysics,* vol. 31 (September 1977).

Riker, William H. *The Theory of Political Coalitions.* New Haven, Conn: Yale University Press, 1962.

Schössler, Dietmar, and Erich Weede. *West German Elite Views on National Security and Foreign Policy Issues.* (M.S.)

Von Neumann, John, and Oscar Morgenstern. *Theory of Games and Economic Behavior.* 3d ed. Princeton, N.J.: Princeton University Press, 1953.

Waltz, Kenneth N., *Man, the State, and War.* New York: Columbia University Press, 1959.

———. "Theory of International Relations." In *International Politics.* Vol. 8. *Handbook of Political Science,* edited by Fred I. Greenstein and Nelson W. Polsby. Reading, Mass.: Addison-Wesley Publishing Co., 1975.

Wiener, Norbert. *Cybernetics.* New York: John Wiley & Sons, 1948.

FIGURES

B

9,9	0,10
10,0	1,1

A

FIGURE 1

B

	y	y'
x	2,3	1,1
x'	1,0	3,2

A

FIGURE 2

B

0,0	50,-50
-50,50	100,100

A

FIGURE 3

CHAPTER 2

SYSTEMS ANALYSIS

THE SYSTEMS CONCEPT

The concept of system in many respects is as ambiguous as it is obvious. The often-used term "systems theory" predisposes some to believe that a systems theory either does or can exist in the same way as mechanical theory in physics. Yet no theory of systems exists—or can exist—that will permit derived predictions of human behavior in the way in which Newtonian theory, for instance, can be applied to the solar system. Neither is systems "theory" genuinely a methodology. If one speaks of the methodology of titrating chemicals, he can specify a set of procedures to be applied to the process. In playing games of chance, there are statistical methods for determining the best strategy to employ. No particular methodology belongs to systems theory.

Is systems analysis a metatheory in the sense in which scientific method can be called a metamethodology? In a broad sense scientific method involves the use of public methods for validating—or for invalidating—hypotheses within the contemporary framework of knowledge. The specific methods for accomplishing this are learned through experience. Our beliefs concerning them change over time and are validated, in turn, by praxis, which will be explicated later in this chapter. Moreover, the methods may differ from subject matter to subject matter. Thus, the methods employed in macrophysical theory, in high-temperature physics, in particle physics, in various forms of chemical theory, in biology, and in some of the softer sciences differ, although they do have in common the attempt to employ more or less precise measurement and various techniques of quantification. If systems theory as a metamethodology or metatheory implies only this, then it adds nothing to scientific method in general. Yet, if it implies something beyond this, what can that be?

The term "system" is one that has been used historically by scientists and that is coming into ever-increasing use with the popularity of systems analysis. For instance, "atomic system" and "solar system" are well-known examples of use of the term. If we examine the best-known example—the solar system—the term at first appears to be purely descriptive. It refers to the pattern of the orbital paths of the planets around the sun. The term "system" in this case implies an ordered patterning of elements, the explanation of, and predictions concerning which, are supplied by Newtonian theory, although Kepler's laws earlier provided a partial explanation involving not a general theory of gravitation but a special explanation of one particular empirical solar system.

In the case of Newtonian theory, the concept of system "told" the scientist not to treat planetary motions as independent events unrelated to the complex of sun and planets. (Later it became clear that for certain purposes the solar system could not be treated as a closed system.) As contrasted with the experiments of Galileo, which were concerned only with the path of a falling body, Newton's theory was more dependent upon explicit recognition of the existence of a system.

Technically this is incorrect, for the Galilean problem could be considered a classic two-body problem in which the movement of the earth toward a smaller body is negligible. The assumption that wind resistance does not affect the velocity of the object specifies the assumed system boundary for purposes of scientific explanation. However, despite the formal similarity, conceptually the Newtonian problem requires greater awareness of the existence of a system. Whereas for Galileo the earth and the falling body were obvious objects of inquiry, the astronomers had to distinguish the rapidly moving circles of light as planets from the relatively stationary circles of light as suns and to recognize that the planets bore a relationship to a particular sun. Although the Newtonian mechanical laws apply to all solar systems, the discovery or perception of such laws arises only from an awareness of such systems qua systems.

Scientific theories may be considered systems in another sense. The concepts employed in a set of laws, mass, for instance, and the functions relating them may be considered the internal elements of the system. The assumed conditions under which they operate, for instance, a vacuum, constitute the boundary conditions of the system. This is a theoretical system or, in more ordinary language, a theory and provides a framework for explanation. Although theories have a hypothetico-deductive form, their interpretation and application—as is true of any analytical system—require information not contained in the formal specification of a theory, a subject to which I shall return in my discussion of praxis.

Presumably every theory employing laws contains a complete specification of boundary conditions. However, we can never be sure that we know all the relevant boundary conditions. Thus, we often learn that what we regard as universal is in fact applicable only under a specified set of boundary conditions. We were not aware, for instance, of superconductivity until certain elements were examined under conditions of extreme temperature or pressure. It is possible, even likely, that what we believe to be the most general laws of the physical universe will require a radically different statement under some changed parameter of which we are now unaware. (Of course, it is also true that our explanations often lead us to look for previously unobserved events.)

For the scientist, however, there are relatively minor problems. Even those scientists who are relatively unsophisticated in methodology, and who would be unable to articulate verbally the procedures they are applying, know that they must specify the conditions under which the experiment takes place and the variables upon which the experiment is to be performed. Thus, despite the increasing propensity of scientists to talk about scientific systems, there would probably be no great loss if the term were not used. The standard laboratory procedures of science guard against the most egregious mistakes and minimize the dangers of misconception. Those scientists who hypostatize the results of particular experiments would probably make this mistake anyway even if they used a systems terminology.

The problems that the physical scientist can afford to ignore because they are taken care of by standardized laboratory techniques infest the social sciences and mandate a systems orientation, not for all problems of social science but for those where conscious recognition of the interrelationship of some elements within a complex whole is essential to a correct statement of the problem. One might argue that the requirements previously stated are obvious in the social sciences also. However, the literature of the social sciences is filled with examples of research that do not respond to this methodological orientation. In his chapter in *Diplomatic Investigations,* for instance, Martin Wight (1966) chooses examples from 2,000 years of history to illustrate certain principles of statecraft. That the international systems in which these actions took place may have been radically different is not a question that occurred to him. That the numbers of states, their weapons systems, their economic potentialities, their patterns of alignment, and so forth, may have produced different types of systems within which the cited examples functioned differently was foreign to his analysis and indeed foreign to any analysis before the middle 1950s, when systems concepts made their entry into the international relations literature. He is far from alone.

WHAT A SYSTEM IS

Systems analysis, instead of being considered a theory, should be considered an approach that calls for the development of theories or the elucidation of propositions oriented to those aspects of reality for which the explicit recognition of systems characteristics is useful. Thus, my initial task in this inquiry is to determine the characteristics to be attributed to the term "system."

A system is a set of interrelated elements sufficiently distinguished from their environment by certain regularities to serve as a focus of inquiry. The elements of a system may be concrete in the sense that they are physically distinguishable, or they may be abstract in the sense that they are conceptually distinguishable. Thus a system may consist of points, of numbers, of roles, of organizations, and so forth. These elements may then be related in terms of authority, wisdom, wealth, strength, or any other relevant characteristic of the roles. We may include as parts of the system characteristics such as economic capabilities or information. We may also distinguish as part of the system the behavior that accords with the other elements of the system under specified parameter conditions.

Systems include both elements and functions. Thus the heart pumps blood and the lungs process air. Priests provide absolution, legislatures pass laws, courts apply law. An input into a system that changes its characteristic behavior is called a step function. Thus opium changes the characteristic optic behavior of the biological organism. A successful revolution changes the characteristic behavior (and the characteristic values and normative rules) of a political system. (This is a schematic explanation of the principle that invalidates the search for a universal set of rules that applies to a system regardless of its internal characteristics or boundary conditions. It applies to normative and also to other behavioral aspects of system functioning.)

The choice of a system is, in effect, a choice of a subject matter. There is no "absolute" single system in the concrete world. In principle, the same reality may be analyzed by a variety of systems models. It is an empirical or at least a praxical—rather than a theoretical—matter whether this is useful. This also applies to the choice of which variables are internal and which are external to the system. Later in this chapter, we shall see that a similar analysis applies to the choice of axioms, theorems, and the other elements of theories.

In my international systems theory sketches, the structure of the system is specified when the roles of the system—whether national actors, blocs, leading bloc actors, universal actors, and so forth—functions, capabilities, information, and boundary conditions have been indicated. The six international systems in

System and Process in International Politics (1957) are partial theory sketches that permit research programs of both comparative historical and analytical types.

MEANING, THEORIES, AND PRAXIS

MEANING AND SCIENCE

Science in its theoretical aspects is analytical. However, the entire realm of science is a realm of praxis in which meaning—and not merely observation—plays a major role. The fundamental error involved in ignoring the role of meaning can be elucidated by turning to a nonconscious entity: the computer. We cannot derive the behavior of the computer, including the content of the output tape, from its circuitry unless we know the content both of the internal code of the computer and of its input tape. If we know these, we can then predict the output from the input plus the internal coding. Knowledge of the particularities of the wiring of the computer would be unnecessary for this prediction, although some form of appropriate wiring and a memory system are necessary for the computer's operation. The sequence of operations of the computer depends upon the internal code as well as upon he wiring, so that the activated coding element actually triggers the next operation of the system.

However, the problem is more fundamental even than this. If we knew the content of the coding of the computer, then, given the input, we could predict the output. However, even this depends on the computer's ability to compare the symbols on the input tape with its code and to recognize their identity. Thus, even at this presumably nonconscious level, the computer "knows" the "meaning" of the symbols. However, we still do not know how to relate the output tape to any observation we can make external to the computer unless we know how to identify the output symbols with observations.

To do this, we must have knowledge of their meaning. Thus, at every level of analysis, whther symbolic or referential, meaning is essential. Willard van Orman Quine (1953) was able to demonstrate that the absolute distinction between the synthetic and the analytic cannot be maintained, that extrasystemic meaning is always required for the interpretation and use of formal analytical systems.

Nor is extrasystemic meaning derived directly from sensations. As John Dewey argued, our knowledge of "red" is not derived from a red sensation. Instead, the theory that perceptions are produced by sensations depends on experience. Yet physiology reveals the inadequacies of naive empiricism as adequately as does epistemological theory. Because the normal eye pupil is in continual motion, no set of sensations could present a stationary object as stationary to the brain. Instead the brain must transform the sensations, and this can be confirmed by experiment. Thus, experience always requires the active participation of the perceiving sytstem. And meaning is an essential element without which the process cannot occur; it is not simply an epiphenomenal derivative from sensations.

Moreover, as Quine pointed out, Rudolf Carnap, the leading exponent of purely analytical procedures, was forced to abandon his beliefs in the one-to-one translatability of statements about the physical world into statements about immediate experience. As Quine says, statements about the external world face the tribunal of sense experience not individually but as a corporate body.

We do not start with an invariant set of meanings. Our initial understanding of meanings is subject to change with experience and is variant as changes occur in the realm of praxis. We learn about meaning as we use terms, theories, and logical form. It was the inability of Aristotle's logic to account for such knowledge as "If horses are animals, the heads of horses are heads of animals" that led to the development of inferential logic. Every form of inquiry involves meanings that are validated by use.

"Meaning" has several aspects. "Meaning" is fully conveyed neither by verbal definitions nor by "pointing" denotations. No complex sentence has a one-to-one correlation with perception; and "pointing" merely identifies a case and, therefore, assumes meaning.

Meaning is related to the coding employed by the organism. However, this coding does not link a discrete coding element to a discrete perceptual element in any simple fashion. Stimulus-response theories assume such discrete elements. For a sufficiently stable world and a sufficiently simple organism, or for simple aspects of a more complex organism, this mode of explanation may be sufficient, though not fully accurate. This discrete conception of "coding" reifies concepts, for instance, color, which praxically depends for its meaning on the observing system, the source of light, and designated coding standards (Kaplan 1976, pp. 49ff).

It is likely that coding is field dependent—that it is dependent on many of the characteristics of the experiential and the neurological fields. As these shift, the codings acquire different experiential meanings. In higher organisms this involves the development and modification of concepts, changes in their relationships, and changes in relations between different levels and types of abstraction. In higher organisms, the method by which different "fits" are tried may not be strictly deterministic and the equilibrium that cocurs may not be optimal. However, the field and its codings are stabilized by their complex fit with the experiential world. And, although the pathways to a "fit" may not be predetermined, the equilibrium of a complex of codings is determined by its "fit." Indeed, the resistance of a person to an intellectually better "fit" may depend upon its inconsistency with other elements—for instance, valuational—of his larger field. The "freedom" of the organism in developing concepts within the field is the source of creativity. And its existence probably can be explained by evolutionary advantage.

How an observation is coded—that is, the determination of what elements of observations are "identified" as evidence and what they are regarded as evidence for—depends upon many other elements of the field of knowledge. The transition from Newtonian to Einsteinian mechanics, although involving differences in the concept of mass, substantially retained the older categories of evidence. Yet even within the realm of physics some observations are disregarded as inaccurate because they do not "fit" contemporary theory.

Sufficiently great shifts in the theoretical structure of science may produce great changes in the coding and interpretation of evidence. Except in the twilight zone, however, this does not mean that competing theories cannot be compared "objectively," for the weight of the field of knowledge likely will "validate" the new coding, particularly if, as is likely to be the case, some of the old codings sustain the new theories that require altered codings with respect to other evidence. Thus, it is the revealed inconsistency in the old field of knowledge that shifts the entire field. The pioneer in science, the great theorist, is one who intuitively "sees" the discrepancy earlier and who recognizes first the new mode of integrating the field or at least of restoring substantial consistency to it. However, there is no global theory that accounts for physical reality. There is only a shifting equilibrium in the realm of praxis, including a multitude of theories and of standards of evidence. As information theory tells us, structure is merely more slowly changing process.

Distinctions are not absolute. They are related to use and they change with both the instruments and purposes of use. Newton's "absolute" system was conceived as if it were independent of instrumental techniques. Einstein's system incorporated an essential instrumental aspect in c, the constant for light, which is a major element in the "relativity" of his system. Nonetheless, the Einsteinian equations are determinate with respect to relations among noninstrumental aspects of macrophysical "objects" within inertial systems, and they produce similar but transposed predictions for independent inertial systems. With respect to quantum theory, the relationship between instrument and system of reference is more intimate, with consequences for determinate outcomes that are well known.

In both cases theory refers primarily to the "objects" of inquiry and not to the instruments and operations of inquiry. These are taken into account only insofar as necessary. Science and philosophy of science are not concerned with operational "games" and would not have progressed to the extent they have if they had been so concerned.

Of course, instrumentation cannot be ignored. Reference to the physiological human instrument of inquiry is required to deal with the question of the "objectivity" of the good. Language is also an instrument of inquiry, and the analysis of language, including the use of concepts, is essential to certain aspects of inquiry. No more than in the case of instrumentation, however, can the analysis of language become the object of inquiry, at least with respect to non-linguistic problems.

Let me repeat: the language of inquiry, even—or especially—if important to an inquiry, cannot be divorced from the substance of inquiry without serious failures in analysis. It is not good enough to assert that language "points beyond itself" and to make a comparison of uses that are abstracted from the "object- or process-like" features of the system within which they are used. Comparative analysis is important for certain purposes, and I shall return to that subject in this chapter.

There are no necessary universal meanings for concepts, even in the sense of family relationships. Meaning is generated within the circumstances of systemic "closeness" at the "object level" of inquiry. Attempts to discuss or to analyze comparatively meanings that are divorced from intrasystemic "object level" analysis will soon rise to a level of abstraction that is sterile. It is therefore no accident that the inquiries of so many adherents of the ordinary-language school of philosophers are sterile and boring. "Language games" are "games" in the pejorative sense of the term. Despite their recognition of the lack of isomorphism in the "use" of language, language is hypostatized by them. The analysis of language is essential to certain stages in inquiry—particularly inquiries concerning human behavior—but the philosophy of ordinary-language analysis, at least as most of its exponents use it, is the converse error of Wittgenstein's earlier position—an error that he, if not many of his followers, likely did not make.

THEORY AND PRAXIS

The distinction between theory (explanation) and praxis (assessment) is not absolute, for even the well-confirmed theories and covering laws of physics depend upon substantive assumptions that may later be modified by other information. Assessment and praxis, however, do not obtrude, at least not obviously, in the cases of those theories that are able to treat their parameters as "givens" for important practical purposes, if not for all. The important work of Boltzmann and Gibbs, however, demonstrated long ago that even the laws of mechanics could not be treated as absolutely universal from some theoretical frameworks. Assessment and praxis come to the fore in those cases in which the interdependence between assumptions concerning the boundary conditions of a theoretical area and the determination of how to formulate theory is so strong that choices among identifications of subject matter, boundary assessments and theoretical formulations become problematic in practice.

The Hempelian deductive covering law model gives the best account of how theoretical scientists state particular theories, of how they confirm or disconfirm them, and of how they reason from them—including sometimes the prediction of surprising results. Thus, the covering law model is not merely an ex post facto formalism, although it is not a complete account of scientific inquiry. It comes closest to practice with respect to the formal derivation of a consequence from theoretical assumptions under specified and relatively noncontroversial boundary conditions. It begins to diverge somewhat more as "nonobvious" interpretations are required in the actual use of scientific tools and methods, including but not restricted to the assessment of experimental results as confirmations of prediction sentences.

In theoretical physics, new information, for example, the Michelson-Morley experiment and non-Euclidean geometries, or new observations, may lead either to a reformulation of a theory or to a replacement of one theory by another. Among other differences, this replacement may involve shifts in concepts, for example, mass; changes in axioms, for example, the constant for light; or changes in theorems, as in the geometry of space. Both Newtonian and Einsteinian theory were able to treat their concepts and parameters as "givens" for significant periods of time. The methods of praxis come to the fore during periods of transition in which alternative theories are compatible with experimental evidence. In these cases, choice is determined by consistency with other confirmed elements of science; range, economy, and "centrality" of explanation; "fit"; and so forth.

The social and physical sciences share the characteristics noted above. However, social science, because of its complexity and the rich interconnectedness of its elements, especially with respect to socially or politically relevant and important factors, is predominantly, but not exclusively, a realm of praxis. This is particularly true of ethics, within which the identifications of particular ethical systems, of rules within a system, and of applications as relevant are necessarily contextually determined to a great degree.

The usual case in social sciences is that in which no single theory provides enough of the variance to account for observations, predictions, or explanations. In this case, the reasoning within each relevant theoretical framework has explanatory form; but its adjustment to other frameworks in accounting for actual events is dominated by a different form of reasoning in which consistency plays an important role. Along with the identification of the relevant theories, this assessment occurs in the realm of praxis.

The identification of a theory with a relevant realm of application is crucial. Even in physics, we must be able to distinguish between electrons and planets; otherwise we could not know whether to apply general relativity theory or quantum meachnics. Yet in the social sciences the reification of words such as "state" or "international system" leads us to assume an identity that may not exist for theoretical purposes.

Use of a theory involves explanation. Decisions concerning its superiority over a competing theory involve assessment, and fall in the realm of praxis. Both theory and praxis employ reasoning, but the reasoning process takes different forms in each. Theory in its formal phase closes the system of explanation at its boundaries. Praxis, in addition to the evaluation of the elements of theory, of boundaries, and of evidence, may involve at least partly independent chains of reasoning that are related to different theories. In the latter case, each part of the reasoning process operates within tentatively assumed parameters. However, these tentative parameters usually will differ for the different theories that are being employed. When it is necessary to choose from among alternative theories, there is a segmented series of adjustments in which less "fitting" theories are replaced by more "fitting" theories and in which the surviving theoretical influences are estimated in assessing the case. Thus, in their analytical aspects, explanation and assessment use different but closed forms of reasoning. Closure characterizes the formal aspects of science. Yet the real world is obdurately open. This is one reason why reason can never exhaust particularity.

"Theory" is a term that is both used and abused; and I am aware that much of what I call praxis is merely a somewhat stricter form of what some people call theory. Those elements of praxis that set constraints on how theory may be formulated but that are consistent with substantively different theories might be called metatheory. I regard this kind of "metatheory" as legitimate, and even necessary, for the treatment of the broadest forms of reasoning that deal with matters that are problematic and only loosely connected.

THE QUINE/LAKATOS CONTROVERSY

Imre Lakatos has attacked some important aspects of Quine's position on falsification that are closely related to my distinction between theory and praxis. Quine argues (1953 pp. 40ff.) that with sufficient imagination any theory can be saved from refutation by a suitable adjustment "in the background knowledge in which it is embedded." On the other hand, he adds, no statement is immune to revision by the same procedure.

As Lakatos points out (1970, p. 184), there are both weak and strong interpretations of Quine's position. The weak interpretation asserts only "the impossibility of a direct experimental hit on a narrowly specified theoretical target." It denies only the possibility of disproving a particular and separate component of a theoretical system that is interpreted within the framework of the entire realm of science. Lakatos regards this weak version as unexceptionable but does not regard it as exceptionally important. However, he argues that there is a strong version of the thesis that "excludes any underlying rational selection among...alternatives...." He believes that Quine accepts the strong version because, in the tradition of William James, pragmatism for him is "only psychological comfort..." (pp. 184-85).

Whether or not Quine accepts this strong version in the sense stated by Lakatos—and I doubt that he does—it is clear from the foregoing that I do not. The realm of assessment—and the standards appropriate to it—constitutes an objective method for accepting or rejecting positions. This is within the pragmatistic tradition as I understand it.

I will attempt to clarify the differences between Lakatos's position and mine. Lakatos distinguishes between what he calls heuristic or progressive theories and those that are not. For instance, when it was discovered that the orbit of Uranus did not conform to Newton's predictions, scientists either could have rejected Newton's laws or could have projected the existence of a planet beyond Uranus that would account for the discrepancy. They made the latter choice, and Neptune eventually was found. Lakatos calls this procedure the formulation of a novel auxiliary hypothesis that is progressive because it predicts something new. He distinguishes it from the case of Copernican theory, which in his view merely provides a different explanation from that of Ptolemaic theory without predicting any new facts. He rejects the Copernican methodology.

I believe that the mistake in Lakatos's position lies in his identification of science with theory and in his failure to recognize the realm of praxis or assessment as a specifiable aspect of scientific procedure. Yet the latter is implicitly present in his own position in the form of a research program, whereas in the position of Karl Popper (1965, pp. 44ff.) it is implicit in his formulation that science deals with problems that come to the fore.

Lakatos fails to ask what the problem was that led to the Copernican research program within which Copernicus reformulated Ptolemaic theory even though it gave rise to no new additional predictions. I am confident that a rich history of science would show that, with the initial progress of enlightenment, more attention was being given to the empirical characteristics of bodies, of perspective, and of distances. If this is correct, as I believe could be shown to be the case, then Copernicus's problem would have arisen because of the lack of "fit" of

Ptolemaic theory with other elements of the realm of knowledge. It is the progressive widening of this lack of "fit," I believe, that a century later gave rise to Galileo's problem.

Both Lakatos and Popper leave virtually untouched the problem of identifying problems. However, the very assertion that something is a problem that requires resolution depends on an assessment that refers in some scientific fashion to other elements of knowledge, even if not in strictly deductive form. Falsification, even in Popper's sophisticated sense, is not merely not a sharp criterion but not an exclusive criterion. We must stand on our refusal to identify an atomic system as the same as a solar system in terms of the application of theory. We refuse to regard experiments in microphysics as refutations of the laws applying to macrosystems and insist upon the differences between them even though we could not have provided an entirely precise set of definitions a priori that distinguished them.

The very applicability of the concept of simplicity in our preference for one theory over another depends on a dialectic involving a praxical type of assessment. For instance, if someone claims that he is being persecuted by the authorities, the initial assemption is that he is suffering from a delusion. Suppose, however, that we can demonstrate that people do behave in a hostile manner to him. The delusionary hypothesis can be saved by arguing that it is his conduct that predisposes others to persecutory behavior. We can always save either of the hypotheses by a sufficient addition of ad hoc hypotheses. However, we rest with one or the other on the basis of its fit with a wide range of the evidence that is available at any point in the process. For instance, we do know that persecuted people sometimes produce persecutory behavior by their own hostility. However, if we then find that someone takes part in the persecution who has never met the individual, we are more likely to accept the hypothesis of persecution even though we could save the hypothesis of delusion by asserting that this individual had heard that this was a very nasty person.

It is possible that scientists and philosophers of science pay less attention to the realm of assessment because the problems of identification either of scientific elements or of scientific problems are often so obvious that they escape attention. They may be aware, as Popper is, that all theories contain undefined terms and that these limit the precision with which identifications can be made. But the practical import of this fact seems so limited that little attention is paid to it or to the fact that what is undefined in one theory may "fit" with what is defined in another.

However, in the social sciences, where independent measures are not available across systems, problems of identification and assessment become at least as important as, and usually more important than, theoretical deductions or falsifications. Although every good theory in principle should be falsifiable, there are cases in which the assessment of evidence may validate the use of a theory even when it is not progressive in the sense of Lakatos. In many cases, the problem will be more that of determining what theory to apply than of deciding which among competing hypotheses concerning a specific system is false. Thus, for instance, a psychologist may be more concerned with identifying the personality type of a patient than in deciding between alternative hypotheses about that personality type. Moeover, his assessments concerning that type may depend more on their "fit" with a wide range of supplementary evidence than with any even semistrict falsification. To the extent that falsification is used, it may apply more to the use of evidence for purposes of categorization than to propositions concerning personality type.

For instance, suppose a psychologist must decide whether an individual is using the mechanism of projection. The fact that he accuses another individual of hostility is not proof of projection. Even a wide range of evidence showing that the accuser is a hostile person is not proof, for the hostility of the other, assuming we can show it to exist, may be neither a response to his own hostility nor a falsehood. We must assess evidence from a wide range of circumstances to show that there is neither a hostile pattern nor one that would independently support a hypothesis of hostility, even if counterfactual, for not every false attribution is a projection in the technical sense. There may be a pattern that even nonhostile individuals would characterize as hostile because they would be unaware of mitigating factors. For instance, there might be a case in which a teacher continually rejects work from one student that he would accept from others because he knows this student is capable of much better work. I am sure the reader can construct even better examples. In each case, we may have to indicate the conditions under which we will accept an item as evidence of hostility and we may have a notion of the circumstances that would cause us to reject it. But these also will relate back to a wide variety of other supplementary evidence, definitions, propositions, and theories. The assessment is a highly complex judgment that makes use of concepts such as "fit" and "relatedness" that in turn determine a judgment as to use.

I may be able to illustrate the praxical mode of argument even better by reference to the current controversy over whether dinosaurs were cold-blooded ectotherms or warm-blooded endotherms. There are several arguments that support the recent hypothesis that dinosaurs were endotherms. They were long-limbed. Futhermore, they walked with an erect posture like that of birds or mammals, in which their limbs were held in a nearly vertical posture beneath the shoulder and hip sockets. This type of limb structure permitted greater speed than that of animals whose limbs sprawl to the side. All modern endotherms are erect while all modern ectotherms have limbs that sprawl. Furthermore, dinosaurs existed for 140 million years. Mammals remained very small until the dinosaurs disappeared. Hence dinosaurs were competitively superior to mammals; this indicates that they had a very high rate of activity, which is an endothermic characteristic.

On the other hand, some modern lizards, if startled, are as active as rodents. The duration of a reptile's activity is limited not by its ectothermy but by heart and circulation limits on the supply of oxygen. Although dinosaurs probably had double-pump hearts similar to those of endotherms and although they carried their heads above their hearts, and thus needed high blood pressure, this by itself is not sufficient proof that they were endotherms. Endothermy is not an automatic consequence of a four-chambered heart, which is necessary for such efficiency. Some lizards have such hearts.

There are hypotheses that some dinosaurs were true endotherms and that others were ectotherms that maintained constant body termperature by utilizing heat in the environment. In any event, their large size may have assisted them in retaining heat even if they were not endotherms. Thus, this evidence is also ambiguous. Moreover, there were no small dinosaurs, which supports the ectotherm hypothesis. Endotherms must eat far more than ectotherms in order to maintain their internal temperature; it has been estimated that they require at least ten times as much prey as ectotherms. This ratio is subject to some debate, as is the debate over whether there was enough prey in the area of dinosaurs to support them if they were endotherms. Similar praxical types of arguments are used to evaluate such questions as the availability of prey and the required predator-prey ratio.

Dinosaur bones have a high density of Haversian canals. All modern endotherms are rich in such canals. However, turtles, which are ectotherms, also have such canals. There is a great similarity between Archaeopteryx, which most specialists believe was the first bird, and certain small dinosaurs called theropods. Archaeopteryx had feathers, which indicates it was a bird. On the other hand, some argue that the feathers of Archaeopteryx may have prevented heat loss—an indication that it was not a bird and therefore not an endotherm.

No single one of these arguments is sufficient, even if proven, to establish that dinosaurs were endotherms or to deny that they were ectotherms, or vice versa. Some of the particular arguments are subject to tests which, given the current state of knowledge in various scientific fields, are in principle falsifiable. However, some of the other arguments merely reproduce the praxical form of argument at still a further level. This is the case with respect to the availability of prey. Thus, there eventually is a complex web of arguments that will not fit into any simply linear or hierarchical pattern. As the interconnections within the web become more complex, there will be an evolution in standards of evidence, definitions, and acceptance of undefined terms. The praxical assessment will serve to establish connections and relatedness within the realm of experience.

However, this does not leave us in the uncomfortable position of asserting that certain things are necessarily true of dinosaurs if they are classified as ectotherms and that other things are necessarily true if they are classified as endotherms. Matters are far more complex than this. And it is a great oversimplification to regard this as a tautology or an exercise in definition. This is also true in the case of delusion: a person who is "normal" will occasionally be deluded, and a delusional person in some cases may perceive the environment more accurately than a normal one. Thus, determinations are not based on single features from which further predictions follow as if we had a very simple deductive theory. In the case of the endotherm-ectotherm controversy, the praxical arguments are inconclusive. In other cases, they will tend to exclude one or more of the alternatives and, in this sense, support the remaining alternative(s).

In the endotherm-ectotherm controversy, the evaluation of evidence in the realm of praxis determines whether we identify the dinosaur as one or the other but does not determine what we consider to be an endotherm. If a live dinosaur were available, that determination likely would not be controversial. Sometimes, however, the role of praxis is to determine the range of categories. Is a crystal, for instance, living or nonliving? We can establish definitions that will lead to either conclusion, but our choice of one definition over another will relate to the realm of praxis, that is, to the entire realm of knowledge as it exists at any particular time. And our decision in favor of one definition over another will resemble the indirect type of evidential (praxical) reasoning used to make a decision concerning whether the dinosaur is an endotherm or ectotherm. However, in this case, the dispute will be less over the characteristics of crystals than over the redefinition of what life is. Our concept of life is dependent on the relevant realm of knowledge—a realm that grows more complex, sophisticated, and interrelated as knowledge increases.

There are still other problems, involved in the fit of category and example. Whether, for instance, we call an organization a bloc or an alliance depends on a praxical assessment that employs categories such as "yes," "no," "possibly," or even "more" or "less." Because these are assessments rather than simple theoretical deductions, the inferences we draw are also assessments.

The physical scientist is used to a field of endeavor in which independently determinable measures may be applied across a wide variety of activities. He therefore tends to ignore his own post hoc distinctions, as in the differentiation of macro- from micro-physical phenomena and their applicable laws and theories.

Thus, he fails to understand the appropriate use of techniques leading to identification and assessment. He treats these problems as if they were the simpler laboratory experiments of harder science and isolates single elements of the praxical field in ways that appear to produce a tautology, as when a person is asserted to be a schizophrenic only if he engages in schizophrenic behavior. However, as soon as we understand that the range of evidence and theories employed in the techniques of identification and the range employed in the techniques of analysis of what is being identified are not identical but that they cross-cut in a complex manner, we can see that we are engaged in a scientific activity that lacks deductive certainty but that still permits public and objective communication when properly employed. Identification, properly employed, still leaves open a wide range of hypotheses concerning what is identified. Decisions concerning identification relate back to the entire relevant realm of knowledge in ways that are not identical with the analysis of the object of identification. Later, I will discuss a closely related problem: complementary frameworks of analysis.

The entire framework of science is embedded in this type of praxical assessment. It determines what we accept as evidence, why we insist on some distinctions and not others, why we accept a result as falsification in one case and not in another, and so forth. Popper refers to a form of dogmatism or conservatism that is scientifically justified (pp. 170ff.). This makes of assessment a mysterious process. Assessment justifies changed as well as fixed assumptions and is, I believe, a rational and objective technique, even though it is not simply deductive (or inductive in a simple frequency sense).

Moreover, because assessment occurs in real-world flux rather than in the timeless realm of deductive theory, we cannot completely specify criteria. They continue to evolve as more evidence, including more types, becomes available. Scientific theory is a closed system. Assessment is an open process that may undergo a step-functional change that revolutionizes all relationships and identifications. But this should not surprise us, for the evidence supporting the metatheories of Popper and Lakatos is of the type I call assessment rather than of the type they call theory. In this sense, I think Lakatos should have paid more attention to his own comment on Ptolemy and Copernicus than he did, for in my opinion the truth of Copernican theory, even in the absence of progressive predictions, is an important fact that provides insight into the character of scientific knowledge, involving the relationship between theory and praxis. Copernican theory "fit" together with more contemporary evidence and showed how disparate areas of science could relate to each other. It was progressive in this sense, even if it did not directly give rise to new predictions concerning planetary motions.

The realm of assessment, as I employ that term, is prior to and more important than what Lakatos calls the "research program." As Lakatos describes his position, a research program is a somewhat mysterious product of creative minds. However, the mind's creativity depends upon the continual interaction of its realm of knowledge with the real world. Einstein's relativity theory developed within a framework that included the Michelson-Morley experiment, Lorentz contractions, non-Euclidean geometries, and the anomaly that Maxwell's theory did not fit with the classical theory of relativity. These were the changes in the larger realm of knowledge that produced both the research program of Einstein and the theory that resulted from the research program, including Einstein's demonstration that Maxwell's theory was consistent with the classical principle of relativity provided that the basic concepts of space and time that underlay the entire structure of physical theory were revamped. It is this concordance that explains why the experimental observation of the bending of light around Mercury was regarded as confirmatory evidence of Einstein's theory even though the difference in the predictions of Newtonian and Einsteinian theory was within the contemporary range of experimental error. And, I believe, it was a lack of a similar concordance between it and other physical science evidence, in addition to Einstein's aesthetic bent, that determined his early resistance to quantum theory, despite his own important contributions to it.

This process of reasoning cannot be called falsification even in Lakatos's sense of sophisticated falsificationism. Apart from the perhaps inessential lack of a "direct experimental hit," there was no basic inconsistency between Newton's theory and the experimental evidence until long after the experiment of the bending of light around Mercury. We can speak only of a greater fit between Einstein's theory and the body of physical and mathematical theory or of a great lack of fit between Newtonian theory and those bodies of knowledge.

As Lakatos uses this concept, both Newtonian and Einsteinian theories were methodologically falsifiable. It is a fact that Einstein's theory had excess empirical content over Newton's theory, that this excess content fulfilled Lakatos's criterion for sophisticated falsificationism in that it did not merely follow in the "wake of the facts," and that this aspect of Einstein's theory accounted for most of the interest it aroused among theorists. However, these facts do not account fully for the early acceptance of relativity theory. It is this discrepancy that the concept of sophisticated falsificationism leaves out of account and that makes its prescription for scientific methodology too restrictive.

Accepted theories will tend to come under challenge in the absence of falsification only when this lack of fit becomes apparent. Until then, even apparent direct falsifications likely will tend to be rejected or reinterpreted. New theories will tend to be accepted more easily the less they tend to challenge the general realm of scientific knowledge. And the greater the fit between such theories and the general realm of scientific knowledge, the more ready the scientific community will be to accept apparently confirming evidence for these theories or disconfirming evidence for rivals that are less satisfactory in this respect.

Surely minds enter into the assessment process whether for reasons of creativity, as Lakatos mentions, or because the formulations of positions by real individuals are made by minds that are not identical in terms either of the information they possess or of the ways in which that information is arranged. This, however, is not in essence a pyschological matter, although it does involve "mind sets."

Knowledge necessarily is possessed by minds and necessarily depends upon the content and information processing characteristics of minds. It is the discourse among minds that constitutes the public process of science. Within this public process the reasons for the varying positions are stated and made explicit. Research programs and theories are formulated and compared. As this process continues, communication among informed and literate minds with respect to the structure of the real world may produce a consensus. However, the consensus rests upon public criteria; it is not itself a warrant for a position. Moreover, to the extent that matters are complicated and that research programs are necessarily incomplete, the warrants for positions have a lower probability and the likelihood of a justifiable consensus is reduced.

THE CONCEPT OF EQUILIBRIUM

Theories or theory sketches in the social sciences—more particularly, international systems theory sketches—are most often either explicitly or implicitly equilibrium theories. Although the type of equilibrium used by such theories is complex, I start my analysis with the simplest concepts in order to understand the more complex concepts.

By equilibrium, I mean that two sets of properties are in an unchanging relationship with respect to each other. Equilibria are normally classified as stable, static, and unstable. One may think of a ball in a valley, on a flat surface, and on top of a narrowly peaked ridge as metaphors for these concepts.

Whether an equilibrium is stable or not depends on our perspective. Thus, biological life on earth is stable from the standpoint of men with short lives, and even of nations with longer lives, but unstable from the standpoint of eternity, for eventually the sun will become a nova. The Roman Empire was stable from the standpoint of a Roman of the first century A.D., but unstable from the standpoint of some historians. There is no contradiction here—or retreat into subjectivity—for, given an adequate statement of the character of the inquiry, there are objective, that is, publicly communicable, standards to determine their accuracy.

POLITICAL IMPLICATIONS OF AN EQUILIBRIUM APPROACH

There is a widespread view that scientific concern with equilibrium produces a bias toward conservative politics. Regardless of some mistaken uses of systems analysis, this is absurd. The best safecrackers are those who understand the mechanisms of the safes they burglarize. The best assassins know the weakest parts of the human anatomy, that is, those particular links in the system that are at the same time essential to the equilibrium of the biological organism and vulnerable. By the same token, the best doctors understand the workings of the human organism. And the best defenders of a political system are also aware of its most vulnerable elements.

Every human being wishes some equilibria to persist and some to change. Most healthy but poor people wish their health to persist but their fortune to change. The revolutionary wishes the system he intends to install to persist although he wishes the system he intends to overthrow to disappear. One is always for particular changes and against particular changes; and if he believes this is not so, he is merely being foolish.

However, an important distinction must be made. Systems analyses, as they apply to particular systems, have neither conservative nor liberal—neither reactionary nor radical—implications, for the reasons already given. However, systemic pragmaticism—which infuses Peircean pragmaticism with a systems perspective—has distinct political implications, depending on factual conditions. Whether these are liberal or conservative, evolutionary or revolutionary, depends on the prevailing state of affairs. But the long-term effects of the philosophy are at least evolutionary. As man comes to fuller awareness of the meaning of his own existence, the insights gained from this knowledge produce a disposition to change the world; to leave the realm of necessity and enter the kingdom of freedom, in Marx's words. (The basic methodology, of course, is Hegel's and is developed in his *Phenomenology*.)

THE RATIONALE FOR EQUILIBRIA-ORIENTED APPROACHES

There is a reason for an interest in studying equilibria. The reason, however, is pragmatic rather than ideological. The biologists tell us that mutations are bad, by which they mean that most mutations lack survival value. On the other hand, the existence of man is a consequence of mutation. Presumably, we consider that good. However, whether we consider it good or bad, the fact is that there are fewer workable combinations of genes, or of economic, social, or political elements, than there are unworkable ones. Thus, our scientific task is made more manageable when our inquiry starts with equilibrium. In the first place, there are fewer systems in (relative) equilibrium than in disequilibrium. In the second place, equilibrium is a precondition for recurrent behavior. Therefore, systems in equilibrium provide us with a better opportunity to study them than systems in disequilibrium. In the third place, systems that persist usually must overcome disturbances, which affords us the opportunity to acquire detailed and systematic information about their vulnerabilities.

In trying to construct models or theoretical sketches, we have enormously narrowed the range of permutation if we attempt to explain systems in equilibrium. If we can do this, we can then learn about the vulnerabilities of a system to disequilibrium produced by particular changes at the boundary of the system. As it would be an unmanageable task to attempt to do this for the complete range of possible disturbances—at least for complex systems in complex environments—our task is simplified by restricting our inquiry to those possible disturbances that we believe are more likely to occur.

Although in principle we could construct dynamic models in disequilibrium, there are so many different ways in which we could do so that the a priori probability that we would have hit upon a model useful for any actual system in disequilibrium would seem remote. Thus, equilibrium is a useful focal point for inquiry into the operations of systems. Beyond this, however, and even more important, the differences in types of equilibria manifested by different types of systems provide us with information concerning important aspects of the behavior of systems. The study of valuational behavior is intimately linked to the equilibrial processes of purposeful systems. Thus, it is this aspect of the systems approach that is particularly appropriate in the investigation of problems of values.

TYPES OF EQUILIBRIUM

Mechanical Equilibria

The best-known type of equilibrium is the perhaps inaptly named mechanical equilibrium. We say that a car resting on a flat surface is in mechanical equilibrium. By this we man that the forces that might move it are canceled. These forces are not merely inferred from the resting state of the car; they generally can be measured independently. And their cancellation in this instance can be derived from Newton's laws.

A law is a universal relationship between sets of properties. We shall call a law a "covering law" when it can be expressed in a set of equations whose terms are independently measurable and generally invariant for all systems of application. In this limited sense, all mechanical equilibria can be explained by covering laws. Although the concept of mechanical equilibrium in physics does not convey much significant information—far more information is conveyed by the other specifics of particular theories—it is more than a label and thus conveys more information than a label normally conveys.

Homeostatic Equilibria

When we move to homeostatic systems, such as thermostat-controlled heating systems or the mechanism that controls the temperature of human blood, we have only the information that a label will provide, although all homeostatic systems operate within boundaries set by some mechanical system. For instance, one can determine how much energy is required to raise the temperature of a room a specified number of degrees if one knows the volume of the room, the thermal qualities of the energy source, and the efficiency of the heating mechanism.

No independently measurable system of equalities applies to the thermostatic system, however. Thus, in this case, an explanation of the temperature equilibrium of the room requires reference to the way in which a thermometer operates within a system of relays designed to turn the heater on and off. In this case, "homeostatic equilibrium" is a label designating the type of system and conveys only the amount of information that a label can convey, whereas the explanation of the behavior of the system is not linked to a concept of equality. The label merely tells us that the system is one in which changes in certain specified elements of the system maintain one or more particular elements of the system within a "requisite" range.

This is one reason—the other, and related, reason being the degree of complication of the system—for an important distinction between theoretical analyses in the social and the physical sciences. Many common terms are used in mechanics, thermodynamics, optics, and astrophysics. And their measurement in experiments in each, in general, is made according to a common scale. Generally we can define and identify these terms independently of more complex system variations. And we can, therefore, employ them in covering laws.

The units of social and political analysis cannot be experimented upon in isolation, either in principle or in practice. We cannot define them in a way that employs terms for which there are common measures independent of some varying system contexts and according to which "equality" is empirically meaningful. Because this is so, we cannot develop a measure of system efficiency in processing such variables as we can for engines that use fuels. "Demands" and "supports," for instance, do not exist in the same way as physical units, for their scale lacks meaning independent of the character of the political or social system that processes them, whereas the energy contained in fuel is measurable independent of the efficiency of particular engines. For this reason, covering laws of the type available to physicists are not available to the social scientist.

Because no common measure is available for variables in homeostatic systems, important information is lost as attempts are made to apply common generalizations across different types of generically similar systems. Thus, although "Democratic systems require popular support if they are to function" is a truism, it conveys little information about conditions for support in any democratic system. Moreover, democratic systems often function well without much support; and the proposition tells us nothing about how to distinguish among these cases. Indeed, even nondemocratic systems require support.

As the level of abstraction is raised to statements that apply to all political systems—for instance, "Political systems are in equilibrium when demands and supports are in balance"—we no longer have even a weak truism. In the absence of independent measures that are generally applicable, the statement is vacuous. This does not imply that demands and supports are vacuous concepts but only that their qualitative manifestations in concrete circumstances differ in major ways from system to system. The strength of these manifestations does not have a measure that is independent of experience, either practical or theoretical, with particular types of political systems. Therefore, if statements are to be relatively meaningful, their range of application must be restricted to subtypes of systems. When lower-level generalizations function in a qualitative theory or theory sketch, with specified boundary conditions and specified actors, as in my international systems models, they do convey useful information.

When an author attempts to offer a first-order universal generalization about human behavior, it will usually be the case that he has offered us a definition —perhaps of rational behavior—rather than a proposition or theory. J.C.C. Smart, for instance, developed an act-utilitarian position in which he claimed that one should do what is best in the individual case, regardless of any rule to the contrary, provided that one is altruistic. When I demonstrated that even altruistic individuals, if they made decisions as he recommended, would do social harm (1960, 1961), Smart wrote that they should do whatever would be best if it were done also by everyone in the same circumstances. One would hardly quarrel with that bit of advice; on the other hand, it merely defines rational behavior as behavior that does not do net social harm. It gives us no methods for determining the actions or consequences for which this evaluation would hold.

My colleague T.W. Schultz made a similar error when he argued that modern economic theory applied even to traditional situations (1968, pp. 1-8). The reason that some primitive tribes did not raise additional crops, he said, was that they did not need the money for any purpose. All he proved was that they were acting rationally within the framework of their own system. He did not demonstrate that the economic theories that explain modern economic behavior apply to such systems. In these cases the preferred rule is really a definition of rational behavior. The rule, therefore, is not a proposition that can function within a theory. Rawls's attempt to find a single set of ethical rules for all societies falls victim to this error also. Later in this chapter we shall see that comparative evaluation is required for cross-system generalization.

In an interesting parallel case, the only game-theoretical area for which there is a general solution is the zero-sum game. In this game, the same physical payoff is evaluated identically by all relevant players, thus establishing a utile value for the payoff that is independent of context for purposes of the analysis. In this sense, the general solution to the zero-sum game requires a kind of equivalent to the independently measurable properties that are essential to the applicability of covering laws in physics. Where this is not the case—the non-zero-sum game— no general solution has ever been found; and particular solutions apply only to particular types of non-zero-sum games; and, even so, the solutions may vary with still other aspects of the games.

The failure of rules or common formulations to apply across different types of homeostatic systems is sometimes not understood by incautious students of so-called general theory. They note, for instance, that the growth curves of populations within city limits and of bacteria within enclosed cultures may be similar. They then infer that general transsystem "laws" have been found.

Their mistake is that of reference. The growth curve in this case is a constant that applies to systems with certain characteristics. To the extent that these specific characteristics are dominant—and this will be true only for some concrete realms of application of the mathematical formulas and within specified boundary conditions—the particular interpretation of the formula will provide an explanation for only the relevant facets of the real world. It will not explain other closely connected facets of behavior in the real world.

Thus, such formulas may explain certain features that some political units have in common with some nonpolitical units, whether social or biological. They do not explain either the differences between different types of political units or those aspects of political behavior that are not relevant to these variables. They are thus not general theories but particular theories, such as theories of population growth in enclosed area. And they function only as parameters in studies of political systems qua political systems, or of bacterial systems qua biological systems. This is another reason why general theories cannot explain the behavior of different varieties of the same general type of substantive system. Where they appear to do so, they will be either vacuous or consistent with contradictory applications.

Ultrastable Equilibria

In the case of both mechanical and homeostatic equilibria, the systems have resting states; in the latter case, although ordinary homeostatic systems might be called goal seeking, they obviously are not purposeful as that term is ordinarily used. The system change is completely determined by the environmental change, although, unlike the case of mechanical equilibria, parts of the internal system vary with the external changes while maintaining an unchanged value of a particular internal variable.

Let us, therefore, carry the inquiry one stage forward with the concept of ultrastable homeostasis developed by W. Ross Ashby (1952). Consider an ordinary homeostatic system such as an automatic pilot in an airplane. If the place deviates from level course, the automatic pilot senses this and corrects for it. Suppose, however, that the automatic pilot has been incorrectly linked to the ailerons of the plane so that the correction imposed by the automatic pilot removes the plane even farther from level flight. Conventional automatic pilots would continue to engage the same damaging "correction," thus throwing the plane into a spin. However, it would be possible to build an unconventional automatic pilot that could take note of the fact that its correction only worsened the drift. It could then attempt, either on an ordered or a random basis, some other patterns of activity until it found one that was corrective. This kind of system—called an ultrastable system—can change its own mode of response to environmental disturbances.

Purpose

The ultrastable system exhibits some aspects of what we mean by purpose. Let us look at another machine and then at some hypothetical human behavior to see if we can determine what we mean by the term "purpose" and how we determine its content.

Consider a device with a gasoline-powered motor and a battery-driven set of headlights. When its gas supply begins to run down, it moves itself to a pump and fills itself up. When its batteries begin to run down, it moves to an electric circuit and plugs itself in to recharge. If obstacles are placed in its path, it moves around them to seek either gas or an electric outlet. Perhaps we do not yet wish to call this behavior purposive, but, as in the case of the ultrastable machine, this machine does things that seem to exhibit purpose.

Consider how we might infer contrasting purposes from the behavior of two different men. One man holds down two jobs. Is he seeking extra money to support his family? Is he merely compulsive? Or does he fear the future? Another man, although proclaiming his desire to work, does not apply for work often and fails in his applications when he does apply. Is his verbal claim insincere? Does he fear rejection?

How do we choose among such competing hypotheses? Consider the case of the man who has failed to find work in the example above. Further investigation reveals that he is bright but did poorly in school except with teachers who were very supportive of him. Despite his intelligence, he avoided demanding classes. We incline toward the hypothesis that he feared rejection. Perhaps we do not have high confidence in it, but we base our conclusion on his observed behavior. We may even make this observed behavior count strongly against his assertion that he does not fear rejection but is merely waiting for a better opportunity than has yet appeared.

Another man tells us that he gambles because he enjoys the thrill of winning, but we notice that he almost always loses. A patient on a psychiatrist's couch makes a Freudian slip and perhaps gains insight into a motivation of which he was previously unaware. The insight, if it is such, is reinforced by behavioral observations that in many ways the patient's behavior was more consistent with the motivation indicated by the Freudian slip, although perhaps not in any straightforward way, than with the motivation that he had accepted as an explanation for his own behavior. A salesman may reason with a customer about his products. If this fails, he may develop an "aggressive" sales pitch. Perhaps in some cases the goals are transformed in the process of achievement. A suitor may switch from the pursuit of beautiful women to the pursuit of any woman. A man unsuccessfully seeking the love of his mother might become an artist and seek acclaim instead. We hypothesize that the latter is a substitute for the former.

Let us briefly examine these examples and see what we mean when we attribute purpose to them. In each case there is an attributed resting state: the consequences toward which the motivation would lead. In each case, obstacles were overcome to achieve this resting state. Our mobile machine had this characteristic. Our ultrastable pilot mimics part of the behavior of the salesman who changed his "pitch." Neither machine "mimics" the behavior of the suitor or the painter.

Obviously, conjectures about purpose require a great deal of supporting evidence before we place any confidence in them, but they all possess a consistent form: a conjectured resting state of which the concrete result is a manifestation. These resting states usually are identified through transformations by complicated procedures of inference involving criteria. These resting states are regarded as purposeful because the actor overcomes obstacles to achieve them. Moreover, they have a more or less persistent relationship to his character and personality. That is, they have some (not necessarily fully or transitively) ordered relationships. A man's own statements about what his purposes are have evidential value but are rebuttable by other aspects of his behavior. Even in those cases in which we believe that he is consciously telling the truth as he knows it, and not attempting to mislead us, we may believe on the basis of other evidence that he is misleading himself.

The example of the individual who learned through a Freudian slip what his unconscious or preconscious motivations were is given not to imply that a preconscious purpose is a fundamental purpose, for bringing it to consciousness may reveal childish and irrational linkages that are useful in eliminating it from the system of purposes. It does, however, illustrate one of the essential aspects of human learning about human character. Our purposes are not presented to us on mental demand. We learn about our purposes from our behavior in a variety of situations. Some people may live an entire lifetime without learning that they are potential cowards as a consequence of good fortune in not being presented with situations that would produce cowardice in them.

We often say that our purposes change over time, but what may happen more often is that we gain a more sophisticated understanding both of the external world and of ourselves. Alternatively, an individual may be subjected to such environmental distress that his learning about himself, which helps to shape his character and his behavior (this is a positive-feedback situation), is unfortunately extremely one-sided. In other words, we are dealing with an extremely complex system which learns well or poorly about itself in part by observing itself in behavioral interaction with others and with the environment. Few of us have such a variety of experiences under a variety of circumstances that we can have more than a glimpse into our human potentialities. Usually anyone who believes that he "fully knows himself" will be an extremely truncated compulsive-obsessive type who secures "certainty" of knowledge at the expense of fullness of being.

Differences between Types of Homeostasis

The unconventional automatic pilot is an example of relatively simple conduct in a relatively simple environment. It is capable of changing its own behavior in the same environment in order to achieve a constant goal and of overcoming obstacles to do so. A relatively small number of observations would exhaust the potentiality of such machines and permit us to reconstruct the codes that determine their behaviors.

The ultrastable automatic pilot has a one-to-one correspondence between environment and flight path. The ability of the system to "reprogram" itself distinguishes it from ordinary homeostatic systems. However, alternative goals cannot be chosen, even as a substitute in reaching some higher-order goal.

The informational elements to which such systems respond are small in number, highly explicit, and not subject to ambiguity. Goal transformation through symbolic identification does not apply to them. Nor do the systems control their intake of information as an essential part of their process of goal pursuit. Consciousness and its distinguishable mental operations do not play a role in their "choices."

The human system is conscious and can substitute alternative behaviors in the same environment. It can pursue identical behaviors in the same environment. It can pursue identical behaviors in different environments. And it can transform its goal structure, presumably in terms of some higher-order comparison. I call this type of process transfinitely stable.

How can we proceed in areas of investigation in which the prior statements concerning homeostatic systems are correct? Systems analysis provides a strategy for research in such cases. Let us first examine the matter more generally. It makes sense to say that the field of knowledge, which includes all its elements, functions as a whole with respect to those of its elements that are brought to bear upon particular problems. However, analysis always requires a differentiation of the field into articulated elements. There is no mysterious, hermeneutic process that permits ordered statements about the whole in the absence of such differentiation. A related confusion is the so-called distinction between holistic and elemental approaches. The real problem is one of finding an appropriate research strategy.

WHOLE AND PART IN SYSTEMS ANALYSIS

It has been asserted that systems theorists believe—and apparently some have said—that the whole is greater than the sum of its parts. I must admit that I do not know what that sentence means, but neither do I know what "The whole equals the sum of its parts" or "The whole is less than the sum of its parts" means.

How do we add the parts of a system together? If a frog is cut into pieces, it is no longer a frog, but is it less than the sum of its parts? If we link several paper clips, the resulting chain is flexible whereas the elements of the chain are relatively rigid. The characteristics of the chain are certainly different from the characteristics of the elements considered individually, but are they greater or less? The characteristics of the chain are related to the characteristics of the parts and the style of linkage, but the characteristics of the whole and of the parts may be dissimilar; and "greater," "less," and "equal" may be inapt forms of comparison.

A more general form of the argument states that the systems approach is holistic, that is, that it attempts to predict the behavior of the parts from the behavior of the whole. It is quite true that the operations of a gasoline engine explain the functions of the piston. But it is also true that knowledge of pistons provides insight into the requirements of engines and of the substitutes that would be required if pistons were to be replaced. Similarly, in a perfect market, prices exist as parametric "givens" for every individual buyer and seller. But not every possible sale will be consummated at that price. What is the behavior of the whole from which individual behavior is predicted? More accurately, we would predict that no action by an individual buyer or seller would affect price noticeably in the marketplace. Thus, we might ignore the individual aspects of decision making in examining price (assuming, of course, that no important change occurs at the boundary of the system) but not in the autobiography of a particular seller or buyer. On the other hand in an oligopolistic market, we might need to know the conditions of the individual sellers to predict price equilibrium. Although it is possible that the price equilibrium of such systems may be changed because of accident or inadvertence, the equilibria of such systems are systematically dependent on the motivation of the actors. Therefore, the analyst or theorist is particularly concerned with the system conditions that motivate behavior and how that behavior corresponds with various equilibria.

Therefore, to the extent that the strange words "Predict the behavior of the parts from the behavior of the whole" or "Predict the behavior of the whole from the behavior of the parts" have any meaning at all, it is clear that their meaning depends on the type of system we examine. In a perfect market, we pay less attention to the individuating features of buyers and sellers. In an imperfect market, we must pay more attention. In all cases, we must know which aspects of the boundaries of the system, if they change, will in turn change the motivations of the buyers and sellers either individually or in the mass. We must also know through which type of system these behaviors will be filtered, for the impact of the behavior will depend on the type of systemic filter. Thus, some business systems tend to eliminate "cutthroat" competitors and others to encourage them and to eliminate ethical businessmen.

To the extent that the conceptions have meaning, to argue that systems analysis chooses holistic over elemental methods of analysis fundamentally misconceives the systems methodology. The systems approach does not say that theoretically relevant aspects of individual actors are irrelevant; it says that statements concerning certain classes of behavior must take into account the systemic relationships of the actors. The extent to which information about an individual or system becomes theoretically relevant depends on the characteristics of the system, of the actors, and of the environment in the particular case examined. This cannot be predetermined on the basis of general principles, but only on the basis of research objectives. Also, one must distinguish between whether one is asking for general (theoretical) or particular (applied) information.

Theory and Application

Part of the confusion over the relationship of whole to part may result from the fact that theories are not designed directly to predict particular results. Thus, for instance, Newton's laws do not mention the sun or the earth. All particularities are ignored. However, to predict when an eclipse will occur, specific information about particular bodies must be fitted into the general equations.

Theories of economics, for instance, do not include within their formulations particular transactions. Thus, when dealing with such systems, some students of social science may think that the particular is determined by the system. But what happens instead is that when the particularities of the individual case are stated, their use within the general formulation permits, to the extent that the theory is sufficiently precise, a prediction that can be verified.

Yet one does not need to know much of economics to know that a farmer who suffers from ten straight years of drought is likely to go bankrupt. In this case, the prediction is made empirically on the basis of specific information without any resort to more general theories of economics. All that this shows is that the suit must be cut to the cloth. These matters are not governed by general principles or by engaging debates between scientific schools but by the requirements of the particular cases. An economist who attempted to explain by reference to abstruse theory, the shutting down of a business by a sole proprietor whose only son had died would be recognized as stupid. So would an engineer who thought that the laws of physics had been proved invalid when the engine of his car failed to start in the morning, as would an inventor who explained that his perpetual motion machine failed because one of the parts was rusty.

Whether an explanation is offered in terms of systems of interaction or in terms of actors depends on circumstances. For instance, a manager of a baseball team may explain that he had a runner attempt to steal second base in the late innings because he needed one run to tie the game. This explanation is offered in terms of the strategy of the game. It pays little attention to the particularities of the individual players, although it does refer to the circumstances of the individual game. In another case, however, the manager may explain that the pitcher was taking a long windup and that the catcher had a bad arm, thus making the steal a percentage play. This explanation rests almost, but not entirely, on the particularities of the actors or players. Which explanation is more or less appropriate depends on the conditions of the case and the question that is being put.

For instance, if one wants to explain why banks lend money, the answer is that they do it to earn interest. If one asks why a particular loan is made by a particular officer of a bank, the answer may lie in the credit characteristics of the borrower, in his personal relationship to the lending officer, or in the attempt by the officer to establish a record for loan acquisitions. These two levels of explanation are different but related. For instance, if one inquires into the reasons why a bank became unprofitable and went into receivership, the answer may be, for instance, that too many officers made loans to friends who were bad credit risks in order to embellish their lending records. However, even "deviant" behavior acquires meaning only in terms of role expectations within a system. If we do not know how banking systems operate, and that lending money in certain ways is a regular function, we do not know why a particular act of lending is deviant or why it may not be easy to recognize as such. On the other hand, we cannot explain the deviance except by bringing into account particular features of the situation that the more general account of banking ignores.

Role theory can be used to analyze system change. Actors are embedded in social and political systems in such complex ways that role conflicts often arise for them. Thus, an actor often must choose which set of role norms he will fulfill and which he will neglect or disobey. Moreover, because the actor can detach himself from any particular social system in which he is a participant, he must be motivated to act in ways consistent with its critical limits; and the other actors must be motivated to induce him so to act if the system is to persist.

The actors are embedded in a web of systems. Thus John Jones has both nuclear- and extended-family relationships, a role in the business in which he is employed, a social and recreational role, and perhaps a religious role, among many others. For some sets of environmental circumstances these roles may be not merely consistent but irreconcilable. Thus, if Jones is a teller at a bank and if his wife desperately needs an operation and he can get the money in no other way, he may have to choose between robbing the bank at the expense of his role as teller or failing his wife at this critical juncture. If Jones fails his wife, his family situation may be destabilized. It is unlikely that the failure of one clerk would destabilize the banking system. However, revolutions occur when critical numbers of key individuals respond to the demands of other role functions in the state system. The conflicts that arise in cases of this kind are, along with the environmental changes that stimulate the problem, among the causes of social change. This kind of cross-sectional problem can best be studied by examining how, under various types of environmental conditions, critical roles in different systems make critically inconsistent demands on the critical actors who participate in the relevant set of systems. This is but another form of applied systems analysis or of engineering systems to the real world or of praxis. This helps us to understand why social change is unavoidable if society is complex and the environment varied.

COMPLEMENTARY FRAMEWORK OF ANALYSIS

Many questions of concern to social scientists do not lend themselves to a single or unitary framework of analysis. To illustrate this, I start with a case similar to that usually found in the physical sciences: the adjustment of a single framework of analysis for the initial conditions of application. If President Truman, for instance, had wanted to know whether an atomic bomb would destroy Hiroshima, the engineering theory of the bomb would have provided an answer to the question for him if some "if" clauses had been filled in, such as the bomb's being correctly constructed, being loaded on the plane, arriving at its destination, and being dropped on target. If, on the other hand, the same methodology is applied to President Kennedy's behavior during the Cuban missile crisis, it is unlikely to work. Let me illustrate why. In the former example, there is a single central theoretical logic that could be applied, if initial conditions are given. In the latter case, we have a number of cogent logics. A strategist might argue that Kennedy acted as he did because the United States had conventional and nuclear superiority. A student of international relations might argue that he acted strong because he was afraid that a failure to do so would have produced some other crisis elsewhere, for instance, in Berlin. A student of domestic politics might argue that he acted strong because he wished to win the election. And a student of psychology might argue that he would have backed down to test the principle of unilateral concessions. Each of these conclusions is based on a theory sketch. There is no way that these theories can be combined in a single deductive system. And each of these theories has some validity in general and with respect to the predicted or to-be-explained properties. Although it is possible that an obsessive president might take into account only the variables of one of these theories, it is highly unlikely. They are not conflicting theories. Even if in principle they might give rise to different conclusions, they express complementary logics that the mind can apply simultaneously to the same event—in some judgmental fashion. In *On Historical and Political Knowing,* (1971), I suggested a principle of "restricted choice": "In deciding that choice is restricted in particular ways, we often have no good framework within which accurate weights can be assigned to particular perspectives or within which *ad hoc* relationships among them can be well articulated. Even the process of identification of a particular aspect of an event or of a series of events with the framework chosen to illuminate part of it is an identification based upon criteria subject to question." This is merely a special, but easier-to-understand, case of the general discussion in that book of the fact that initial conditions in social science predictions are derived from a variety of theory sketches and not simply estimated directly, as in the physical sciences.

In applied theory, theory is engineered for specified boundary conditions. In the case of the Cuban missile crisis, a series of complementary theoretical sketches or perspectives is applied. The essentially deductive reasoning within each theoretical sketch is explanatory. The choice of relevant theory sketches and the assessment of their contribution to the outcome are within the loose equilibrium of the realm of praxis. In that realm, assessments are made according to considerations of consistency and "fit."

COMPARATIVE METHOD

It is well known that our knowledge both of scientific "truths"—for example, Newtonian versus Einsteinian mechanics—and of the methodology of science increases with our scientific experience. In the same way, our knowledge of our nature, of our society, and of our human and social possibilities increases with our comparative knowledge about these. Just as most formulations of the mind-body problem misunderstand the character of human knowledge by trying to derive mental from physical behavior, other reductionist theories of knowledge are likely to be wrong (although this is not necessarily true in every case). Physics may set constraints within which biology operates, but important aspects of biology are not derivable from theories of mechanics, or vice versa.

The world of physics, however, possesses one undeniable advantage over most other scientific arenas. Studies concerning its variables can be conducted, at least tentatively, as if there were no "contamination" from other sources. In the complex world of human behavior this is not true. Varieties of theoretical schemata must be applied to human behavior, and this cannot be done in any simply deductive form. Complexity, ultrastability, and the contextual meaning of systems variables contribute to this difficulty. (Even the multi-body problem in physics requires an iterative procedure employing the two-body formula that produces an answer only for a particular case.) Therefore, either explanation is only partial or the elements of explanation from different theoretical realms are linked together in particular explanations that do not permit singular deductive chains and that depend instead on consistencies among theoretical perspectives, partial relatednesses, judgment, and looser modes of analysis. The relevant realm is that of praxis. Thus, there is a partial quality about explanations of real historical events that is supplemented even by leaps of intuition.

Examples of cases where comparative knowledge is essential to understanding or explaining behavior are readily available. For instance, consider an old-style Chinese merchant who charges more per item to the customer who wishes to buy his entire supply because he must be compensated for his loss of face when other customers find his store unable to provide service. He responds differently from the merchant in a modern American community because of differences in the two systems. The south Italian villager discussed by Edward and L.F. Banfield (1958) is amoral in his behavior with nonfamily members, whereas the English villager generally observes moral standards. Westerners tend to help others during periods of natural catastrophe, but old-style Japanese did not. Their behavior was not understandable unless one was familiar with the burden of obligation this would have placed on a person who was helped and the strain this would have produced within the Japanese society.

Still other examples of the ways in which comparative knowledge assists us in understanding behavior are provided by studies of cultural differences within the same society. For instance, early sociological studies showed great differences between the behaviors of racial groups. Later investigators studied the effects of income level on behavior and discovered that many of the differences attributed to race by the earlier studies were greatly reduced or disappeared when a more complex system of classification was employed.

These examples indicate the extent to which our generalizations about behavior are based on observations limited either to particular groups or to particular classification systems. It is the extension of the frame of reference that permits us to place these behaviors within the framework of the constraints that produce them, to compare them systematically, and to derive conclusions from these comparisons. Such comparisons, in addition to impressing us with the range of human variability in behavior, also permit us to determine the factors that produce the differences and, in this sense, to understand human or social behavior far better. The differences no longer appear as reified absolutes.

Changed environmental or changed social conditions are likely to produce corresponding changes in behavior. All elements, including behavior, function together within a system. But the system cannot properly be understood only in its own terms. Only in the comparisons of systems with each other do we gain a fuller understanding of the functions being filled by different combinations of social and cultural practices. It is also within this framwork that we are able to determine that some of the practices represent secondary-type gains in the same way as do certain types of individual behavior.

Examples of societal secondary gains include, for instance, putting female children out to die of exposure or eating aged parents. Anthropological studies have shown that, in societies in which aged parents were eaten, the parents tended to accept these practices as good and even to insist on them, just as in India the widow of a prince used to insist on *suttee* (her fiery immolation on the bier of her husband). In the example of the infant children and the eating of the aged parents, our inference that these societal values represent secondary gains is based on evidence that such practices occur only under conditions of great poverty.

Most Westerners would assume that the older Japanese practice of refusing to aid a victim of a catastrophe also represented a secondary-type gain. However, this is far more difficult to demonstrate, for a conclusion with respect to this practice is not related to an environmental fact in the same simple way as in the other examples. Moreover, it may be the internal relationships of the elements of the system, rather than an environmental condition, that are essential to analysis.

The relationships between the human organism and the social and cultural environment is extremely complex. There is no reason to believe that a univocal and transitive order of values in macrosocial systems is possible even in principle, let alone in practice. Moreover, because the elements of a social system bear some relationship to each other—as, in the Japanese case, where the refusal to aid a victim of catastrophe was related to the extensive role of "obligation" in the Japanese system—even in those cases in which our judgment affirms that some social systems on the whole are better than others, particular practices in them that cannot be grafted on to foreign systems may be more "in tune" with human nature than the corresponding practices of "better" systems.

It is obvious that, to the extent such evaluations are possible, they require extensive knowledge of how the elements of social and cultural systems fit together and of how they respond to environmental conditions. Moreover, we must never forget that human beings are information-using systems and that their beliefs concerning these relationships are essential elements of the systems studied.

We may thrill to, and understand, the great Greek plays and biblical accounts, but our understanding of society and of human nature in general, as well as of its manifestations under particular conditions, is always subject not merely to advances in techniques within particular disciplines but also to increases in our knowledge of human possibility as these are revealed by choices under novel conditions. Neither man nor society is a book to read at one sitting. We may not yet understand the depth to which either may plunge or the heights to which either may rise.

REFERENCES

Ashby, W. Ross. *Design for a Brain*. New York: John Wiley & Sons, 1952.

Banfield, Edward C. and L.F. Banfield. *The Moral Basis of a Backward Society*. New York: Free Press, 1958.

Kaplan, Morton A. *Justice, Human Nature, and Political Obligation*. New York: Free Press, 1976.

————. *On Historical and Political Knowing: An Inquiry into Some Problems of Universal Law and Human Freedom*. Chicago: University of Chicago Press, 1971.

————. "Some Problems of the Extreme Utilitarian Position." *Ethics* 70 (April 1960): 228-32; "Restricted Utilitarianism." *Ethics* 71 (July 1961): 301-2.

————. *System and Process in International Politics*. New York: John Wiley & Sons, 1957.

Lakatos, Imre. "Falsification and the Methodology of Scientific Research Programmes." In *Criticism and the Growth of Knowledge*, edited by Imre Lakatos and Alan Musgrave. Cambridge: Cambridge University Press, 1970.

Popper, Karl. *Unded Quest: An Intellectual Autobiography*. Glasgow: William Collins Sons, 1976.

Quine, Willard Van Orman. *From a Logical Point of View*. Cambridge, Mass.: Harvard University Press, 1953.

Schultz, T.W. "Production Opportunities in Asian Agriculture: An Economist's Agenda." In *Symposium on Development and Change in Traditional Agriculture: Focus on South Asia*. Asian Studies Center Occasional Paper. East Lansing: Michigan State University, 1968.

Wight, Martin. "The Balance of Power." In *Diplomatic Investigations*, edited by Herbert Butterfield and Martin Wight. Cambridge, Mass.: Harvard University Press, 1966.

CHAPTER 3

THE SYSTEMS APPROACH TO INTERNATIONAL POLITICS

INTRODUCTION

It is not uncommon for new approaches to a subject to be misunderstood. Sometimes the misinterpretations develop into creative contributions to the literature. At other times confusion is introduced into problems that should have been transcended earlier. One interesting instance of this involves common misinterpretations of my use of game theory. In his article on the use of mathematical reasoning in the study of politics, Richard Fagen, for instance, correctly noted that my "use of the game theoretical model is analogical and suggestive rather than rigorous and deductive. Since both his critics and his defenders seem to forget that at times, it is profitable to quote Kaplan himself on this point" (1961, p. 896).

Misinterpretations similar to those clarified by Fagen concern more central problems in international systems research. Thus it is often asserted that *System and Process* (1957) is an example of a precise deductive system, of a "scientism" that ignores the "if...then" character of scientific statements, of general theory, or even of the teleological use of models. I should regret it if I were responsible for these misconceptions, and no doubt I failed to communicate clearly enough. Short clarifications of these misinterpretations may be useful.

The discussion of the character of deductive theories begins on the first page of the preface to *System and Process,* which describes the ideal type of strictly deductive theory. The last sentence of the paragraph that contains this description reads: "If 'theory' is interpreted in this strict sense, this book does not constitute a theory." This thought is developed two paragraphs later: "If some of the requirements for a theory are loosened: if systematic completeness is not required; if unambiguous interpretation of terms and laboratory methods of confirmation are not required; then this book is, or at least contains, a theory. This theory may be viewed as an initial or introductory theory of international politics." I should now prefer to call the models of chapter 2 of *System and Process* "theory sketches" and to emphasize my later statement (on p. 21 of that book) that they are "heuristic models." The preface then relates why the systems framework was chosen: for explicitness of categories so that the framework of reference will not shift as new "facts" are brought in; for the integration of variables that do not fall within a single discipline; for a degree of explicitness that helps to reveal incompleteness; and for the generation of hypotheses by indicating structural similarities to other subject matters.

System and Process also attempts to be explicit on the "if...then" character of scientific statements: "Scientific laws state only what will happen if something else happens...if one body strikes another, x will happen. Whether one body will strike another is a separate problem" (p. 6). The subject was discussed in greater detail in the preface:

> For instance, can a theory of international politics be used to predict a specific event or action like the Hungarian Revolution of October 1956? The answer probably must be negative. Yet why make such a demand of theory?
>
> There are two basic limitations upon prediction in the physical sciences which are relevant to this problem. In the first place, the mathematics of complicated interaction problems has not been worked out...the scientist cannot predict the path of a single molecule of gas in a tank of gas.
>
> In the second place, the predictions of the physical scientist are predictions concerning an isolated system. The scientist does not predict that so much gas will be in a tank, that the temperature or pressure of the tank will not be changed by someone, or even that the tank will remain in that experimental room. He predicts what the characteristic behavior of the mass of gas molecules will be if stated conditions of temperature, pressure, etc., hold.

The engineer deals with nonisolate systems in which many free parameters play a role...but many aspects of exact design stem from experiments in wind tunnels or practical applications of past experiences rather than directly from the laws of physical science.

The theory of international politics normally cannot be expected to predict individual actions because the interaction problem is too complex, and because there are too many free parameters. It can be expected, however, to predict characteristic or modal behiavor within a *particular* [italics added] kind of international system.

The real question concerns the degree of articulation, precision, and theory that the subject matter permits. *System and Process* hypothesizes that macro-structural theory is possible in international politics as it is in comparative politics or in comparative society. Thus, international systems with different alignment patterns should manifest different behaviors. The same generalizations should not apply indifferently to them. And it should be possible both to give reasons for the differences (theory) and to relate the theories of different systems to different actual historical systems (articulated confirmation).

Thus, the use of comparative models in *System and Process* reflects an effort to move away from general theory to comparative theories of different systems. This point was succinctly stated by Charles Kindleberger, according to whom *System and Process* "tries to treat international politics piecemeal by partial-equilibrium methods. Contrast is furnished by such a contemporaneous book as——which tries, brilliantly but ineffectively in my judgment, to construct a single general-equilibrium system in which collective security and balance of power are interwoven" (1958, pp. 83-84).

Perhaps one other important observation should be made. Several writers have asserted, either in agreement or in opposition, that I hold multipolar systems to be more stable than bipolar systems. Inasmuch as I have never used the term "multipolar," I find it difficult to recognize the source of this confusion. It is true that my "balance of power" system is multipolar as others use the term, and that I do refer to it as more stable than the loose bipolar sytem. However, the unit-veto system would also be multipolar in this sense, and I regard it as less stable than the loose bipolar system. Differentiation of international systems merely by number of actors—although number does play a role in system behavior—ignores too many other elements of system structure to be useful either theoretically or descriptively. Attempts to base hypotheses merely on numbers of actors thus do not seem to me to be useful. Too many other parameters that influence both behavior and stability are likely to vary for that research schema to be meaningful or productive.

RESEARCH LESSONS

International systems models are macromodels of international politics. They are not models of the foreign policy process or of regional or intranational systems or of relationships between regional and international systems. The type of model that will prove useful depends on one's research aim, that is, on one's subject matter and on the questions one is asking. In my Chicago workshops we have been able to apply the models, however, in a variety of ways that we did not anticipate, for instance, to the Chinese warlord system. However, the application of the models to any particular system requires a reasoned analysis. We cannot simply apply a model on the basis of a few superficial resemblances, and we must distinguish between those elements of an existential international system to which the model clearly has reference and those for which there is no a priori reason to expect explanatory power. For instance, to expect that the loose bipolar model would explain behavior within the African subsystem when it is designed to explain the overarching system of international politics would be equivalent to expecting a model of monopolistic competition to explain the economics of the garment trade on the East Coast of the United States. Yet the monopolistic model might (or might not, depending on the facts of the case) be a relevant model for exploring the economy of the United States. If we confuse different aims, different structural levels of analysis, different levels of complexity, different levels of abstraction, different degrees of concreteness or descriptivity, and the differences between the theoretical and the descriptive, we will hopelessly muddle our efforts to advance the state of the discipline.

Systems models are merely tools for investigating reality. In the words of *System and Process,* "these systems are hypothetical only" (p. 2). Indeed, one might emphasize that the models developed in *System and Process* are quite crude; they are based at best on plausible reasoning. For instance, the injuction in the essential rules of some systems to increase capabilities does not specify by how much or under what risk conditions. Similar ambiguities necessarily occur elsewhere in the general statements of the models. For instance, it is virtually impossible to discriminate with words between the behavior of a system of nine actors and a system of seven.

Only when we were able to play out realizations of the "balance of power" model on a computer were we able specifically to link outcomes to the parameters that produced them. The theory itself is not mathematicized, and it is not clear that this is possible. A realization of a model or theory involves building the features of the theory into the computer program as parameters of that program. These parameters can then be varied to explore the sensitivity of the computer program to changes in the parameters. Thus it is possible to explore changes in the number of players, and so forth. If the outcome in unstable, we can ask how to reintroduce stability, and by what changes in the parameters. We also must ask ourselves what relation each change has to the initial verbal model and why it helps shed light on that model, for the objective of this work is not merely to produce a stable computer realization. Computer analysis is used not to prove any specific propositions but to explore the interrelationships of propositions concerning the strategic structure of the model of the international system. For instance, consider the proposition: "Would a 'balance of power' system operate differently were the actors security oriented or hegemony oriented?" To explore this, we constructed a pilot computer model instructing the national actors of the international system to optimize over each war cycle according to the appropriate utility schedule designed for them. We discovered that, if there was a hegemony-inclined actor in the system, the system became unstable. Initially, a balance-oriented actor was the victim of this instability. Pursued to the end, however, it became clear that according to the logic of the model the hegemony-inclined actor would never succeed in becoming the greatest actor in the system and would eventually be eliminated by the remaining balance-oriented player. Thus there was an inconsistency between short-run optimization and long-run optimization for the hegemony-inclined actor. Consequently, for the pilot model, if hegemony-inclined actors could optimize over the long run, they would behave the same way that more conservative security-oriented players do. This, however, is a conclusion not about the real world but about the logic of the model. Therefore, the next step was to explore the conditions under which the hegemony-inclined actor could succeed in obtaining hegemony. Introducing imperfect information, uncertainty, and nonsimultaneous commitment to war is believed to have permitted success for the hegemony-inclined actor.

We can explore further counterdeviancy measures that would be sufficient to prevent the hegemony-inclined actor from exploiting his deviant tendencies. Which of these alternative models is relevant to particular real-world situations is a matter to be determined by careful analysis and is not subject to arbitrary fiat.

The general literature asserts that in a system of five states wars will tend to be three against two and that wars of four against one will tend to destabilize the system. In our initial pilot runs, the wars were almost invariably four against one; yet some of our systems remained stable for hundreds of war cycles with no indication that continuation of the runs would produce instability. We then had the problem of modifying our model to produce the three-two wars that are more characteristic of history. There are probably at least two ways to accomplish this: by reducing the cost of wars or by permitting side payments within coalitions.

The two examples illustrate how systems theory utilizes computers. The computer is used to explore the relationships between assumptions. It is thus capable of assigning outcomes to causes, at least with respect to the structure of theory we have established to account for the real world of international politics. Thus, if we attempt to make inferences concerning the real world of international politics, we at least know how and why our hypotheses are related to our premises. We also have a ground for asserting that the real-world outcome may be related to the assigned cause if, in exploring the external world, we find those conditions that produced the same outcome in the computer model and no other conditions (at least that we can think of) that would counteract this outcome were we to place these conditions in the computer model.

A second problem that we faced was the paucity of historical information about international systems and their behavior. To overcome this deficiency, *System and Process* recommends among other methods a series of case studies based on the hypotheses flowing from the models (p. xvi). Although historical scholarship may have successfully answered many questions of interest to historians, the questions a political scientist should pose to these data are largely unexplored in literature. We did not know the characteristic behavior of the Greek city-state system, for instance, or how it differed from behavior in the Italian city-state system. Nor did we have any good ideas as to why the differences occurred. We did not understand how the patterns of alignment differed or why they differed. We did not know how or under what conditions wars were waged or peace made. It was indeed difficult even to ask questions such as these, for they flow more naturally from the kinds of models employed in international systems theory than from the case-specific questions historians ask or even those that political scientists ordinarily ask.

NATURE OF THE MODELS

The models employed in *System and Process* utilize five sets of variables: the essential rules, the transformation rules, the actor classificatory variables, the capability variables, and the information variables.

The essential rules of the systems state the behavior necessary to maintain equilibrium in the system; thus they are essential. The transformation rules state the changes that occur in the system as inputs across the boundary of the system that differ from those required for equilibrium move the system toward either instability or the stability of a new system. This is necessarily one of the least-developed aspects of the model; fully developed, however, it would provide alternative models of dynamic change.

The actor classificatory variables specify the structural characteristics of actors. These characteristics modify behavior. For instance, "essential national actor," "uncommitted national actor," and "universal actor" names actors whose behavior differs as a consequence of structural characteristics. The capability and information variables require no comment here.

There are three kinds of equilibria in such systems. There is an equilibrium within the set of essential rules. If behavior occurs that is habitually inconsistent with one of the essential rules, one or more of the other essential rules also will be changed. If the set of essential rules is changed, changes will occur in at least one of the other variables of the system. Or, conversely, if changes occur in one of the other variables of the system, then changes will occur in the essential rules also. If changes occur at the parameter of the system, changes will also occur within the system, and vice versa.

The models are not equilibrium models in the Parsonian sense, however. They are ultrastable, or even multistable, in Ashby's sense. Thus they respond to change, when it is within specified limits, by maintaining or restoring system equilibrium. Equilibrium does not have an explanatory function within such systems. Rather, it is the equilibrium that is to be explained; and the model itself provides the explanation by indicating the mechanisms that restore or maintain equilibrium. The actors do not behave consonantly with the essential rules merely to maintain equilibrium but because they are motivated under the specified system conditions to do so. The statement that changes within the system will cause changes beyond the system is a (theoretically useful, rather than merely empty) tautology in terms of the theory. Whether these will be consistent with continued equilibrium, however, is an open question. Extrasystemic changes will produce changes inside the system. This also is a tautology. However, whether the system will be able to restore its equilibrium is an open question.

Such equilibrium models necessarily abstract from a far richer historical context. The theories therefore can be used for the derivation of consequences *only* under explicitly stated boundary or parameter conditions. For instance, the statements concerning alignment patterns of the "balance of power" model in *System and Process* apply only at the level of type of alignment; they do not specify the actual actors who participate in specific alignments. And they specify even this broad consequence only for stated values of the exogenous and endogenous variables. The first attempt to bring the models closer to the richness of history occurs in chapter 3, where the models are varied for specified differences in the internal political and regulatory structure of nation states (these latter in principle could be derived from comparative macromodels of national systems). The motivations of nation states, as dealt with in this chapter, may differ from the initial first-order approximations as stated in chapter 2. Thus, as we come closer to reality—and this is still at a high level of abstraction—we lose generality. We begin to employ procedures closer to the step-by-step engineering applications of physical theory than to the generalized theoretical statements of physical theory.

Even these gross characteristics of national actors are far removed from their historical complexity: "Any attempt to describe the actual actor systems would founder under the weight of the parameters which individualize these systems—even when their structural characteristics are similar. Such things as capability factors, logistic factors, and information, including history of the past, are specific to the system..." (p. 54).

When we include the important factors that, from the standpoint of theory, are contingent, such as personality factors, economic and political conditions, technological developments and inventions, and other intranational and transnational factors, the complexity becomes so great that serious efforts to discuss them all systematically and relate them all to models would become lost in the detail. If we want to apply the macromodels to concrete cases, that is, to historical microevents, we must choose just those factors and just those values that we have some reason to believe operate in the particular instance we wish to understand and to explain. The chapters in *System and Process* on integration and disintegration, on values, and on strategy also attempt to bring to bear on the analysis in a highly generalized way some additional factors required to engineer the models closer to specific reality.

THE THEORY SKETCHES

"Balance of Power" Model

The "balance of power" model has the following characteristics:

1. The only actors in it are essential national actors, and thus there is no role differentiation in the model. This is a somewhat counterfactual assumption, for during portions of the historical "balance of power" period there were other organizational forms, such as the Danube Authority and the League of Nations.

2. The goals of the essential national actors of the system are oriented toward the optimization of security and they are not constrained from such optimization by any internal characteristic. By this we mean that essential national actors will prefer a high probability for survival, even though this excludes the possibility of hegemony, to a moderate probability for hegemony combined with a moderate probability for elimination as a major actor. Most analysts would argue that Napoleon and Hitler did not operate according to this assumption. It is possible, although far from

obvious, that the model would function differently were the assumption relaxed. There is sufficient factual validity to the assumption for large and interesting periods of history, however, to more than justify its use as a first approximation.

3. The weaponry in the system is not nuclear.
4. There are stochastic and unpredictable increases in productivity that, unless compensated for, in time might destabilize the system. Therefore, each actor seeks a margin of security above its proportionate share of the capabilities of the system.
5. There must be at least five essential national actors in the system. A two-actor system would be unstable. If either of the two actors gained a clear margin of superiority, it would be tempted to eliminate the other in order to guarantee that the other would not eliminate it, if through some combination of circumstances the ratio of capabilities were reversed. In a three-actor system, if there were a war of two nations against one, the victorious coalition would have some incentive to limits its demands on the defeated actor. To eliminate the defeated actor would throw the victors into an unstable two-actor system. Under the assumptions, this result would be undesirable, unless one actor could gain such advantage from the elimination of the third that it could eliminate the second actor. But this result would also give the second actor an incentive to combine with the third against the first unless it misunderstood its own interests. In one of a long series of subsequent wars, if one of the victorious actors sees some advantage in eliminating the first actor, it is now dependent on the ability of the only remaining actor to recognize that its own interests require it to oppose this. However, this other victorious actor now must recognize recursively that its interests require such opposition only if the losing actor subsequently behaves rationally in all subsequent wars. This is a hazardous assumption.

Although the prior considerations are not conclusive, they cast strong doubt on three as a lower bound for stability in a "balance of power" system. If there are at least five actors, however, it seems plausible that the argument for limitation on war would hold because of the geometric increase in the number of potential stabilizing alliances.

Arthur Burns (1957) regards five as the upper as well as the lower limit, because the geometric increase in permutational possibilities in systems with more than five actors would confront them with problems of enormous computational complexity. I disagree with Burns because I regard a model that includes information in this particular form as a misleading heuristic tool. Not only is it true that situational factors—

including but not restricted to tentative proposals for alliance—would enormously simplify decisional problems, but the qualitative aspects of the rules would do so also. Because it would be too costly and empirically impracticable to calculate what a maximal alliance would be, the actors would search for alliances that meet certain qualitative standards —these being related to the essential rules—and would tend to stick to them, in the absence of some major change in the real-world situation. In his analysis of my account of a "balance of power" system, William Riker (1962) gives reasons for believing that I am right in arguing that five is not an upper bound. Since then we have developed a point theorem that appears to support this conclusion.

It is easy to see that there must be an upper bound beyond which the system's characteristics do not motivate the actors to behave consistently with the essential rules. If there were 100,000 national actors, there would be no reason to limit wars or to worry about the availability of alliance partners. I choose an unnecessarily high number to avoid controversy, although a number under twenty likely would suffice to produce the same conclusion.

Because of structural characteristics of the system that are partly related to the numbers factor, it is clear that the system is more sensitive to disturbances arising from lack of understanding, miscalculation, or other extrasystemic influences at lower numbers than at higher, as long as the number is below the upper bound.

6. Each actor, even though of essential national actor status, is likely to require allies to obtain its objectives. Thus it desires to maintain the existence of potential future alliance partners.

7. Each essential national actor has one and only one boundary with every other essential national actor. I am aware that this is a counterfactual assumption that cannot be realized on any two-dimensional map system, although the computer model incorporates it. It functions in this theory somewhat as the assumptions in economics that information and movement are free and that all assets may be made liquid without cost. We shall see when I discuss Franke's Italian city-state system what modifications are necessary when the peculiar peninsular geogrphay of Italy is taken into account.

The characteristics specified above give rise to the following essential rules of conduct:

1. Act to increase capabilities but negotiate rather than fight.
2. Fight rather than pass up an opportunity to increase capabilities.

3. Stop fighting rather than eliminate an essential national actor.
4. Act to oppose any coalition or single actor that tends to assume a position of predominance with respect to the rest of the system.
5. Act to constrain actors who subscribe to supranational organizing principles.
6. Permit defeated or constrained essential national actors to reenter the system as acceptable role partners or act to bring some previously inessential actor within the essential actor classification. Treat all essential actors as acceptable role partners.

Rules 1 and 2 follow from the need for a margin of security in a world in which capabilities change stochastically. Rule 2 is essential to maintain the availability of future coalition partners. Rules 4 and 5 recognize that deviant actors may destabilize the system by their actions or by the actions of their followers or cohorts within other nations. Rule 6 is also related to the need for potential alliance partners and warns against restricting one's own choices unnecessarily.

These rules are not descriptive rules. They are prescriptive rules. That is, under the governing assumptions, states would follow these rules in order to optimize their own security. Thus there is motivation to observe the rules, abstracting from other considerations, but no requirement to do so. Under the appropriate boundary conditions, however, states would follow the rules and the model would be both predictive and descriptive.

If the essential national actors follow the specified rules under the specified system conditions, some of the consequences are obvious and others are not so obvious. Alliances will tend to be specific, of short duration, and to shift according to advantage rather than according to ideologies (even within war). In wars essential national actors will tend to have limited objectives and to observe the rules of war and the doctrine of nonintervention.

Alliances will tend to be of short duration because permanent alliances would undermine the "balancing" characteristics necessary for the security of the essential national actors. Thus alliances will have specific objectives as determined by short-term interests. And to use a phrase current in the eighteenth and nineteenth centuries, essential national actors will be disposed to act in terms of interest rather than in terms of sentiment. In short, there is in this system a general, although not necessarily implacable, identity between short-term and long-term interests.

The limitation of war in the "balance of power" system requires no further discussion.

I shall mention only a few of the expected norms of international law. One would expect belligerents to behave in ways that maintain the essential rules of the system, since the rules are required for the security of all essential actors, including belligerents. Behavior during war or territorial occupation that infuriated the enemy population might preclude the possibility of that actor as a future ally. Although this might not be the only constraint operating to enforce the rules of war, nonetheless it is an important factor tending in that direction.

The rule against intervention in the domestic affairs of another actor, a rule violated on many occasions, also tends to be sustained under conditions of the model. If the intervention—for instance, in favor of rebels—were to succeed, there might be a permanent alliance between them or a tutelage of one over the other. This arrangement would injure all the other actors in the system and tend to draw their active opposition. For this reason the intervention would likely be unwise or unsuccessful. And if for any reason the intervention were unsuccessful, the actor in which the intervention took place might have a serious revulsion for the intervening actor that would make it a permanent enemy of that actor. Although these reasons are not absolutely compelling, they are strong enough to make likely general observance of the rule of nonintervention in the "balance of power" system.

By and large, in *real-world* revolutions states did not tend to intervene on the side of the government either. Rather, they maintained normal state relations and trade with the established government. If the rebels grew strong enough, then the rules of belligerency applied; other states behaved neutrally toward the belligerents, at least with respect to shipping articles of war or trade goods. The reasons for this are similar to those given above; intervention would have had potentially destabilizing consequences for the system and would have elicited opposition from the other members.

For like reasons, recognition of new governments or new states tended to follow universal norms in the "balance of power" system. Was there a definite territory? Did the government control the territory? Was there reasonable support from the population or at least the absence of large overt opposition? If the answers were yes, then the government or state tended to be recognized, regardless of the form of government or its friendship for or antipathy toward particular states. Although the act of recognition itself was political, so that the fulfillment of the above criteria did not absolutely require the act of recognition, there was, with notable exceptions, fair concordance between rule and practice. Moreover, since nonrecognition was a political act, its consequences for international law were less than massive, the nonrecognized state merely being denied access to the privileges stemming from comity. Failure to recognize a state or government did not turn it into an outlaw, remove its obligations under international law, or free other states to behave toward it without regard for international law. Even before the facts establishing the legitimacy of a government were clear, other states were in effect bound by the rules of international law in their conduct toward the nonrecognized government or state. Intervention in its affairs would have been contrary to the rules of the system. Recognition may have been a political act and a negotiating tool in getting the new government or state to recognize its obligations under the rules of the international community, but it was not a weapon in a cold war designed to undercut its existence.

THE LOOSE BIPOLAR MODEL

A second model, which has some relevance to present-day international politics, is the loose bipolar system. This model contains two blocs, each led by a leading bloc actor. There is role differentiation in this model; in addition to blocs and bloc members are uncommitted actors not joined to blocs and universal organizations, such as the United Nations. The weaponry in this model is nuclear—at least for the contemporary time period. In an age of efficient logistics and great organizational capacity, nuclear weaponry is an essential element of the system. For unless factors of scale precluded it, we would expect one of the blocs to overwhelm the other unless deterred by nuclear weapons.

This system operates according to the following simplified set of essential rules:

1. Blocs strive to increase their relative capabilities.
2. Blocs tend to be willing to run at least some risks to eliminate rival blocs.
3. Blocs tend to engage in major war rather than to permit rival blocs to attain predominance.
4. Blocs tend to subordinate objectives of the universal actor to objectives of the bloc but subordinate objectives of rival blocs to the universal actor.
5. Nonbloc actors tend to support the universal actor generally and specifically against contrary objectives of blocs; and vice versa.
6. Nonbloc and universal actors tend to act to reduce the danger of war between blocs.
7. Nonbloc actors tend to be neutral between blocs except where important objectives of the universal actor are involved.
8. Blocs attempt to extend membership but tend to tolerate the status of nonbloc actors.

Rules 1 to 3 reflect the uncertainties of a bipolar system and the need for at least a margin of security. Rule 4 is related to the need within the system for mediatory functions. Particularly in the nuclear age, mediatory activities help coordinate conflicting blocs and achieve agreement short of nuclear war. This is similar to many other types of bargaining situations in which optimal solutions are facilitated by the mediatory process. On the other hand, although the blocs should support these processes, each bloc should also take advantage of opportunities to obtain a somewhat favorable outcome. That is, maneuvering will take place that is related to situational advantages. Moreover, it is desirable, even apart from the need for mediatory functions, to subordinate the goals of one's opponents to those of the universal organization and to subordinate the goals of the organization to those of the bloc, provided it can be done with minimal inconsistency.

Universal organizations are major supports for the interests of actors not belonging to blocs—the greatest protection for them insofar as they can be protected by universally applicable rules of conduct. Therefore, nonbloc members have an interest in subordinating both blocs to the universal actor. This would become difficult, perhaps impossible in the event of a major war. And minor wars might escalate into major wars. Hence rule 6 that nonbloc actors act to reduce the danger of war between the blocs. The nonbloc actors cannot properly fulfill this function unless they remain neutral between the blocs. Lack of neutrality would impeed their mediatory functions and their support for the universal actor. On the other hand, a neutrality that threatened to undercut the universal actor would injure their interests. Thus rule 7. Rule 8 emphasizes the fact that, although extending bloc membership is important to the bloc, the mediatory role is sufficiently important for the bloc to tolerate nonbloc membership—and, under appropriate conditions, even to support it.

The consequences of the rules are straightforward and for the most part have already been stated: Blocs are long term, are based on permanent and not shifting interests, and have ideological components. Wars, except for the fear of nuclear escalation, would tend to be unlimited. The fear of nuclear war, however, has a strong dampening effect on war. The universal organization tends to support mediatory and war-dampening activities. With respect to international law, there are few restrictions on intervention and these arise mainly out of the fear of escalation.

Some of the reasons for these consequences may now be stated. Blocs tend to be long term and based on permanent interests. There is a tendency in a bipolar system for a bloc to support its leading member even on issues where there is a temporary divergence of short-term interests. Moreover, there is a tendency for ideological congruity within the blocs, for the kind of close association involved requires either organizational uniformity, as in the Communist bloc, or the kind of public support and cultural similarity that helps to support NATO. If one bloc were organized according to long-term interests, and other actors were not, the bloc might well gain its way on most important issues by splitting the opposition issue by issue.

There would be a tendency in this system for wars to be unlimited; neither bloc would regard the other as a potential coalition partner. The greatest inhibitor of a central confrontation lies in the nuclear component and perhaps in certain factors of scale that would make administration of the world an extremely difficult, if not impossible, task.

As for the rule of intervention in international law, at least some of the constraints present in the "balance of power" system would not be operative in a loose bipolar system. The opposition to intervention would come from the other bloc and would not have the same massive quality as in the "balance of power" system, where most major actors could be expected to oppose it. Fear of confrontation and escalation would nevertheless inhibit intervention to some extent. In areas where one bloc had easy access and the other did not, intervention would not be unlikely. Where both blocs had relatively similar access, they might agree to insulate the area from bloc competition or alternatively they might decide to compete for it. The decision would depend on the specifics of the situation; the model cannot be expected to give rise to a specific prediction on this point. One factor inhibiting intervention would be the fear that the erosion of this particular rule of law might tend to erode the general system of law. Although this fear might be a factor in decisions concerning intervention, the consequences feared would not be so direct or massive that it would prove overriding. Moreover, most interventions would be indirect and covert.

One would expect the use of force to be permissible in this system. The same factors that permit intervention also operate to permit the use of force, the Charter of the United Nations to the contrary notwithstanding. Historically, Palestine, the Congo, Cyprus, Greece, Korea, Vietnam, Suez, Hungary, and various other episodes firmly illustrate the erosion of the so-called rule of law enunciated in the Charter. The bipolarity of the system tends to focus competition between the blocs and to produce a resort to force in those circumstances where one of the blocs has a clear preponderance of capabilities. The rule can to some extent be enforced against nonleading nations, as in the Suez case, or even as in the Pakistan-India case; but it runs into greater difficulties in the India-China case.

To some extent this conclusion stems from the fact that the bloc leaders have no desire for the continuance of a war that neither side supports, especially since any armed conflict might lead to a central confrontation, even if only with low probability. The bloc leaders see no reason to risk even the lowest probabilities of nuclear war if there is some convenient way of avoiding it and if the bloc leaders get no clear gain from the use of force. Where the universal organization tends to dampen armed confrontations and to mediate quarrels among nonleading states, it therefore tends to reinforce the interests of the bloc leaders.

Recognition of states or of governments is based not on the criteria of control within a region with reasonable support from the people but, in large part at least, on the consequences of the act of recognition for bloc policy. Thus, not recognizing East Germany, North Korea, or Communist China was, during the height of bipolarity, part of a program of political warfare designed to erode the positions of these governments. This did not mean that nonrecognized states or governments were entirely without rights within the system or that unprovoked major acts of military warfare against them were permitted, even during the height of bipolarity. Yet whereas in the "balance of power" system the objective of nonrecognition is to secure the compliance of the nonrecognized state or government with the norms of the system, in the loose bipolar system the objective of nonrecognition is to weaken the international position of the nonrecognized state or government and, under favorable circumstances, contribute to its demise.

TIGHT BIPOLAR SYSTEM

The tight bipolar international system represents a modification of the loose bipolar system in which non-bloc-member actors and universal actors either disappear entirely or cease to be significant. Unless both blocs are hierarchically organized, however, the system will tend toward instability.

There is no integrative or mediatory role in the tight bipolar system. Therefore, there will tend to be a high degree of dysfunctional tension in the system. For this reason, the tight bipolar system will not be a highly stable or well-integrated system.

UNIVERSAL SYSTEM

The universal international system might develop as a consequence of the functioning of a universal actor organization in a loose bipolar system. The universal system, as distinguished from those international systems previously discussed, would have a political system as a subsystem of the international social system. However, it is possible that this political system would be of the confederated type, that is, that it would operate on territorial governments rather than directly on human individuals.

The universal international system would be an integrated and solidary system. Although informal political groupings might take place within the system, conflicts of interest would be settled according to the political rules of the system. Moreover, a body of political officials and administrators would exist whose primary loyalty would be to the international system itself rather than to any territorial subsystem of the international system.

Whether or not the universal international system is a stable system depends on the extent to which it has direct access to resources and facilities and on the ratio between its capabilities and the capabilities of the national actors who are members of the system.

HIERARCHICAL SYSTEM

The hierarchical international system may be democratic or authoritarian in form. If it evolves from a universal international system—perhaps because the satifactions arising from the successful operation of such a universal international system lead to a desire for an even more integrated and solidary international system—it is likely to be a democratic system. If, on the other hand, the hierarchical system is imposed on unwilling national actors by a victorious or powerful bloc, then the international system is likely to be authoritarian.

The hierarchical system contains a political system. Within it, functional lines of organization are stronger than geographical lines. This highly integrated characteristic of the hierarchical international system makes for greater stability. Functional cross-cutting makes it most difficult to organize successfully against the international system or to withdraw from it. Even if the constitution of the system were to permit such withdrawal, the integration of facilities over time would make the costs of withdrawal too high.

UNIT-VETO SYSTEM

Consider a world in which some twenty-odd actors have nuclear systems capable of a not incredible first strike. That is, each actor would have a nuclear system that would not completely reduce enemy forces in a first strike but that nonetheless might reduce enemy forces so much, if everything went according to plan, that a war begun by a first strike might be contemplated. However, even a successful first strike would then leave an actor launching such an attack, because of its depleted arsenal, vulnerable to attack by a third actor—an attack that might not be unlikely either if its own attack had been without provocation or if the other actor were malevolent. In any event, the vulnerability of the attacker to subsequent attack by a third actor would tend to inhibit such a first strike except in the most provocative circumstances.

In the "pure" model—that is, excluding economic, political, and ecological reasons for cooperation—there would be little need for specific alliances in this world. To the extent that alliances would occur, one would expect them to be of a nonideological nature. Actors might ally themselves in pacts establishing an obligation to retaliate against any "aggressor" who launched a nuclear attack exceeding certain specified proportions against an alliance member.

In this system one does not expect large countervalue or counterforce wars. If nuclear weapons are used at all, they will tend to be used in limited retaliations for purposes of warning or in other strictly limited ways. The wars that do occur will tend to be nonnuclear and limited in geographic area and in methods of fighting. Sublimited wars will occur more often than actual wars.

The system, however, might seem to have some potential for triggering wars or for catalytic wars. That is, if one actor engages in a counterforce attack, this might trigger an attack on it by a third actor. Or an anonymous attack or accident might catalyze a series of wars. These possibilities cannot be denied, particularly if tensions within the system become high. Nonetheless, first strikes and accidental wars are unlikely because credible first-strike forces will not exist and because adequate command and control systems will be available Furthermore, from a purely strategic point of view, this world would be more stable than a two-actor nuclear world. Even if one actor thought that it had gained a sufficient strategic nuclear advantage to attempt a first strike against a particular enemy, that strike would make it exceptionally vulnerable to the remaining nuclear actors, who would now see it as dangerous in the long run but temporarily clawless. Such a system might even possibly slow down the qualitative arms race, for one motive that drives it forward strongly in a two-actor nuclear system is the fear that the other actor might gain a qualitative advantage that would permit a not incredible first strike capability that might be used either militarily or as a bargaining club in a crisis.

Because nuclear systems will be relatively stable against accidents, an anonymous attack will be a theoretical possibility but not a practicable one unless many actors develop Polaris-type forces—that is, forces such that an attack cannot be attributed to a particular actor. Even so, it would seem difficult to identify the rational motive for attack in such a world. An anonymous attack would not seem to have any reasonable political motive, since, by definition, the aggressor could not identify himself and thus secure the benefits arising from threats. Numerous nervous rivals would remain, and the attack might very well trigger a holocaust.

Because of the adequacy of nuclear systems and the relative unimportance of alliances, when contrasted with the "balance of power" international system, interventions would not be as ominous as in that system and therefore would not be as strongly interdicted. But since the gains resulting from such interventions would be far less important than in the loose bipolar system, they are unlikely to become characteristics of this system. The danger of escalation, moreover, would tend to limit them. If universal organizations exist in this system, they would act as mediators, as would noninvolved actors, whether nuclear or nonnuclear. In general, though, the universal organization would have fewer and less important functions than in the loose bipolar system. Nations equipped with nuclear forces in the unit-veto system will tend to be self-sufficient and to reject outside pressures, even if coming from universal organizations. In particular, the functions of the universal organization dealing with political change will tend to be minimized. This will be reinforced by the disappearance of the colonial question as an important issue in world politics.

The foreign policies of the great nuclear actors will tend to be isolationist. Alliances, as specified, will recede in importance. Hegemonial ambitions will be curbed—primarily by an obvious inability to achieve them. Protective functions will tend to be shifted to "other" shoulders, when aggression does occur, since no "natural" assignment of this function will be possible. (That is, almost any one of the nuclear powers could play the role; there is no particular pressure on any particular nation to assume it.) This is parallel to the situation between the two world wars when the League of Nations sought to control aggression. The onus of stopping aggression could always be shifted to other shoulders and was not undertaken by any nation or combination of nations until very late in the game. At the time of Korea, on the other hand, in the loose bipolar system, if aggression was to be halted, only the United States was in a position to do it. Thus, the fact that the system singled out a particular nation for this role served to reinforce the performance of the role function.

The domestic corollary of the above would involve publics suspicious of foreign actors, relatively uninterested in the morals of quarrels or in social change external to the actors, and lacking the assurance necessary for an articulated goal-oriented foreign policy. This would contribute to instability.

MIXED EMPIRICAL MODELS

A number of mixed models follow that may be considered variations either of the loose bipolar system or of the unit-veto system. The variations will occur under conditions that are not consonant with maximum stability for either kind of system. Although not equilibrium systems, they correspond with conditions that conceivably might persist for critical periods of time. In this sense they might be considered to have some sort of local stability. They are worth exploration, since they indicate some potential lines of development from the existing situation. Still, for purposes of model construction we simplify and reduce the number of variables involved. We look for those conditions that make for maximum stability within the limitations of the somewhat destabilizing constraints that we do place on the models. Other variants could easily be constructed.

VERY LOOSE BIPOLAR SYSTEM

This model has elements of great inherent instability and would not be presented at all except that it has striking resemblances to contemporary international politics. In the loose biplar system, the nations playing different roles are not differentiated in terms of history, culture, state of economic development, color, and so forth. In the real world, the uncommitted nations, by and large, are ex-colonies, in particular, ex-colonies of nations belonging to NATO, are in bad economic circumstances, are attempting to modernize and develop, belong, by and large, to the so-called colored races, and possess ideologies that make them hostile to much the NATO bloc stands for. Increased nuclear stability has reduced the fear of central war, except as a consequence of escalation. This has tended to dampen international crises of the classical military kind but has created a shelter for guerrilla and sublimited wars as well as for rare limited wars in areas where escalation is not likely. The blocs have weakened, although they still exist. Large areas of accord and common interest between the United States and the Soviet Union appear to have arisen. Meanwhile Communist China appears to many as a potential threat to the USSR; and friction has increased significantly between China and the Soviet Union. There has also been a limited degree of nuclear diffusion.

In this system, the universal organization is used in ways consonant, but not identical, with the revolutionary drives of many of the uncommitted nations. Within the universal organization both blocs will compete for the support of the uncommitted states with respect to the issues of decolonization and of racial equality. In this competition the bloc, which for the most part supports the status quo, will, by and large, be outbidden. The conservative bloc will be more effective in those areas in which it can intervene directly, or even indirectly, with military force and economic support.

The competition for the support of the uncommitted actors in part will be shifted from that between the United States and the USSR to that between the USSR and China. This will likely coincide with the quasi-legitimization of intervention against existing "conservative" governments by revolutionary governments.

This system will be characterized by the search for arms control and for accommodation between the blocs and by the opposition to bloc policy by important members of both blocs. There will be a fragmentation, or at least weakening, of bloc structures. In the area of law, the rule of nonintervention will be breached even more than in the loose bipolar system. The universal organization will be used primarily to control the path of political change rather than primarily as a mediatory instrument. As a consequence, it is likely to have forced upon it more and more difficult problems that are not unlikely to be beyond the competence of the organization. They will likely involve strong conflicts of interest between the bloc leaders and may reach such magnitude that the support of the bloc leaders for the universal organization may be called into question. Extreme self-restraint on the part of the bloc leaders will be required if the system is not to become unstable and if, in particular, the universal organization is to remain viable and continue to perform its mediating functions.

DÉTENTE SYSTEM

The "détente system" world assumes that some of the favorable projections as to changes within both the Soviet and American systems will occur. Soviet society will become more open and the United States less defensive of the international status quo. Although no responsible, reasonable, and cautious social scientist would predict these changes, it still would be interesting to see if we can picture the kind of system that might occur if these changes did take place. In general, we assume the amelioration of the Soviet system, the domestication of the Chinese system, or at least the inability of the Chinese to create difficulty, and stability in much of the uncommitted world.

This is a world in which the United States and the USSR are still strongly competitive but in which the competition is not conflict producing. Tensions are relaxed and important arms control agreements reached. As a consequences, the United States and the USSR support nuclear forces capable only of mostly finite deterrence and there are portents that the forces are being reduced to those required for minimum deterrence only.

As a consequence of this détente system, the internal organization of the two blocs loosens up. Some of the Soviet satellites begin to take occasional positions on foreign policy agreeing with those of the West rather than with the USSR. Fissures within the Western bloc increase. Eurocommunism is on the rise. This creates difficulties for the USSR with respect to eastern Europe and for the United States with respect to the long-term stability of NATO. Although most issues tend to find groupings revolving around the USSR and the United States, the alignments have some tendency to differ from issue to issue. And on some issues the United States and the USSR are in agreement and differ with China or one or more Western states.

The foreign policies of the United States and the USSR tend toward liberal interventionism. Anticolonialism is carried to completion. The United States quits backing oligarchical but anti-Communist states. The USSR learns how to live with non-Communist new nations and ceases its support of national liberation movements. China on some occasions supports conservative regimes.

In the area of law, nonintervention in the internal affairs of other states is stressed. This is a necessary corollary of the détente system. Although some of the rules of international law are changed to accord with new values—on the subject of expropriation, for instance—in general the rules of international law are strengthened and enforced. They are extended to outer space and celestial bodies.

The universal organization plays a strong role in the governance of space, celestial bodies, and the polar regions. It aids in extinguishing colonialism and regulating arms control measures, and takes a leading role in the dampening of international breaches of the peace.

Breaches of the peace—or even wars—may occur in this system, but they will not involve the United States and the USSR, at least in direct confrontations with each other. Such wars will tend to be local, to be strictly limited in objectives, to involve minor nations, and to be strictly nonnuclear. Where this threatens not to be the case, the United States and the USSR will likely cooperate within limits to prevent occurrences that might escalate. And, if they do not cooperate in this endeavor, at least they will not seriously interfere with each other's actions to prevent or dampen such events. They will usually work through the universal organization in these cases.

UNSTABLE BLOC SYSTEM

The world of "the unstable bloc system" is a world in which developments contrary to those assumed for the détente system world have taken place. This is a world in which tension has increased and in which the United States and the USSR are highly suspicious of each other. Arms control agreements are minimal in this world. Third-area conflicts are extensive. There are local outbreaks of violence. And national liberation movements continue to be a problem. Qualitative developments have made nuclear systems cheaper and easier to acquire.

The nuclear systems of the United States and the USSR vary in strength from mostly finite deterrence to not incredible massive retaliation. Four or five other states have nuclear systems, but these are good for minimum deterrence only. All nuclear powers possess strategies calling for limited strategic reprisal under appropriate circumstances. But obviously it is easier and safer for the United States and the USSR to use this strategy, even against each other, and certainly against the small nuclear powers, than it is for the small nuclear powers to use it against each other. It is conceivable—but not credible—that the small nuclear powers would use limited strategic reprisal against one of the large nuclear powers. The chance is much greater that the small power attempting this would be left to its fate and that the retaliation then applied against it would not trigger off the other larger nuclear power. Thus the deterrent value of such a threat by a small nuclear power—unless led by an apparent madman—would not be great.

Alliance policy in this system is highly dependent on military capability and policy. If the United States' posture, for instance, is clearly not adequate for deterrence against aggression directed at countries other than the United States, the strains on its alliances during periods of crises might prove overwhelming, except in those cases where its allies' capabilities, in addition to its own, might produce the requisite deterrence.

In general, bloc alignments would be subject to two conflicting pressures. The fact of crisis in a basically bipolar world would give the blocs greater reason for being and greater cohesion. The additional fact, however, that the United States, or any other nation, might hesitate before inviting nuclear destruction on its own territory provides an opening for nuclear blackmail. That such blackmail might be dangerous and that it is unlikely to be practiced except under conditions of very great provocation does not negate this consideration. Moreover, the threat need not be overt. The fact that blackmail is operative in a situation is enough to help shape expectations, attitudes, and national policies. How the two conflicting pressures factor out depends on an interplay of considerations difficult to consider in the abstract.

The foreign policies of the United States and the USSR in this model will tend to be interventionist. They will respond to the basic clash of interests and not to a general concordance of interests as in the détente system. United States policy will tend toward conservatism, that is, toward the support of status quo conservative regimes. Change will tend to be viewed as a threat, despite some plausible arguments to the contrary.[1] There will be a consequent alienation of a considerable portion of the intellectual elite within the United States and in the other NATO states. Soviet policy will be oriented toward national liberation movements despite a desire not to "rock the boat" in the dangerous nuclear age. Additional "Czechoslovakias" or other comparable events may occur that will disillusion Soviet intellectuals. Relations between the USSR and China will influence Soviet policy.

Although most breaches of the peace in this system will not involve direct confrontations between the United States and the USSR, such confrontations are not entirely unlikely in this system. Moreover, there is a distinct possibility that nuclear weapons will be used in some limited fashion. If so, the use will probably be of the limited-reprisal variety.

The role of the universal organization will be primarily mediatory and adapted to dampening the consequences of outbreaks of violence. Although each bloc will support political changes contrary to the interest of the opposing bloc, efforts to secure a constitutional majority in the universal organization will generally prove ineffective. The universal organization will not acquire authority over outer space, celestial bodies, and serious arms control measures.

Intervention in the internal affairs of other nations will be rampant in this system and will be limited primarily by the fear of nuclear escalation. This system will not be noted for the growth of international law. If anything, there will be retrogression. Existing standards will be eroded and will not be replaced by generally agreed-upon norms.

INCOMPLETE NUCLEAR DIFFUSION SYSTEM

I now consider another variation of the "unstable bloc system." This system is similar to the previous one, except that fifteen or twenty nations, in addition to the United States and the USSR, will have nuclear forces. But these forces will be of the small, vulnerable variety. My analysis stresses only those features of this world that differ from the unstable bloc system.

The United States and the USSR will have nuclear forces that are not capable of first strike against each other but that do give some significant advantage if used first. The smaller nuclear nations will possess what is ordinarily called minimum deterrence. This is similar to the French idea of "tearing an arm off." These forces would, in fact, deter most attacks against the homeland, but not all, particularly in extremely provocative situations. Their triggering capability would be quite small. And they would be quite vulnerable to surprise attack, particularly by one of the major nuclear powers.

Alliances would be possible between major and minor nuclear powers or among minor nuclear powers. But the former type of alliance would be inhibited by the small state's possession of nuclear arms. Possession would by itself be a sign of independence and distrust. Moreover, the large state would fear commitment by the small state's nuclear use. It would want to insulate itself from a chain of actions that it could not control. And, although a general alliance among most of the small states possessing nuclear forces might create a reasonable deterrent, unless there were exceptional political or cultural circumstances the alliance would be very susceptible to nuclear blackmail and splitting tactics. Otherwise the discussion of the unstable bloc system is applicable with respect to alliance conditions.

Although wars in this system would tend to be limited, as in the unstable bloc system, the degree of tension and the possibility of escalation would also be greater. Limited and direct confrontations between the United States and the USSR might occur in non-European areas. A central confrontation in Europe might also occur, but here the danger of escalation beyond the limited-war category would be very great. And for this reason the factors operating against a central confrontation would tend to be very great.

The mediatory functions of the universal organization would be more important than in the unstable-bloc-system world and would tend to be more stressed, although it would also prove very difficult to use them successfully. Outside of mediatory functions, the universal organization would have even fewer functions than in the unstable-bloc-system world and would handle them less successfully on the whole.

The legal system would function even more poorly than in the unstable-bloc-system world, and intervention in the internal affairs of other states would be even more extensive. Foreign policy would be as in the détente system world, but the conservative interventionist nature of American policy would be even more pronounced. Soviet policy would tend to be more revolutionary. The alienation of some intellectuals would be increased, but the obvious dangers of the situation would also create a countercurrent of chauvinism leading to a highly dangerous bifurcation of intellectual opinion within both blocs and within the leading nation of each. Governments and their supporters would lack assurance and might become susceptible to ill-considered actions. There might be a swing between excessive caution and excessive adventurism.

ENGINEERING THE MODEL

As I have already pointed out, the models constitute closed systems, while the real world in which they are to be applied is an open system. An example of the difficulties encountered in extrapolating from a model to the real world may be helpful. We would expect that, in a "balance of power" system, alliances would be short-lived, based on immediate interests, and neglectful of existing or previous alliance status. The rigid alliance systems of the European great nations between 1871 and 1914 and the relatively unlimited nature of World War I would seem, superficially at least, inconsistent with the prescriptions of the "balance of power" theory. We could, of course, resolve the problem by analyzing the period from 1871 to 1914 in terms of a rigid "balance of power" system. This type of solution, however, if adopted uniformly, would require us to analyze every characteristically different state of the world in terms of a different systems model, thus depriving the concept of "system" of much of its theoretical meaning and turning it into a primarily descriptive device. The alternative procedure is to decide whether the underlying theory of the "balance of power" system can be used to explain the observed discrepancies.

We do not, of course, assert that if the theory of the "balance of power" system can account for the behavioral differences from 1871 to 1914, it therefore is *the* true explanation of the observed behavior. Other factors undoubtedly played important roles in producing both the specific sequence of events and the general form that the sequence took. We will merely have established that the asserted irregular behavior does not invalidate the theory and that the theory may be useful for relating a wider range of phenomena than is possible without such a theory. This may increase the confidence we place in the theory and its explanatory power.

The reconciliation of theory and behavior follows. If we recognize, as there is reason to believe that Bismarck foresaw, that the seizure of Alsace-Lorraine by Prussia led to a public opinion in France that was ineluctably revanchist, this parameter change permits engineering the theory in a way consistent with the developments that followed. As long as Germany was unwilling to return Alsace-Lorraine to France, France would be Germany's enemy. Thus France and Germany became the poles of rigid opposed alliances, as neither would enter— or at least remain in—the same coalition regardless of specific common interests. The chief motivation for limitation of war in the theoretical system is the need to maintain the existence of other essential actors as potential future allies. For the foreseeable future, however, neither France nor Germany was the potential ally of the other. Consequently, neither had an incentive—as would normally be the case in a "balance of power" system—to limit its war aims against the other. What had been an incentive for limitation became instead a disincentive.

Many historians explain the breakdown of the historical "balance of power" system in 1870 by emphasizing nationalism. This is misleading. Although it is true that the nationality problem of the Dual Monarchy interfered with that actor's ability to function as an essential national actor, nationalism functioned at the actor rather than the systemic level. To the extent that nationalism played a role in Bismarck's inability to act with external rationality on the Alsace-Lorraine problem or that it interfered with appropriate French responses, again it functioned at the actor rather than the systemic level. And it did so for reasons that were accidental in terms of the system. That is, in principle, all the actors could have been nationalistic without instability. It was only as policies were applied in the real world that conflicts between regime considerations and external rationality arose.There was nothing in principle that required the existence in a real but nationalistic world of a problem akin to that of Alsace-Lorraine or a state such as the Dual Monarchy. That is why the effects of nationalism on the breakdown of the "balance of power" system were indirect and accidental from a systems standpoint. Nationalism, in combination with other intranational and situational factors, explains why a parameter took the value it did. It does not identify it as inconsistent with equilibrium in the absence of a macrotheory of the international system or explain why it had the consequences it had for the system. Only a macrosystems theory permits that identification and explanation.

The European system after 1870 is also a good example of how analysis at both the macro- and the micro-level can be used in engineering an example of a particular case. The effort by Bismarck to build a Germany that would be a major, and even possibly the most important, national actor in the international system was not in itself destabilizing. However, the effort to build the type of domestic support that enabled him to block the emperor's policies after Sadowa and to pursue his other objectives made it impossible for him to allow France to keep Alsace-Lorraine although he was aware of the problems the seizure would cause. The reinsurance treaties by Bismarck were part of an effort by Bismarck to jury-rig a system that he knew had lost some degree of stability. However, in the crucial case of Alsace-Lorraine his domestic base of support precluded the external rationality that is a condition for stability in the model. French public opinion then made it impossible for France to behave with external rationality. What occurred thereafter is consistent with what the theory predicts under this set of parameter conditions. However, as the real world is far more complex than any systems model, the theory sketch does not provide a complete explanation. A complete explanation would require, in addition, discussions of the stability problems of the Dual Monarchy and the peculiar conditions of the pre-World War I mobilization system, and also of many other conditions.

The engineering problem is merely a variant form of the normal testing problem. The theory sketches can be used in the way in which theories are supposed to be used. That is, seemingly discordant behavior can be explained through application of the theory or theory sketch, as in the case of the Alsace-Lorraine situation and the European system after 1870. On the other hand, seemingly concordant information is not in itself confirmatory, for one must be able to show that the situation sufficiently corresponded with the conditions under which that behavior is to be expected. Thus, for instance, in the case of Franke's Italian city-state system (1968), the first phase of the system exhibits behavior consistent with the essential rules. However, further analysis shows that this behavior results from the lack of a state apparatus that survived the death of a duke, deficiencies in logistical capabilities, and other extrasystemic reasons. In the absence of international theories or theory sketches, it would not be possible in any coherent manner even to make these distinctions. Moreover, when we use such theory sketches we are able to search more systematically and more coherently for the parameters that produced or reinforced various states of equilibria or disequilibria. Thus more coherent research programs are possible.

HOW MANY MODELS?

This discussion of the problem of engineering a theory may help indicate the circumstances under which a theory can be extended or a different theory called for. Where the theory can be adapted to the changed parameters economically within the explanatory framework that the theory provides, it is not necessary to develop a new theory merely because the behavior looks different. Where such adaptation cannot be made, a different theory will be needed. Since many of the adaptations depend on ingenuity and insight, it is possible that one theory will later be recognized to do the job that two theories were once required for. On the other hand, additional evidence may later cast doubt on a reconciliation between theory and behavior that once seemed adequate. In some cases, alternative theories may seem equally adaptable. And in still other cases, non-international factors—for instance, domestic politics—may so dominate an international event that a theory of international politics may have only marginal explanatory power or perhaps none at all.

Designations of systems in terms of theoretical models are, then, not descriptive. The years between 1870 and 1914, for instance are referred to as a "balance of power" period because the theory of the "balance of power" explains the observed behavior, which differs from that postulated by the model, by adjusting the theory for the change that French public opinion caused at the parameter. There are analogues to this elsewhere in political science. The British system during World War II is generally considered a democratic system (or whatever comparable terminology one prefers) under conditions of wartime stress; presumably, democratic behavior would be restored with the return of peace. This emphasis on theoretical equilibrium models does not mean that statements of variations of the models would not be useful for at least some analytic purposes, or that these variations must not be descriptive. But such models should be distinguished from the more important theoretical models that serve as the core of explanation.

The six theoretical models, or systems, of *System and Process* are equilibrium models. The more complex real world goes through phases for which these models are useful explanatory tools. *System and Process* (p. 21) leaves open whether the phases of the real world to which the different models are applied should be considered real system changes or merely different equilibrium states of one ultrastable international system. Thus, in *System and Process* the transformation rules for the theoretical models suggest possible conditions for each of the models under which a world analyzable in its terms could be transformed into worlds analyzable by each of the other models.

Whether the real-world system is presumed to have undergone system change or equilibrium change[2] depends on the reversibility of the process. The transitions between the types represented by the six models would seem to be not easily reversible—that is, to involve more system ramifications than intramodel variations and consequently to require more than restoring the original value of the variable whose change precipitated the transformation if the previous system is to be restored. Variations of the model, that is, variations that can be explained by the same theory, would seem to be more easily reversible.

In any event, the two levels of analysis must be kept distinct. In a question of the relationships between a model or theory and observed events, we consider systems the same (of the same type) if the same theory or model explains behavior. In a "concrete" situation (when we ask if an external real-world system has changed), the question of reversibility becomes dominant. The world is said to have undergone a system change if the change from one model type to another is irreversible; otherwise there is merely equilibrium change.

The Italian city-states during their "balance of power" phase and nineteenth-century Europe are both examples of "balance of power" systems although there is no historical continuity; whereas in 1945 or thereabouts there emerged the bipolar system, which is considered distinct from the "balance of power" system for purposes of theoretical explanation although there is historical continuity. In the latter case, both analytical and "concrete" system changes have occurred, for we believe that nuclear weapons have introduced irreversible changes into the world.

The changes of systems types in real cases may be abrupt, in which case there is no doubt when they occur, or they may be gradual, in which case there may be transitional periods when resemblances to one or another model is a matter of more or less rather than of yes or no. The analogy is to the transition between a "normal" personality system and a "psychotic" personality system, usually one of shading in which the designation of the boundary line between the conditions, although important for a number of purposes, depends on the application of criteria that may be subject to legitimate disagreement. Conceivably, although we have not yet discovered such cases, one theory might be applicable to certain selected aspects of the international system and a second to different aspects, just as certain aspects of the economic market are best explained by models of perfect competition and other aspects by models of imperfect competition. In any of these cases, the problem is practical, but the theoretical models are essential for both analysis and explanation.

Each historical system occurs in its specific set of environmental circumstances. In some cases the differences in circumstances do not produce behavioral irregularities or require explanations linked to variations at the parameters.

In other cases the variations at the parameter may make for either less or more stability in the system than would otherwise have been expected. Take, for example, the mercenary system in the Italian city-state system; here we need to examine the ways in which the two systems are linked. The mercenaries had an incentive to behave consistently with the essential rules of the system, for instability would have undercut their own role. If there had been a roll-up, mercenaries would not have been needed in the system. And occasionally mercenaries did transform themselves into rulers in an Italian city-state—another incentive to maintain the system. Thus the operation of a mercenary system adds nothing to our model at the level of generalization that the model employs. On the other hand, it adds quite specifically and importantly to an understanding of the historical Italian city-state system. If, however, our investigations were to show that historical "balance of power" systems were stable only when some additional kind of actor were operating (not the mercenary system itself, for it is not universal to "balance of power" systems), it would be useful to modify the systems model so that it would not be stable without this factor.

We could also attempt to incorporate such changes into our machine realization of the "balance of power" system. If the new factor increased the stability of the realization in the absence of still other changes, it would increase our confidence in the explanation of the historical system. If it decreased stability, it would then raise questions about the historical explanation. We would also ask ourselves which parameters of the realization model we should change in order to restore stability when this added factor impaired stability, and which we should change so that the new factor is required for stability when it improves the stability of the system. This might, depending on the circumstances, lead us to change either the historical explanation or the model of the "balance of power" system This is by no means as easy as it may sound; it is more a programmatic intention than an accomplished fact. Still it serves to illustrate the ways that feedback and learning may occur between the historical analysis, the verbal models, and the operations of the computer realizations.

Our perspective on the nature of international systems theory has been clarified in several ways since the earliest formulations. Although our present views are consistent with those expressed earlier, we have refined their expression. We are more cautious than we were originally about assuming the dominance of international factors in events of international importance.

The theory sketches have distinctive heuristic power even for cases we had earlier excluded, for instance, the classical Greek period. On the other hand, we understand that the models do not explain the behavior of that period but enable us to demonstrate that behavior which superficially conformed with the essential rules either of a "balance of power" or of a bipolar system was in fact produced by extrasystemic factors such as the narrow citizenship base of Sparta, which severely limited its external capabilities, and logistic problems in extending rule. The stability of the early phase of the Italian city-state system is also explained by extrasystemic factors.

THE WORKSHOP RESULTS

We used the Chicago workshop to produce historical studies to provide comparative materials. Systematic comparisons may provide a refinement of inference and theoretical structure. The articles by Chi (1968) on the Chinese warlord system and Franke (1968) on the Italian city-state system provide illustrations of the potentialities for this kind of comparative research. I here recapitulate some of the comparisons that emerged and their importance for an understanding of the theories of the systems.

In the process of forming regional groupings—before the regional actors could enter into strong interactions with each other—the Italian system produced at least five and the Chinese system only three strong actors at any one time. The Chinese case also contrasts in this respect with the system resulting from the breakdown of Alexander's Macedonian Empire. The Italian and the Macedonian systems were stable and the Chinese unstable. We hypothesized that the factor of number played a role in the contrasting stabilities.

The logistics of the Italian system were bad in terms of striking at the heart of an opponent, while after the initial phase of the system the logistics of the Chinese system were good. The existence of rail lines permitted rapid penetration of enemy territory. Since the enemy force had no real support in the countryside, the attacker could disperse it easily. The Macedonian case accords more with the Italian than the Chinese. Although armies could be and were transported long distances, these campaigns required long preparation and time for completion. The defenders had ample time to recoup.

The Italian cities had the support of their citizens, who did not view their governments as alien or external impositions. The Chinese warlords, however, conquered their territories and treated them as mere resources. Although they exercised the functions of government, they exploited their domains. In this sense, the warlord system was not based on fixed territories and populations. Except for Ptolemaic Egypt, however, the Macedonian system was even less territorial than the Chinese, with more rapid interchanges of territory and fewer connections with the indigenous populations. Yet it was stable and the Chinese was not.

No capital city had legitimacy as the seat of government nor was any public official national ruler in the Italian system. The Chinese system devolved from a unified state, however, and all warlords paid lip service to the myth of unity and to Peking as the seat of Chinese government. Moreover, the belief in eventual unity was a source of weakness for the warlords. Control of Peking therefore conferred some values in internal politics and also in relations with foreign governments. Successive warlords captured Peking; with its effective organization and ideology, the Kuomintang gained support as the potential unifier of China after the capture of Shanghai (until then the warlords had been unaware of Kuomintang potential for reasons that cannot be recounted here). The Macedonian system also had a central symbol of legitimacy and unity; and there were putative successors to Alexander. When for other reasons none could succeed in unifying the empire, legitimacy devolved to the generals who gained recognition as kings. All three systems contrast with the French. Paris had legitimacy as the seat of France and the ruler of Paris as king. Usually the king was stronger than any other noble. Even when he was not, however, the other strong nobles could not permit any one of their number to displace the king, for this would be too threatening to their own ambitions. Thus the French king, whose central logistical position was inherently superior and who potentially had access to superior assets, could afford to bide his time—whether or not he consciously did so—until conditions were ripe for unification.

In all the international systems studied so far, the success of hegemonial attempts depended as much on the individual abilities of a particular ruler as on the resources of the city or nation he headed. Attempts at hegemony might be cut off either by the aging of a city ruler or by his replacement by an ineffective successor. Thus the international system was given respite in many cases. In the Chinese case, on the other hand, with its good logistics, failures of leadership might, and did, permit an effective actor to take over. Time worked against stability. The Macedonian case was closer to the Italian and was, of all the international systems, the most dependent on the qualities of leadership. In none of the Macedonian actor systems, with the exception of Ptolemaic Egypt, was there anything approaching an independent bureaucracy that could keep the wheels of government running effectively despite deficiences of top leadership. The Roman system of choosing consuls provides strong contrast to these systems. Although not all consuls were great generals, all were experienced; and they were rotated rapidly under the guidance of a continuing senate. In all systems studied the actors who threatened the stability of the system were subsystem dominant and directive.

The Italian system was stable until members of the system invited the intrusion of France. The Macedonian (Greek) system was quasi-stable until members of the system got involved with Rome. The Chinese system persisted only for a very short time and was rolled up by a peripheral actor with a superior form of organization and ideology. In three of our historical cases—the Kuomintang roll-up of China, the Macedonian roll-up of Greece, and the later Roman roll-up of Greece—a peripheral actor rolled up what might be regarded from some perspectives as a central system. Toynbee hypothesizes that such roll-ups are examples of classical civilizations conquered by ruder and more warlike systems. The Macedonians clearly were ruder and more warlike than the Greeks and also possessed a superior military organization. It is difficult to say whether the Romans, whose genius lay in law, were less civilized than the Greeks, whose genius lay in philosophy. Clearly the Kuomintang leaders were culturally more advanced than the more traditional Chinese warlords. Moreover, the Roman roll-up of Italy constituted a roll-up by a central rather than by a peripheral actor. We are more impressed by the fact that in each of the three cases where a "peripheral" actor conquered a "balance of power" system, it did not participate in the wars of that system until the system had run itself down. Although the actors within the "balance of power" system maintained reasonable relative positions, the series of wars ran down the absolute resources of the system while the "peripheral" actor either husbanded its resources or actually gained resources as a consequence of military gains in outside systems. Then, when for one reason or another the "peripheral" actor became involved in the affairs of the "central" system, it was able to roll it up.

The Italian, Chinese, and Macedonian systems were all highly dependent on personal or group interrelationships that theoretically should have been inconsistent with stability. Both the Chinese and Macedonian systems rested on ties that stemmed from common military service or schooling. The Italian system was cross-cut by Guelph-Ghibelline rivalries. Yet only the Chinese collapsed, and it is unlikely that personal relationships that interfered with external rationality played any significant role in the collapse.

There was no nationalism in the Italian example. Loyalties extended to the city. There was a latent Chinese loyalty to the nation, however, that worked to the advantage of the Kuomintang and later of the Chinese Communist Party. The Macedonian satraps thought of themselves as Macedonians, even after the devolution of loyalties. Rome's extension of her system of law and, under some circumstances, of citizenship was undoubtedly of some aid in the Roman conquest of the Italian boot—particularly so in view of the dangers stemming from barbarian inroads.

The Italian city-state system was stable enough so that none of the states had any incentive to acquire potentially destabilizing weapons at considerable cost. This was not true of the Chinese system, where comparative advantages were magnified. Thus there was an acceleration of the scale and scope of war in the Chinese system. Demetrius went to great expense in the Macedonian system to build his fleet in an effort to roll the system up. He failed, however.

The mercenaries helped to stabilize the Italian system. A roll-up would have undercut their interests by reducing the need for mercenaries. Moreover, after long sieges of war, the defenders often found themselves in a position to buy the mercenaries off. Mercenary leaders also did not like to expend their soldiers, for they were their capital.

Note that the systems I am discussing were regional or local international systems embedded in the general international system but apparently sufficiently insulated for long periods to permit independent treatment. A series of comparative studies of both regional and general international systems would help us fit the parameters of international systems much better than we presently can, and better understand the interactions between parameters and system. Such studies might provide clues to future possibilities by giving us a clearer understanding of the range of possibilities and of the factors that sustain one possibility rather than another. Such studies might also help us understand better the process of political unification. If we were to focus these studies on the normative aspects of the system, we would probably learn more about them also. History is still a huge blank from the perspective of information relevant to informed (international) political analysis. Much remains to be done before we are able even to attempt an intelligent evaluation of what we might learn.

FOOTNOTES

1. For some of these arguments, see "United States Foreign Policy in a Revolutionary Age" in Kaplan (1962).
2. See Kaplan (1957, pp. 6-8) for a set of definitions distinguishing equilibrium change, system change, and system dissolution.

REFERENCES

Burns, Arthur L. "From Balance to Deterrence." *World Politics* (July 1957).

Chi, Hsi-cheng. "The Chinese Warlord System as an International System." In *New Approaches to International Relations,* edited by Morton A. Kaplan. New York: St. Martin's Press, 1968.

Fagen, Richard R. "Some Contributions of Mathematical Reasoning to the Study of Politics." *American Political Science Review* 55 (December 1961): 896.

Franke, Winfried. "The Italian City-State System as an International System." In *New Approaches to International Relations,* edited by Morton A. Kaplan. New York: St. Martin's Press, 1968.

Kaplan, Morton A. *The Revolution in World Politics.* New York: John Wiley & Sons, 1962.

————. *System and Process in International Politics.* New York: John Wiley & Sons, 1957.

Kindleberger, Charles P. "Scientific International Politics." *World Politics* 10 (October 1958): 83-84.

Riker, William H. *The Theory of Political Coalitions.* New Haven: Yale University Press, 1962.

CHAPTER 4

DIPLOMATIC HISTORY
AND INTERNATIONAL SYSTEMS

In chapter 1, it was shown that when a theory is applied to the real world we must be able to identify those features of the real world that make the theory relevant and those initial conditions that permit us to derive a specific conclusion. In chapter 2 it was argued that the historical interpretation of particular events usually requires a multifaceted approach. No single theoretical schema is likely to apply. The theoretical and praxical problems of interpretation require emphasis. Diplomatic historians tend to make serious mistakes at all three levels.

Many historians who study the immediate post-World War II period commit failures of analysis related to their lack of comprehension of the irreversible breakdown of the previous "balance of power" system as a consequence of the devastation of the war, the Russian geopolitical dominance of the Eurasian land mass, the annihilation of the military depth of western Europe as a consequence of military and technological innovation, and the economic, political, and military factors that rendered problematic the development of an at least temporarily stable loose bipolar system in the absence of remedial and protective measures by both the Soviet Union and the United States. Historians have a tendency to make abstract arguments that are unrelated to concrete factual conditions, including the condition of choice in different types of international systems.

The historian often is misled by the specificity of the question he asks. He notes correctly—if he notices it at all—that when we move from international systems to diplomatic history, we move from theories to the real world and from macrostructural-dominated situations to microevent-dominated situations.

Macrotheory, however, still may be helpful to the historian in understanding—as to the statesman in anticipating—why particular policies are stabilizing or destabilizing or in disentangling intrasystemic causes from extrasystemic causes, a technique in which the field of historical analysis is particularly weak. In addition, the diplomatic historian has a tendency to emphasize those causative factors that fit his thesis and to interpret his data in ways that are too "obvious."

The historian too often uncritically assumes that facts are simple things. Quotations mean what they say, regardless of the sophistication of the speaker, the context in which the statement was made, the forum within which it was delivered, and the general historical milieu. Historians rarely raise counterfactual conditions as a mode of exploration of what appears to be evidence.

Nonetheless, it is an elementary fact that we have not yet learned how to program a computer so that it can perform the simple recognition operations that a child is capable of when he distinguishes his parent from some other individual. Information does not become evidence for any complex thesis in the absence of a radically more difficult process of identification that places it within a pattern that alone can give it adequate meaning. And diplomatic historians tend to be naive in their treatment of evidence.

Let me choose one well-known example from the early history of the cold war to make this point explicit although the events occurred before and during World War II. The Department of State of the United States published a set of translated diplomatic documents entitled *Nazi-Soviet Relations: 1939-1941*. The documents were reasonably complete, adequately translated, and presented in chronological order. The editor of the volume placed no interpretation on the documents and allowed the reader to draw his own conclusions. The documents showed that Germany offered the Soviet Union a partnership in the war and the right to expansion in the Persian Gulf area. The Soviet Union responded favorably but demanded instead large Nazi concessions in eastern Europe that the Germans resisted. The negotiations dragged on, and eventually broke down. Eventually Germany attacked the Soviet Union. The reader is left with the unstated, but almost surely intended, hypothesis that the Soviet Union had no objection to entering the war on the German side and that negotiations toward this end failed only because its demands were too great. This unstated hypothesis is not unreasonable, and it may even be correct; but it lacks the iron objectivity that the editor and most readers assumed, given the then current beliefs.

If Stalin had assumed that a Russian Communist future in a Nazi-dominated Europe would be insecure—and he would have been a fool if he had not—this would have been a sound reason for avoidance of an alliance with Hitler. Suppose, however, that Stalin had been afraid that a direct rejection of the German demands would have led to an immediate German attack on the Soviet Union for which it was ill-prepared. Might not it then have been a reasonable strategy for him to hold out the hope of successful negotiations for as long as he could while refraining from offering terms that the Germans were likely to accept? Even the fact that the Russians later took the territories that they demanded from the Germans is not strong evidence against this hypothesis, for the demands would not have been plausible unless the Russians had had some real interest in them. I use this example to make the point that even the most seemingly obvious case may be far more complex than many assume and that the seemingly most objective evidence, even in cumulative detail, may be misleading.

Let me take two recent books to illustrate how the historian fails properly to cope with his problems. Consider Robert M. Slusser's *The Berlin Crisis in 1961* (1973). First of all, let me report that Slusser is a highly intelligent man with a very sophisticated mind, and that he has an intensive knowledge not only of Soviet diplomatic history but of Soviet government and Communist party life, including its esoteric practices. His profound grasp of Communist theory and practice becomes manifest in his use of his documentation, which he weaves into a genuine interpretative pattern. I would not lightly dismiss any conclusion he reaches in the area of his competence, even when the weight of evidence is not clearly in its favor.

However, Slusser uses the Berlin crisis to demonstrate that Khrushchev was not as solidly in control of the Kremlin in 1961 as most professional observers believed and that on a number of issues decisions were made that did not accord with his wishes. With respect to these large details of his thesis, his evidence is impressive and convincing. On the other hand, it should not have been as surprising as it was to many observers. The Soviet system encourages factionalism and conspiracy despite the fact that these activities are heavily penalized within it. There are natural resistances in the sytsem to an accumulation of power by the first or the general secretary. Even as late as 1934, Kirov mobilized a majority against Stalin on the question of death sentences for party comrades. The Leningrad affair and the doctors' plot are incomprehensible unless one assigns inordinate weight to Stalin's presumed paranoia, in the absence of resistance to Stalin's policies or the possibility of an accumulation of power by secondary figures in the regime that presented a potential threat to Stalin's control of it.

With respect to more secondary details, Slusser's evidence that Kozlov was at the center of the anti-Khrushchev activity and that on some issues he was joined by Mikoyan to prevent an accumulation of power by Khrushchev is also convincing.

When he moves beyond these broad details and a few of the minor points that can be established relatively easily, the author is on weaker ground. He maintains his interpretation of events with skill and always has an ad hoc—and possibly correct—explanation for a seeming discrepancy. However, I am going to use an example in which it is relatively easy to demonstrate that there is an alternative, and probably correct, hypothesis that does not fit his schema of explanation to show the dangers that are inherent in his technique. He argues that Khrushchev was taking a position for more consumer goods (clearly correct) and that he was an opponent of larger military expenditures, including large-scale testing of nuclear weapons. In Slusser's account of Khrushchev's interview with C.L. Sulzburger, Khrushchev said that Russia would not test the 100-megaton bomb but only the trigger for it. Slusser then uses the fact that the tests began while Khrushchev was in the Crimea (on a perhaps enforced vacation) as evidence that his enemies, led by Kozlov, made this decision against his wishes. However, even apart from the fact that the series of tests required long planning, Khrushchev came back in time to prevent the explosion of the large bomb. Therefore, Slusser argues that he was overruled by the Politburo on the question of restricting the tests to a trigger for the weapon but managed to reach a compromise in which only a fifty-megaton weapon was tested. In the first place, even the initial plausibility of the argument rests on the assumption that Khrushchev used the word "trigger" in the same way as a weapons' specialist would use it. There is nothing in Khrushchev's use of language to suggest that he is a precisionist. Thus, the explosion of a fifty-megaton bomb—which would have been a 100-megaton bomb if the lead casing had been made of fissionable material instead—might have been viewed by Khrushchev as a trigger for the larger weapon. Furthermore, Slusser reports but barely notices statements by Russian representatives at the United Nations that they failed to explode the 100-megaton weapon because of the environmental consequences. However, he should have paid attention to this argument, for such a weapon would have had environmental consequences not much different from those of the famed Krakatoa explosion, which shook the world. Technical discussions of these consequences may well have convinced the entire Politburo, including Kozlov, of the inadvisability of a test of a 100-megaton weapon. Beyond this, no American weapons expert doubted that the larger bomb with a fissionable casing would have worked on the basis of the actual test. On the other hand, the testing of a trigger mechanism (in a technical sense) for the large bomb would not have been an adequate test for such a weapon and would not have convinced external observers—or the Russians—of Russia's ability to construct a workable weapon of that type. Thus, it is quite likely that technical information concerning the infeasibility of a test series either restricted to a trigger or expanded to the large bomb convinced Khrushchev and all other politburo members by the time the decision was made.

Slusser usually presents us with the evidence that fits his thesis but not with the evidence that does not. That he does an extraordinarily superior job of this should not blind us to the fact that this is not an adequate method for testing hypotheses. He labels Khrushchev anti-China and Kozlov pro-China. But he gives us no basis for understanding why each man takes this position. He shows, as an example of Kozlov's pro-China position, that in North Korea Kozlov used a phrase implying that all the Socialist countries would approach communism together. Khrushchev employed the same phrase in his address to the Twenty-second Congress. However, Slusser argues that he did this because of a Politburo decision and that another sentence in his address that seems to lead to a different conclusion reveals his actual attitude. On the other hand, the fact that Kozlov used the earlier phrase only, and not the later qualifying phrase, in North Korea may be more responsive to the setting in which his talk was given than to anything else. Slusser is not as clearly wrong here as he is on the bomb test series. However, because he provides no account of the nature of the dispute between the two individuals, we have no way of interpreting, except through indirect semantic evidence, the seriousness of the dispute between them. For instance, in the reputed conflict between Khrushchev and Kozlov over Berlin, it is plausible that the entire politburo may have agreed on a last test of the strength of a Western riposte in Berlin. Perhaps the Soviet military and the East Germans had been arguing that the signal that the issue was terminated had been a mistake. In this case, the real reason for the new move would have been less to secure a Western retreat— although this might have been an acceptable bonus—than to satisfy the military and the East Germans that their proposed policy was too dangerous. If so, the last Berlin "push" will not fit Slusser's thesis.

Again, in ascribing serious differences in policy to Khrushchev and Kozlov, Slusser tells us nothing about the internal dynamics of the Soviet system that leads men into opposed positions. Beria's consumerism and his attempt to reach a compromise over Germany in 1953 were among the factors that permitted an effective coalition to form against him. On the other hand, once Malenkov was in office, he turned to consumerism as well. This enabled Khrushchev and others to form an effective coalition against Malenkov. Was Koslov attempting the same strategy against Khrushchev?

To what extent were their positions genuinely opposed? To what extent did they only appear to be opposed for reasons of power jockeying? If to a consid-erable extent they only appeared to be opposed, Kozlov may have had no serious interest in pushing the Soviet Union toward the brink of war with the United States. There is nothing in the volume that permits us to raise these questions in a systematic manner. Yet they are essential elements of the picture. There is no account of the general world situation or of that within the Soviet bloc. That Slusser's thesis stands up as well as it does is a tribute to his ingenuity and knowledge. However, he has clearly overstated his case and very well may have missed some essential factors in the absence of which the information he presents us with is not adequate as evidence.

Thomas G. Paterson's book *Soviet-American Confrontation* (1973) might be called an entry in the second wave of revisionist literature. Briefly, the argument of the author is that the United States brought on the cold war through its attempt to use economic aid as an element of coercion and because it believed it was essential to create a world in which the American principles of free trade and economy could operate. Let me immediately distinguish this book from the more reprehensible entries in the first wave, such as Gar Alperovitz's (1965). Paterson makes a modest effort to be fair-minded and rarely engages in major distortions of the so-called objective evidence to make his point. Moreover, although he calls the United States arrogant, he does not seem to doubt that it was interested in a durable peace. But he regards its decision makers as prejudiced and unsophisticated. Therefore, he believes they triggered unfortunate actions by the Soviet Union that produced the cold war.

Let us first of all admit the obvious. American decision makers started with certain ideological perspectives. They did believe in free trade. They did believe that nationalization should not occur without compensation. They often used economic strength as a bargaining tool. They often misinterpreted the behavior of other nations and sometimes behaved in unnecessarily irritating ways. They were often simpleminded in their statements, although I do not believe that the diplomacy of the first Truman administration can genuinely be called unsophisticated. This certainly caused friction with the Soviet Union. Moreover, the two countries clearly had some opposed interests.

What it is incumbent on Paterson to show is that the factors he emphasizes produced the cold war and that, had this been understood by American decision makers, they could have avoided the cold war by adopting policies that were prudent. I find nothing in the book that can properly be called evidence for his thesis. There are some minor inadequacies in his evaluation of evidence that I will not spend much time on. For instance, his footnoting of American military superiority in the early postwar period flies in the face of the actual evidence. We had no stockpile of atom bombs. Most of our military aircraft were incapable of flying in combat status. And General Marshall was discussing with military officers the question of whether in the event of a Soviet attack the Allied forces would be able to evacuate Europe successfully or whether they would simply be captured. The assertion by Paterson that what the United States saw "as signs of Russia's generally aggressive behavior Russia saw...as defensive measures to protect Soviet security and its rightful fruits of victory over the axis, and if necessary for reconstruction and industrialization" (p. 102) is footnoted: " 'The Russian Sphere in Europe: Economic Planning in Eastern Europe,' *The World*

Today, III (October, 1947), 432-45.'' Paterson may be correct. But even an informed opinion would have had more relevance than such a footnote.

These, however, are relatively minor quibbles compared with the major defects of documentation in the volume. Surely some of our actions irritated the Russians. However, they had been even more irritated by the Nazis prior to the Munich Pact. Yet, the day after Munich, Potemkin, the undersecretary of the Foreign Office, told Coulandre, the French ambassador, that this meant a fourth partition of Poland. It gravely underestimates Stalin to believe that Soviet foreign policy was determined by irritation. Moreover, the argument that American actions triggered reprehensible Russian deeds that otherwise would not have occurred is a rather elastic device. We can always find some such trigger. But we can also always find some Russian action that triggered the American action. Policies are often interrelated, but they are seldom mindless in the sense that Paterson's hypothesis suggests. Paterson ignores the enormous body of evidence concerning our difficulties in trying to get the Soviet Union to behave as an ally should during the war. The Russians were very difficult to deal with. The case of the Polish Sixteen is merely one instance of this.

The case of the Polish Sixteen involves an immediate postwar episode in which the British and Americans urged Stalin to meet with sixteen members of the democratic underground. Stalin agreed, but the underground members were reluctant, for they feared Stalin. Finally, in response to Allied pleas, Stalin provided the sixteen with NKVD permits. With these permits in hand, the sixteen entered Russia only to disappear. It was months before the United States could find out even that they were in jail, and it could not secure their release. This egregious, even monstrous, violation of Allied comity by Stalin certainly would have justified far harsher responses than Truman took; and he might well have taken them except for the fact that he was so thoroughly committed to maintaining the postwar alliance in the service of peace.

Paterson presents numerous quotations from American leaders to demonstrate that they had an unsophisticated picture of the world. To some extent, this is true. Yet he makes no real effort to reconstruct their view of the world in a decision-making sense. Nor does he do that for the Russians either, except to keep insisting that our actions triggered memories of the post-World War I period. To suggest, as the author does, that economic aid to Czechoslovakia might have strengthened the democrats and prevented the coup of 1948 or that it might have led the Soviet Union to desist, suggests a simpleminded view that all the documentation in the world of the kind the author presents will do nothing to sustain. No doubt some Czech leaders thought and hoped that aid would permit them to preserve Czech autonomy. But some Czech leaders also asked Ambassador Steinhardt for a promise of American military assistance before the coup on the thesis that this also would serve the same purpose. Leaders in a desperate situation often place inordinate emphasis on last-ditch hopes and bitterly resent a lack of response. Extensive quotations of this type prove nothing in the absence of a far more complex argument than Paterson provides. Nor does Paterson take into account the decisions reached in the autumn of 1947 in the Zhdanov-dominated first Cominform meeting at which the economic program for eastern Europe was determined. Confidential polls showed that even before the implementation of such a program in Czechoslovakia, the Communists had lost enough of their popular support to threaten their dominance in a succeeding coalition government. Any effort to impose such a program as the Cominform meeting required—and the Soviet Union insisted on it—would have severely threatened the position of the Communist party in Czechoslovakia if free elections had been permitted. American aid to the Soviet Union or to Czechoslovakia would not have affected this conclusion. And this likely is what necessitated the Czechoslovak coup from the standpoint of both the Soviet Union and the Czechoslovak Communist Party.

The author adduces as evidence for his assertion that economic aid would have produced such results as avoiding the cold war his (heavily documented) rediscovery of the fact that Soviet control in eastern Europe was far more flexible prior to 1947 than later. That is certainly true and was so well known that the famous "salami" thesis was used as early as 1947 to explain it. Except perhaps for Bulgaria, economic reconstruction—essential to the Soviet Union—would have run into very great difficulty in the absence of moderately popular non-Communist elements in the governments. During this period of time, effective Soviet control was maintained through Soviet armed force and control of the interior ministries in the various countries. According to the "salami" thesis,[1] the autonomy of the non-Communist popular-front forces would be whittled away a slice at a time. Thus the former editor of the Royal Institute's annual survey, Peter Calvocoressi, argued that the Czechoslovak coup had been planned since 1945. Long before Vietnam and the first wave of revisionism made alternative hypotheses academically fashionable, I wrote a study of the Czechoslovak coup designed to show that the case for the "salami" thesis could not be proved and that an alternate thesis that a series of interactions in the developing international system led to the coup was more acceptable. I must admit that it never occurred to me to suggest that something as simple as economic aid might have averted it. Moreover, I am less than enchanted with the author's fairness when he underplays Stalin's role in demanding that Czechoslovakia withdraw from the Marshall Plan. He cites Hubert Ripka in his footnotes. He, therefore, should be well aware that Klement Gottwald, the Communist prime minister, had had a preliminary meeting with Stalin after which he informed the other members of the Czechoslovak delegation that Stalin was furious and that he had demanded Czechoslovakia's withdrawal from the Marshall Plan. Only someone who does not boggle at taking quotations out of context could have written this account of the Czechoslovak coup.

Paterson does make one apparent systematic effort to use more than simple repetitive documentation—as if repeated samples from the Sahara would show that the earth is made entirely of sand—to make his case. He compares the Czechoslovak, Yugoslav, Polish, and Finnish cases to attempt to show that the presence or absence of American economic assistance or pressure was the decisive factor in their fates. Although he does speculate that the Finnish willingness to fight and the absence of access to Soviet records might affect his conclusion, these speculations are not integrated in his argument and function only to forfend criticism that he ignored these factors.

Paterson's argument proceeds in such a vacuum that he soon forgets his main argument that American aid would have fostered national independence in eastern Europe and notes of the fact that United States aid to Yugoslavia occurred only after its split with the Soviet Union: "Tito could not be bribed. Although he toned down his criticism of the United States and improved relations with Turkey, Greece and Italy, he did not support American foreign policy and repeatedly asserted his commitments to socialism, nonalignment, and independent coexistence" (p. 141). To the extent that Paterson seems to be arguing that American economic pressure drove eastern European states closer to the Soviet Union, Yugoslavia is a clear exception to his argument. American diplomatic and economic pressure was greater against Yugoslavia than against any other eastern European state. Continued overflights of Tito's summer palace at Bled were intended to be threatening, as were the charges over the Stepanic case and the so-called slave labor cases. In fact, in the case of the other famous split—China—American pressure against China was also inordinate. Moreover, aid to Poland after 1956 coincided with internal retrogression and increased closeness to the Soviet Union in foreign policy, whereas Rumania, to which American citizens were not permitted to travel, acquired the greatest autonomy within the bloc and Hungary, subjected to similar pressures, developed the greatest liberalism.

To the extent that Paterson's argument is supposed to account for Finland's independence and the Czechoslovak coup, he ignores the relevant comparative evidence. In every eastern European state except Czechoslovakia and Finland, the Red Army was physically present and the Communists controlled the police and the armed forces. Czechoslovakia, but not Finland, had been "liberated" by the Red Army. Its premier was a Communist. The police were under Communist control. The army had Communist leadership. Before the coup, civilian "action" squads had been armed by Communist Interior Minister Nosek; and, even apart from the historic unwillingness of the Czechs to fight, the Communists were in physical control. These factors were absent in Finland; and the presence or absence of economic assistance or pressure had nothing to do with it.

The important differences in the Yugoslav and Chinese cases that distinguished them from the other eastern European nations were that the Red Army was not present and that the national Communist party leaderships had been unified and had gained independent control within the individual nation. In every other state, there was a three-way split between the Russian exiles, the Western exiles, and the local resistance that Stalin manipulated. Although I have only adumbrated what an analysis of this subject would involve, it does make clear that Paterson did not engage in a genuine, as opposed to a merely pro forma, comparative analysis.

Other revisionists argue that the Marshall Plan was nothing but a device to ensure the success of capitalism. They ignore all the documented evidence that Marshall, Acheson, Nitze, and others who formulated the plan were primarily concerned with the stability and non-Communist independence of western Europe. They ignore the fact that the Congress that came in in 1946 was Republican and heavily conservative and that the administration had to argue that the Marshall Plan was good for business if it was to get conservative votes for it. Even so, that argument was unsuccessful, for the conservative pro-business Congress did not want to spend that kind of money for anything and would have preferred to spend it in the United States if it were to spend it at all. The Marshall Plan went through only after a perceived increase in the Russian threat and the linking of the Marshall Plan to the threat of war.

Could the cold war have been avoided? Obviously this question cannot be given a definitive answer. But another, and more serious, question is whether, even on the basis of more sophisticated evaluations of foreign policies than Western leaders had made—and of information available to Paterson but not available at the time—prudent leadership would have tested a hypothesis of avoidance. Would a prudent American leadership have run the risk that western Europe might have fallen under irreversible Soviet domination? If not, then the Marshall Plan was a necessity, and it is unfair for the author to characterize it as anti-Russian. Should a prudent Stalin have run the risk that more flexible systems in eastern Europe might have produced anti-Communist governments? I have always doubted that (unless he had converted to democratic beliefs), and I do not think that the issue of American aid would likely have influenced his decisions or the potential threat to western Europe posed by Soviet control of eastern Europe. Perhaps I am wrong on this point, but there is nothing in the extensive documentation and footnoting of the author that permits a serious investigation of this question.

Historians such as Paterson argue on the basis of hindsight and assume that their policies would have avoided the costs of actual policies. They ignore the fact that for statesmen the future is uncertain. The policies of other states are not entirely clear. They may even change in response to new opportunities for gain or for the avoidance of loss, to pressures from internal opponents who suggest that they are not serving the interests of the state or making the most of opportunities, or for other reasons. Statesmanship is fallible and its guideline is prudence, except where conditions are desperate. Policies often have unintended consequences, although our historians, most of whom did not live through the period, seem so sure that they would have done so much better. And they so blithely ignore the irreversibly catastrophic consequences that might have resulted if policies had been based on their hypotheses and if those hypotheses had proved to be wrong.

Our leaders were to some extent simplistic, subject to "group think," and uninventive. They probably could have done better to some extent. They could have avoided some of the worst excesses of interpretation. But could they have avoided some kind of cold war? I doubt it. It was inherent in the situation. Europe was "up for grabs." If either Russia or the United States dominated it—whether militarily or politically, whether by conquest or by pressure from propinquity—the results would have been the same: calamity for the side that lost. The instability of the postwar situation mandated this condition: destruction, population loss, fear and failure of will, economic catastrophe, and extremely unpopular political systems in eastern Europe. Whatever mistakes of policy or misinterpretation that may have led to the excesses of the cold war, the cold war was embedded in the structural situation of world politics. The decline of the cold war was less a response to new leadership than a response to a new situation in which opportunities for either side to take all of Europe or to cause monumental threats to the other had much diminished. To a great extent, it was the success of the policies of the forties and fifties that produced the détente of the sixties and seventies. The limitations of detente, and the historical assurance that structural conditions in the world do not permit a return to the excesses of the cold war, are among the major factors permitting a return to greater competitiveness in relations between the United States and the Soviet Union.

My short account of these two books is an illustration—and I believe a representative one—of the shortcomings of diplomatic history. Diplomatic historians, on the whole, are unsophisticated in the interpretation of evidence, untrained in the study of international relations, and largely interested in substantiating a thesis—the credential that gains them professional recognition.

Consequently, they select evidence that fits their thesis.

Discrepancies are explained by *ad hoc* hypotheses. The evidence that would suggest countertheses is usually not presented. They do not know how to ask counterfactuals such as: would the Marshall Plan have been proposed if it had not been good for business? Suppose, however, that the historical evidence had been kinder to the revisionist thesis, that a perceived increase in the Soviet threat had not been necessary for passage of the Marshall Plan, and that the argument that the plan was good for American business had been sufficient to gain Congressional passage. Even then, the argument that the Marshall Plan was adopted because it was good for American business would have to establish the similarity of Congressional and Executive motivations and that it was adopted independently of concern for political or social instability in western Europe. Otherwise, one could not show that the good of American business was a sufficient factor for proposal and adoption of the Marshall Plan. Only by including such counterfactual considerations in analysis is it possible even to attempt such a complex interpretation as the motivation behind the Marshall Plan.

There are other lacunae in most historical analyses. The large context, such as that of the international political system, or the world views of the leaders of opposing countries, is seldom presented. Very seldom is there a serious investigations of the alternative policies available to leaders and an assessment of the risks and opportunities of these alternative courses.

What does such scholarship represent? At its worst it is part of a dons' game. "Become famous by presenting a different thesis no matter to what extent the evidence must be manipulated" is the motto. If theses are too inconclusive or difficult to understand, people do not notice them—and publishers do not wish to publish them.

Slusser is more serious than this and has something to contribute to knowledge. Even though I suspect his concentration on a single focus of analysis, he employs that focus expertly. I respect his intelligence and knowledge sufficiently to take any hypothesis of his seriously. In the case of Paterson, his book is a crashing bore because he has no real comprehension of any aspect of his subject matter. Despite his accumulation of footnotes, there is no significant evidence for anything in the book except his diligence in collecting debaters' points with which to discomfit opponents. However, it is unfair to criticize him for this, for he is merely adhering to accepted contemporary standards of scholarship, which in the field of diplomatic history are every bit as superficial as they are in the field of criticism in international relations theory.

FOOTNOTES

1. If memory serves me correctly, the term may even have been used first by Bela Rakosci, the Hungarian Communist party secretary.

REFERENCES

Alperovitz, Gar. *Atomic Diplomacy.* New York: Simon and Schuster, 1965.
Paterson, Thomas G. *Soviet-American Confrontation: Postwar Reconstruction and the Origins of the Cold War.* Baltimore: Johns Hopkins Press, 1973.
Slusser, Robert M. *The Berlin Crisis of 1961: Soviet-American Relations and the Struggle for Power in the Kremlin.* Blatimore: Johns Hopkins Press, 1973.

INDEX